Flowers and Their Messages

THE MOTHER

Flowers and Their Messages

SRI AUROBINDO ASHRAM
PONDICHERRY

First edition 1973
Sixth edition 2019

Rs 325
ISBN 978-93-5210-184-9

© Sri Aurobindo Ashram Trust 1973, 2019
Published by Sri Aurobindo Ashram Publication Department
Pondicherry 605 002
Web https://www.sabda.in

Printed at Sri Aurobindo Ashram Press, Pondicherry
PRINTED IN INDIA

Editor's Note

Flowers and Their Messages is primarily a book of the Mother, where Sri Aurobindo's touch is undoubtedly felt. The spiritual significances of flowers are, we believe, a completely new way of looking at them. It may also be called a book of the Integral Yoga, for the Mother used flowers as an aid in our self-development to realise the highest possibilities that await us. A conscious and intimate relationship with flowers can help us to experience a beautiful communion with the Divine. Sri Aurobindo once remarked: "The plants are very psychic but they can express it only by silence and beauty." Here the Mother has made of that beauty an eloquent and potent expression.

This revised and enlarged edition has in the Introduction a few more passages from the writings of the Mother and Sri Aurobindo. The section 'Nature, the Mother and Flowers' traces her sensitivity to Nature and her intuitive work of giving the spiritual significances of the flowers that were offered to her. Two other lists have been inserted: the first is a compilation of some of the names previously used by the Mother; the second gives the corresponding name to hibiscus flowers first given for Auroville. We have added one more flower that Mother named but was not included till now. This Hibiscus appears on page 115.

As in earlier editions the order of botanical names is followed, but these are often shortened by giving only the generic name. In the case of the conifers and the orchids however, the family name is used, since the Mother named the family as a whole. For the few scientific-minded readers, there is on page 297 a short list of alternative botanical names corresponding to the ones used in this book.

The Mother once remarked during a conversation that she could transmit a state of consciousness more easily to a flower than to a human being.

When the first edition of this book was in preparation she said: "This is a book for those who want to know what flowers tell us."

It is our joy to share this gift of the Mother with all who cherish and treasure flowers.

Contents

Introduction — Words of Sri Aurobindo and The Mother	I-XIX
The Mother's Flower Significances	1
Previously Used Names	257
Flowers Named for Auroville	258
The Symbolism of Colour	259
Flowers Game	261
Classified List of Significances	268
Index of Common Names	288
The Hibiscus Group	292
Alternative Botanical Names	297
References	298
Glossary	301
Glossary of Philosophical and Psychological Term	305
Nature, The Mother and Flowers	310
The Mother: A Life Sketch	312

Flowers are the moment's representations
of things that are in themselves eternal

SRI AUROBINDO

Lo! here are flowers and benedictions!
Here is the smile of divine Love!
It is without preferences and without
repulsions.
It streams out towards all in a generous
flow and
never takes back its marvellous gifts!

INTRODUCTION

Love and Aspiration in Plants

The trees rise towards the sky, beautiful symbol of Nature's aspiration towards the light.*

*

The flowers are the prayers of the vegetal world. The plants offer their beauty to the Supreme.*

*

It is not certain whether the plant makes an effort or not. And in any case, it has an aspiration; plants grow because they aspire for the light, for the sun, for the open air.

And it's a kind of competition. If one goes into a wood, for instance, into a park where there are many different plants, one can observe very clearly that there is a sort of competition among plants to pass each other and reach the light and open air above. It is indeed quite wonderful to see.

*

The movement of love is not limited to human beings and it is perhaps less distorted in other worlds than in the human. Look at the flowers and trees. When the sun sets and all becomes silent, sit down for a moment and put yourself into communion with Nature: you will feel rising from the earth, from below the roots of the trees and mounting upward and coursing through their fibres up to the highest outstretching branches, the aspiration of an intense love and longing,—a longing for something that brings light and gives happiness, for the light that is gone and they wish to have back again. There is a yearning so pure and intense that if you can feel the movement in the trees, your own being too will go up in an ardent prayer for the peace and light and love that are unmanifested here.

*

The unselfish movement, uncalculating, is one of the most beautiful forms of psychic consciousness in the world. But the higher one rises in the scale of mental activity, the rarer it becomes. For with intelligence come all the skill and cleverness, and corruption, calculation. For instance, when a rose blossoms it does so spontaneously, for the joy of being beautiful, smelling sweet, expressing all its joy of living, and it does not calculate, it has nothing to gain out of it: it does so spontaneously, in the joy of being and living. Take a human being, well, apart from a very few exceptions, the moment his mind is active he tries to get some advantage out of his beauty and cleverness; he wants it to bring him something, either men's admiration or even much more sordid gains yet. Consequently, from the psychic point of view, the rose is better than human beings. Only, if you climb a rung higher and consciously do what the rose does unconsciously, then it is much more beautiful. But it must be the same thing: a spontaneous flowering of beauty, uncalculating, simply for the joy of being. Little children have this at times (at times, not always). Unfortunately, under the influence of their parents and the environment, they learn to be calculating when yet very young. But this kind of wish to gain by what one has or does is truly one of the ugliest things in the world. And it is one of the most widespread and it has become so widespread, that it is almost spontaneous in man. Nothing can turn its back on the divine love more totally than that, that wish to calculate and profit. Do flowers love? This is their form of love, this blossoming. Certainly, when one sees a rose opening to the sun, it is like a need to give its beauty. Only, for us, it is almost unintelligible, for they do not think about what they do. A human being always associates with everything he does this ability to see himself doing it, that is, to think about himself, think of himself doing it. Man knows that he is doing something. Animals don't think. It is not at all the same form of love. And flowers, so to speak, are not conscious: it is a spontaneous movement, not a consciousness that is conscious of itself, not at all. But it is a great Force which acts through all that, the great universal Consciousness and the great Force of universal love which makes all things blossom in beauty. You know, crystals which are formed in matter already obey a movement of love; but this becomes quite perceptible in the vegetable kingdom, in the tree and plant. It is the need to grow to get more light. All these trees which are always growing higher —always growing, the smaller ones trying to catch up with the taller, the taller ones trying to climb yet higher; you put two plants side by side, they both try to find an orientation that gives them the maximum light possible—that is the need to grow, to get more air, more light, more space.

*

Have you never watched a forest with all its countless trees and plants simply struggling to catch the light—twisting and trying in a hundred possible ways just to be in the sun? That is precisely the feeling of aspiration in the physical—the urge, the movement, the push towards the light. Plants have more of it in their physical being than men. Their whole life is a worship of light. Light is of course the material symbol of the Divine, and the sun represents, under material conditions, the Supreme Consciousness. The plants have felt it quite distinctly in their own simple, blind way. Their aspiration is intense, if you know how to become aware of it.

Consciousness

Those who have studied the vegetable kingdom in detail are well aware that there is a consciousness there. For instance, plants need sunlight to live—the sun represents the active energy which makes them grow—so, if you put a plant in a place where there is no sunlight, you see it always growing up and up and up, trying, making an effort to reach the sunlight. In a virgin forest, for instance, where man does not interfere, there is this kind of struggle among all the plants which are always growing straight upwards in one way or another in their effort to catch the sunlight. It is very interesting. But even if you put a flower-pot in a fairly small courtyard surrounded by walls, where the sun doesn't come, a plant which normally is as high as this (gesture), becomes as tall as that: it stretches up and makes an effort to find the light. Therefore there is a consciousness, a will to live which is already manifesting.

*

We must suppose in the plant and the metal also a force to which we can give the name of consciousness although it is not the human or animal mentality for which we have hitherto preserved the monopoly of that description.

Not only is this probable but, if we will consider things dispassionately, it is certain. In ourselves there is such a vital consciousness which acts in the cells of the body and the automatic vital functions so that we go through purposeful movements and obey attractions and repulsions to which our mind is a stranger. In animals this vital consciousness is an even more important factor. In plants it is intuitively evident. The seekings and shrinkings of the plant, its pleasure and pain, its sleep and its wakefulness and all that strange life whose truth an Indian scientist [Jagadish Chandra Bose], has brought to light by rigidly scientific methods, are all movements of consciousness, but, as far as we can see, not of mentality. There is then a sub-mental, a vital consciousness which has precisely the same initial reactions as the mental, but is different in the constitution of its self-experience, even as that which is superconscient is in the constitution of its self-experience different from the mental being.

*

How to develop our consciousness in order to work in a better way with plants and flowers?

First you must learn to be silent; then note carefully what happens in the consciousness.*

Material Nature

Mother, certain flowers come in a particular season; does this mean that during that season a greater force is at work?

This is a question which is difficult to answer. But I have made a rather interesting experiment in this way. I don't know if you remember—if you were there—if you remember the time when flowers used to be counted; you see, it was a kind of agreement between me and Nature. To each of these flowers I had given a particular value, not only its significance but its value. For example—it was understood —I had made an agreement with Nature. Take, for instance, the "transformation" flowers; note that if one is quite attentive, one will see that in different seasons one flower is replaced by another with a similar or close significance, and you can go all round the year in this way—if you know how to make use of things! There are also permanent things which are always there.... But flowers, for example, like the "transformation" flowers, have a season, quite a long one, but still a season. The "realisation" flower has a fairly long season, but it doesn't come at the same time as the "transformation" flower.... They... how shall I put it?... overlap. One begins before the other finishes. But the seasons when they come abundantly are not the same, and all flowers are like that. Yes, it is arranged. This answers your question, doesn't it? These are shades in the meaning and it is possible that some seasons are more favourable; one may lay greater stress on one movement than on another. But each of these flowers had a numerical value, and I used to write it down; I had them counted, because I was noting the numerical value. I stopped when my pages... I had long pages like this, you see (*Mother stretches out her arms to indicate the length of the pages*), because I was totalling up the numerical values. I had my reasons for it, it was not just like that.... I did a great deal of work with it.... I had to stop because it was taking too much time. You see, when I had to write figures on a paper at least as long as this, and then later, suddenly it had to be still bigger, it was impossible! (*Mother stretches out her arms again.*) So I had to stop. I stopped because of this. But not only did I have a numerical value and did some work upon it, there was also the meaning of the flower. Well, it was an agreement like this: the numerical value corresponded to something that it was understood Nature would give me for my work, but the significance of the flower also was something agreed upon between me and Nature. For example, take "transformation". When there was a computation—it was sometimes by thousands during the season, you know—well, it represented (it was an understanding with Nature) that the same number of men would be transformed.... And it was even much better than this. It was that when I gave somebody one, two, three, four, five flowers I gave him at the same time the power to transform as many elements within him. But naturally, for this to work in all sincerity, it had not to pass through the head; because when their head starts working—not always in the right way—men spoil everything. That is why I never used to say anything about this. It was the same thing for all flowers, "aspiration", for example: the "aspiration" flowers which used to come in large basketfuls, you know; there were thousands and thousands of them, all counted.... Well, each one represented an aspiration; and even now, sometimes, when I have flowers like "prayer"... I have at times told you when I distribute "prayer" flowers, "It is a prayer. Be careful, this prayer is granted." I did that, you remember, don't you? And I told you, "Take care of your 'prayer'. Pray only for what you want should be! Take great care! Because this prayer is granted. I give the flower, but at the same time the possibility of [. . .] the prayer you will make. Well, it will be granted." It was very interesting, in the sense that I always used to tell Nature, "You know, if you don't want me to have these things, you need not give them to me." There were fluctuations, there were times when things came in abundance, when I insisted; there were times when they stopped abruptly, why one couldn't tell, one did not understand.... She did not agree to give us... Other things, on the contrary, she gave in great abundance. But all this is what goes on behind the scene, behind the stage....

The Care of Plants and Flowers

Flowers are very receptive and they are happy when they are loved.

*

Why do plants fall ill and what can we do to help them?

When man does not meddle, the illness of plants seems to be accidental. But man's action has upset the life of plants, even as that of animals, of course.
    Men have upset the life of plants and animals, and supermen have upset the life of men.*

*

There are many plants we are trying to grow here which suffer because of our climate. How can we help them to grow and blossom here?

Naturally, plants which like cold climates would grow in greenhouses. Also by planting forests one could have a regulating action on the climate.

Growth of consciousness in the atmosphere will surely have an effect which it is difficult to describe beforehand.*

*

Plants have feelings, they are alive, they should not be treated brutally.

*

As a rule plants suffer if they are kept shut up in a room.

*

Just imagine, there are plants which are vain! I am speaking of plants one grows for oneself. If one pays them compliments by words or by feelings, if one admires them, well, they hold up their head—with vanity!

*

Look, it's Enthusiasm, see how beautiful it is! It must be put in water right away, otherwise....
It needs vital force and water is vital force. It is lovely! What fantasy!

*

Sweet Mother, what should we do with the flowers which you give us every day?

You ought to keep them as long as they are fresh, and when they are no longer so, you must collect them and give them to the gardener (any gardener you know), so that he can put them in the earth to produce other flowers. Yes, one must give back to the earth what it has given us, for otherwise it will become poor.

*

Can I remove the branches of shrubs which are overhanging and causing inconvenience to the inmates?

I cannot say yes or no, as all depends on the way it is done. It is not only the welfare of the inmates that must be taken in consideration but also the welfare of the shrubs.

*

I do not like clipped and trimmed plants, it looks too artificial.

*

The only thing I insist upon is care, gentleness and consideration, as you would have for a living being—for plants are living and *they feel and suffer.*

*

When a plant is tired or sick give it rest for a few days, in a proper place, and it will recover. Repotting is always a blow and to give a blow to a sick plant is just the way of finishing it.

*

In preparing the beds ...it may be found necessary to cut away some roots of the trees.

This is not possible. No roots of trees must be cut. Apart from that – if the trees are respected, you can prepare these [beds].

*

Yesterday I took out a considerable quantity of soil...to see if any worm was at its root. If you like, I will now take out the whole lump of roots and inspect it.

There would be no use in doing that. Besides, plants must not be disturbed too much – like people, they need quiet to get strength and grow.

*

Innumerable like ideas, flowers are joyous companions.*

Dreams, Beings and Forces

What do flowers and gardens in our dreams signify? Sometimes in dreams one sees flowers which don't exist.

This happens undoubtedly in the subtle physical. But it may also be possible that these flowers exist physically on the earth in a place you don't know.

What do these flowers symbolise?

These symbols are most often individual and different people have different significances. It may happen that certain people have written books and those who read them adopt their symbology. But then it is a purely mental question. You give a certain meaning to flowers; for instance, to a rose—we have a certain meaning for the rose. As we have given this meaning, in your dreams you see the same symbolism. If you tell me one of your dreams I could explain it to you. You see, a flower must spontaneously tell you something, then that would be symbolic for you. But that may be what we have already decided.*

*

Are there subtle beings that are in an intimate relation with flowers?

That is possible, even probable. There are children who have experienced this and related it.

Is it possible to become conscious of these beings and work in harmony with them?

Yes. It is a question of nature and capacity.

Is it possible to develop this capacity and how to do it?

Certainly one can develop the capacity if one takes sufficient interest in this to put in the time and necessary effort. Naturally, it will be more or less difficult according to each one's nature.

To become conscious of one's dreams helps to do this. A silent and still concentration helps also.*

*

Are there forces directly hostile to vegetal nature? Are insects a manifestation of these forces?

There do not seem to exist forces consciously and voluntarily hostile to the vegetal kingdom. Insects do harm because they feed on plants, but in this way they serve them also; both things are there, good and bad, without any conscious will. They do good, they do harm, without knowing it.*

*

Mother, does a plant have its own individuality and does it also reincarnate after death?

This may happen, but it is accidental.

There are trees—trees especially—which have lived long and can be the home of a conscious being, a vital being. Generally it is vital entities which take shelter in trees, or else certain beings of the vital plane which live in forests—as certain beings of the vital live in water. There were old legends like that, but they were based on facts.

The plants serves as home and shelter, but the being is not created by the plant itself!

Contact with the Psychic

The plants are very psychic but they can express it only by silence and beauty.

The beauty of a flower: form, colour, scent and something else which is indefinable.

The soul of a plant or an animal is not altogether dormant—only its means of expression are less developed than those of a human being. There is much that is psychic in the plant, much that is psychic in the animal. The plant has only the vital-physical evolved in its form, as it cannot express itself, the animal has a vital mind and can, but its consciousness is limited and its experiences are limited, so the psychic essence has a less developed consciousness and experience than is present or at least possible in man. All the same, animals [and plants] have a soul and can respond very readily to the psychic in man.

Directly there is organic life, the vital element comes in, and it is this vital element which gives to flowers the sense of beauty. It is not perhaps individualised in the sense we understand it, but it is a sense of the species and the species always tries to realise it. I have noticed a first rudiment of the psychic presence and vibration in vegetable life, and truly this blossoming one calls a flower is the first manifestation of the psychic presence. The psychic is individualised only in man, but it was there before him; but it is not the same kind of individualisation as in man, it is more fluid: it manifests as force, as consciousness rather than as individuality. Take the rose, for example; its great perfection of form, colour and scent expresses an aspiration and a psychic giving. Look at a rose opening in the morning at the first touch of the sun, it is a magnificent self-giving in aspiration.

*

How can flowers help us in our life and in our yoga?

Flowers teach us the charm of silence and also the self-giving that demands nothing in exchange.*

Love of flowers is a valuable help for finding and uniting with the psychic.

You have written: "Love of flowers is a valuable help for finding and uniting with the psychic." Could you explain this more in detail?

Since flowers are the manifestation of the psychic in the vegetal kingdom, love of flowers would mean that one is drawn by the psychic vibration and consequently by the psychic in one's own self.
 When you are receptive to the psychic vibration, that puts you in a more intimate contact with the psychic in your own self. Perhaps the beauty of flowers too is a means used by Nature to awaken in human beings the attraction for the psychic.

What is the best way of opening ourselves to the deep influence of flowers?

It is to love them. If you can enter into psychic contact with them, then that would be perfect.

How can one enter into a psychic contact with flowers?

When one is in conscious contact with one's own psychic, one becomes aware of an impersonal psychic behind the whole creation and then, through this, one can enter into contact with flowers and know the psychic prayer they represent.

What is this impersonal psychic you spoke of?

By impersonal psychic I mean the psychic region which does not belong to any individual in particular—the psychic region which is in the creation, as air is in the earth's atmosphere.

What is this psychic prayer that flowers represent?

The psychic, when it manifests in a plant, in the form of a flower, is in the form of a wordless prayer; it is the élan of the plant towards the Divine.

We have flowers with such significances as ~Greed for Money~, ~Passion~, ~Vanity~, ~Chatter~, etc. How do these flowers represent a psychic prayer?

These flowers offer their bad vibrations for transformation.*

Do the strong-scented flowers represent a more ardent psychic prayer than the unscented ones?

Their nature gives itself more generously and more integrally.

And is there the same difference among plants and trees?

No, that is like the difference among animals; some are big, some are small. But everywhere it is like that... in minerals, in animals, in men. Each manifests its own nature and these natures are innumerable.*

Psychological Perfection

Mother shows the white Champak flower she
is holding in her hand. She has named the
flower "Psychological Perfection".

Who remembers this?
(*Counting the petals*) One, two, three, four, five psychological perfections. What are the five psychological perfections?

For they can be changed. And in fact, to tell you my secrets, every time I give it to someone, they are not always the same psychological perfections. That depends on people's needs. Even to the same person I may give at different times different psychological perfections; so it's not fixed. But the first time this flower was named "Psychological Perfection" (I remember very well it was at a gathering up there where Prosperity[1] now is, where I go on the first of the month; there was a gathering and we had decided the five psychological perfections), at that time they were noted down, but as for me it is something very fluid—I told you it depends on the circumstances and needs—I don't remember what was chosen the first time.

So, if someone knows it, he can tell us, we'll compare.

I am not sure.

You are not sure. Is there anyone who is sure?

Aspiration, devotion, sincerity and faith.

That makes only four, so far.

And surrender.

Surrender? Someone told me something else.
(*To a disciple*) You, do you know? Well, then, come and tell us.

In English, Mother?

Ah, no, my child, this is a French class, not in English!

Faith, sincerity, aspiration, devotion, surrender.

But that's what he just said. (*Turning to another disciple*) You —a little while ago, you told me "faithfulness".

I said that, but it's not faithfulness, instead of faithfulness it's faith.

But why should there not be faithfulness? I didn't put it down, because I didn't try to recall anything, I simply wrote down what seemed to me the most important and most general. But it may be put in various ways.

In any case, what is always there, in all combinations and to whomever I give it, the first among them all is sincerity. For if there is no sincerity, one cannot advance even by half a step. So that is the first, and it is always there.

But it is possible to translate it by another word, if you prefer it, which would be "transpar-

---

1. "Prosperity" is the place where, on the first of every month, Mother used to distribute to the disciples what they needed for that month.

ency". I shall explain this word:

Someone is in front of me and I am looking at him; I look into his eyes. And if this person is sincere or "transparent", through his eyes I go down and I see his soul—clearly. But —this is precisely the experience—when I look at somebody and see a little cloud, then I continue, I see a screen, and then sometimes it is a wall, and afterwards it is something quite black; and all this must be crossed, and holes bored in order to go through; and even then I am not sure if at the last minute I may not find myself before a door of bronze so thick that I shall never get through and see his soul; so, of such a person I can immediately say that he is not sincere. But I can also say, figuratively, that he is not transparent. That is the first thing.

There is a second, which is obviously, as indispensable if you want to go forward; it is to have faith. Or another word, which seems more limited but is for me more important, because (it is a question of experience) if your faith is not made of a complete trust in the Divine, well, you may very easily remain under the impression that you have faith and yet be losing all trust in the divine Power or divine Goodness, or the Trust the Divine has in you. These are the three stumbling-blocks:

Those who have what they call an unshakable faith in the Divine, and say, "It is the Divine who is doing everything, who can do everything; all that happens in me, in others, everywhere, is the work of the Divine and the Divine alone", if they follow this with some kind of logic, after some time they will blame the Divine for all the most terrible wrongs which take place in the world and make of Him a real demon, cruel and frightful—if they have no trust.

Or again, they do have faith, but tell themselves, "Well, I have faith in the Divine, but this world, I see quite well what it's like! First of all, I suffer so much, don't I? I am very unhappy, far more unhappy than all my neighbours"—for one is always far more unhappy than all one's neighbours—"I am very unhappy and, truly, life is cruel to me. But then the Divine is divine, He is All-Goodness, All-Generosity, All-Harmony, so how is it that I am so unhappy? He must be powerless; otherwise being so good how could He let me suffer so much?"

That is the second stumbling-block.

And the third: there are people who have what may be called a warped and excessive modesty or humility and who tell themselves, "Surely the Divine has thrown me out, I am good for nothing, He can do nothing with me, the only thing for me is to give up the game, for He finds me unworthy of Him!"

So, unless one adds to faith a total and complete trust in the Divine Grace, there will be difficulties. So both are necessary....

Now, we have put "devotion" in this series. Yes, devotion is all very well, but unless it is accompanied by many other things it too may make many mistakes. It may meet with great difficulties.

You have devotion, and you keep your ego. And then your ego makes you do all sorts of things out of devotion, things which are terribly egoistic. That is to say, you think only of yourself, not of others, nor of the world, nor of the work, nor of what ought to be done—you think only of your devotion. And you become tremendously egoistic. And so, when you find out that the Divine, for some reason, does not answer to your devotion with the enthusiasm you expected of Him, you despair and fall back into the same three difficulties I was just speaking about: either the Divine is cruel—we have read that, there are many such stories, of enthusiastic devotees who abuse the Divine because He is no longer as gentle and near to them as before, He has withdrawn, "Why hast Thou deserted me? Thou hast abandoned me, O monster!..." They don't dare to say this, but think it, or else they say, "Oh! I must have made such a serious mistake that I am thrown out", and they fall into despair.

But there is another movement which should constantly accompany devotion.... That kind of sense of gratitude that the Divine exists; that feeling of a marvelling thankfulness which truly fills you with a sublime joy at the fact that the Divine exists, that there is something in the universe which is the Divine, that it is not just the monstrosity we see, that there is the Divine, the Divine exists. And each time that the least thing puts you either directly or indirectly in contact with this sublime Reality of divine existence, the heart is filled with so intense, so marvellous a joy, such a gratitude as of all things has the most delightful taste.

There is nothing which gives you a joy equal to that of gratitude. One hears a bird sing, sees a lovely flower, looks at a little child, observes an act of generosity, reads a beautiful sentence, looks at the setting sun, no matter what, suddenly this comes upon you, this kind of emotion—indeed so deep, so intense—that the world manifests the Divine, that there is something behind the world which is the Divine.

So I find that devotion without gratitude is quite incomplete, gratitude must come with devotion.

I remember that once we spoke of courage as one of the perfections; I remember having written it down once in a list. But this courage means having a taste for the supreme adventure. And this taste for supreme adventure is aspiration—an aspiration which takes hold of you completely and flings you, without calculation and without reserve and without a possibility of withdrawal, into the great adventure of the divine discovery, the great adventure of the divine meeting, the yet greater adventure of the divine Realisation; you throw yourself into the adventure without looking back and without asking for a single minute, "What's going to happen?" For if you ask what is going to happen, you never start, you always remain stuck there, rooted to the spot, afraid to lose something, to lose your balance.

That's why I speak of courage—but really it is aspiration. They go together. A real aspiration is something full of courage.

And now, surrender. In English the word is "surrender", there is no French word which gives exactly that sense. But Sri Aurobindo has said—I think we have read this—that surrender is the first and absolute condition for doing the yoga. So, if we follow what he has said, this is not just one of the necessary qualities: it is the first attitude indispensable for beginning the yoga. If one has not decided to make a total surrender, one cannot begin.

But for this surrender to be total, all these qualities are necessary. And I add one more—for so far we have only four —I add endurance. For, if you are not able to face difficulties without getting discouraged and without giving up, because it is too difficult; and if you are incapable... well, of receiving blows and yet continuing, of "pocketing" them, as they say—when you receive blows as a result of your defects, of putting them in your pocket and continuing to go forward without flagging—you don't go very far; at the first turning where you lose sight of your little habitual life, you fall into despair and give up the game.

The most... how shall I put it? the most material form of this is perseverance. Unless you are resolved to begin the same thing over again a thousand times if need be... You know, people come to me in despair, "But I thought it was done and now I must begin again!" And if they are told, "But that's nothing, you will probably have to begin again a hundred times, two hundred times, a thousand times; you take one step forward and think you are secure, but there will always be something to bring back the same difficulty a little farther on. You think you have solved the problem, you must solve it yet once again; it will turn up again looking just a little different, but it will be the same problem", and if you are not determined that: "Even if it comes back a million times, I shall do it a million times, but I shall go through with it", well, you won't be able to do the yoga. This is absolutely indispensable.

People have a beautiful experience and say, "Ah, now this is it!..." And then it settles down, diminishes, gets veiled, and suddenly something quite unexpected, absolutely commonplace and apparently completely uninteresting comes before you and blocks your way. And then you say, "Ah! what's the good of having made this progress if it's going to start all over again? Why should I do it? I made an effort, I succeeded, achieved something, and now it's as if I had done nothing! It's indeed hopeless." For you have no endurance.

If one has endurance, one says, "It's all right. Good, I shall begin again as often as necessary; a thousand times, ten thousand times, a hundred thousand times if necessary, I shall begin again —but I shall go to the end and nothing will have the power to stop me on the way."

This is most necessary. Most necessary.

So here's my proposal: we put surrender first, at the top of the list, that is, we accept what Sri Aurobindo has said—that to do the integral yoga one must first resolve to surrender entirely to the Divine, there is no other way, this is *the* way. But after that one must have the five psychological virtues, five psychological perfections, and we say that these perfections are:

      Sincerity or Transparency
      Faith or Trust (Trust in the Divine, naturally)
      Devotion or Gratitude
      Courage or Aspiration
      Endurance or Perseverance.

One form of endurance is *faithfulness*, faithfulness to one's resolution—being faithful. One has taken a resolution, one is faithful to one's resolution. This is endurance.

There you are.

If one persists, there comes a time when one is victorious. Victory is to the most persistent.

Flowers are Mediums of Transmission

When I give flowers, it is as an answer to the aspiration coming from the very depths of your being. It is a need or an aspiration, it depends upon the person. It may fill a void or else give you the impetus to progress, or it may help you find the inner harmony in order to establish peace. Do you understand?

Be like a flower. One must try to become like a flower: open, frank, equal, generous and kind....

A flower is open to all that surrounds it: Nature, light, the rays of the sun, the wind, etc. It exerts a spontaneous influence on all that is around it. It radiates a joy and a beauty.

It is frank: it hides nothing of its beauty, and lets it flow frankly out of itself. What is within, what is in its depths, it lets it come out so that everyone can see it.

It is equal: it has no preference. Everyone can enjoy its beauty and its perfume, without rivalry. It is equal and the same for everybody. There is no difference, or anything whatsoever.

Then generous: without reserve or restriction, how it gives the mysterious beauty and the very own perfume of Nature. It sacrifices itself entirely for our pleasure, even its life it sacrifices to express this beauty and the secret of the things gathered within itself.

And then, kind: it has such tenderness; it is so sweet, so close to us, so loving; its presence fills us with joy; it is always cheerful and happy.

Happy is he who can exchange his qualities with the real qualities of the flowers. Try to cultivate in yourself their refined qualities.

I give you flowers so that you may develop the divine qualities they symbolise. And they can directly transmit into the psychic all that they contain, pure, unalloyed. They possess a very subtle and very deep power and influence. Do you understand? Now, it seems to me that you wish to become like a flower or cultivate these qualities. And, you know, each flower symbolises an aspect, an emanation, an aspiration and a progress in the evolution of the earth.

*

On the plane of Matter they [plants] are the most open to my influence—I can transmit a state of consciousness more easily to a flower than to a man: it is very receptive, though it does not know how to formulate its experience to itself because it lacks a mind. But the pure psychic consciousness is instinctive to it. When, therefore, you offer flowers to me their condition is almost always an index to yours. There are persons who never succeed in bringing a fresh flower to me—even if the flower is fresh it becomes limp in their hands. Others, however, always bring fresh flowers and even revitalise drooping ones. If your aspiration is strong your flower-offerings will be fresh. And if you are receptive you will be also very easily able to absorb the message I put in the flowers I give you. When I give them, I give you states of consciousness; the flowers are the mediums and it all depends on your receptivity whether they are effective or not.

*

When one is given [by the Mother] a flower of Silence, does one also acquire it?

It is when the Mother puts her force into the flower that it becomes more than a symbol if there is receptivity in the one who receives.

*

Flowers are extremely receptive. All the flowers to which I have given a significance receive exactly the force I put into them and transmit it. People don't always receive it because most of the time they are less receptive than the flower, and they waste the force that has been put in it through their unconsciousness and lack of receptivity. But the force is there, and the flower receives it wonderfully.

I knew this a very long time ago. Fifty years ago.... There was that occultist who later gave me lessons in occultism for two years. His wife was a wonderful clairvoyant and had an absolutely remarkable capacity—precisely—of transmitting forces. They lived in Tlemcen. I was in Paris. I used to correspond with them. I had not yet met them at all. And then, one day, she sent me in a letter, petals of the pomegranate flower, "Divine's Love". At that time I had not given the meaning to the flower. She sent me petals of pomegranate flowers telling me that these petals were bringing me her protection and force.

Now, at that time I used to wear my watch on a chain. Wrist-watches were not known then or there were very few. And there was also a small eighteenth century magnifying-glass... it was quite small, as large as this (*gesture*).... And it had two lenses, you see, like all reading-glasses; there were two lenses mounted on a small golden frame, and it was hanging from my chain. Now, between the two glasses I put these petals and I used to carry this about with me always because I wanted to keep it with me; you see, I trusted this lady and knew she had power. I wanted to keep this with me, and I always felt a kind of energy, warmth, confidence, force which came from that thing.... I did not think about it, you see, but I felt it like that.

And then, one day, suddenly I felt quite depleted, as though a support that was there had gone—something very unpleasant! I said, "It is strange; what has happened? Nothing really unpleasant has happened to me. Why do I feel like this, so empty, emptied of energy?" And in the evening, when I took off my watch and chain, I noticed that one of the small glasses had come off and all the petals were gone. There was not one petal left. Then I really knew that they carried a considerable charge of power, for I had felt the difference without even knowing the reason. I didn't know the reason and yet it had made a considerable difference. So it was after this that I saw how one could use flowers by charging them with forces. They are extremely receptive.

Do flowers retain the forces always, even when they decay?

Decay? No my child; when they dry up, yes. Decayed flowers are just nothing. Decomposition takes place, so the thing disappears. Perhaps it brings energy to the soil, that's quite possible; but still, when it decays it is good only to make manure to grow other flowers. But if it dries up, it is preserved; it can remain for quite a long time.

*

Those small [Blessing] packets which I give on Kali Puja day are made to be preserved for one year. For a year they keep their force intact and I renew them every year to make sure that... I know that there isn't one in ten among you who makes a proper use of it... but still, I give it on the off-chance for those who know how to use it. It is prepared to keep the force for one year. And when I give the new one, you can dispose of the other. Usually it has fallen to dust. Not always.... But these little packets keep their charge of force exactly for one year.

The Significances of Flowers

Sweet Mother, how do you give a significance to a flower?"

By entering into contact with it and giving a more or less precise meaning to what I feel... by entering into contact with the nature of the flower, its inner truth; then one knows what it represents.*

*

Each flower has its special significance, hasn't it?

Not as we understand it mentally. There is a mental projection when one gives a precise meaning to a flower. It may answer, vibrate to the touch of this projection, accept the meaning, but a flower has no equivalent of the mental consciousness. In the vegetable kingdom there is a beginning of the psychic, but there is no beginning of the mental consciousness. In animals it is different; mental life begins to form and for them things have a meaning. But in flowers it is rather like the movement of a little baby—it is neither a sensation nor a feeling, but something of both; it is a spontaneous movement, a very special vibration. So, if one is in contact with it, if one feels it, one gets an impression which may be translated by a thought. That is how I have given a meaning to flowers and plants—there is a kind of identification with the vibration, a perception of the quality it represents and, little by little, through a kind of approximation (sometimes this comes suddenly, occasionally it takes time), there is a coming together of these vibrations (which are of a vital-emotional order) and the vibration of the mental thought, and if there is a sufficient harmony, one has a direct perception of what the plant may signify.

In some countries (particularly here) certain plants are used as the media for worship, offering, devotion. Certain plants are given on special occasions. And I have often seen that this identification was quite in keeping with the nature of the plant, because spontaneously, without knowing anything, I happened to give the same meaning as that given in religious ceremonies. The vibration was really there in the flower itself.... Did it come from the use that had been made of it or did it come from very far, from somewhere deep down, from a beginning of the psychic life? It would be difficult to say.

*

Have flowers a power in the occult world?

Yes, they have an occult power; they can even transmit a message if one knows how to charge them with it.

Can the flower transmit other messages, apart from the significance you have given it?

It is not impossible, but the person who sends the message must have a great power of formation.

Is the power of formation purely occult or can a mental or vital power of formation also transmit messages?

The mental power of formation can certainly transmit messages. But for these messages to be received and understood, the person to whom they are sent must himself be very receptive mentally and particularly attentive.

When we offer flowers, with what attitude should we offer them? Does it matter if we do not know the significance?

This depends completely on the person who gives the flowers and on his state of consciousness. The same answer may be given to both the questions. According to the degree of consciousness of people, what they do has or hasn't a deep significance.

If our flower-offering depends on our state of consciousness, does it help us to learn the significances of flowers even if it is purely mental to begin with?

Yes, surely.*

The Fragrance of Flowers

The fragrance of flowers is physical Nature's offering to the Divine, her most subtle offering.

*

It's largely the fragrances that have made me give flowers their significance. I find these studies quite interesting; it corresponds to something really true in Nature.

Once, without telling me anything, someone brought me a sprig of tulsi [*Ocimum sanctum*]. I smelled it and said, Oh, Devotion! It was absolutely a... a vibration of devotion. Afterwards, I was told it is the plant of devotion to Krishna, consecrated to Krishna.

Another time, I was brought one of those big flowers (which are not really flowers) somewhat resembling corn, with long, very strongly scented stalks [Spiritual Perfume]. I smelled it and said, "Ascetic Purity." Just like that, from the odour alone. I was later told it was Shiva's flower when he was doing his tapasya.

These people have an age-old knowledge which they have preserved. In other words, it is something concretely true: it doesn't depend at all on the mind, on thought or even on feelings—it is a vibration. . . .

Yes, this flower is Shiva, doing his tapasya.

And interestingly enough, its smell is fantastically attractive to snakes; it makes them come from far away to nest in the shrubs. And as you know, the serpent is the power of evolution, it is Shiva's own creature; he always puts them on his head and around his neck because they symbolise the power of evolution and transformation. And snakes like this flower; it often grows near rivers, and wherever there is a cluster of the plants you are sure to discover snake nests.

I find this very interesting, for we didn't decide it should be like this: these are conscious vibrations in Nature. The fragrance, the colour, the shape, are simply the spontaneous expression of a true movement.

*

Is there a relation between the perfume of a flower and its significance?

Certainly there should be one but so far I have not studied it.

How can one begin to study this relation? What is the first step?

Study and experience. You take a flower with a strong and definite perfume. You breathe in this perfume, trying to find what thought or image it evokes. If you find something, you compare it with the significance given to the flower.

It is a long and detailed work. After some hundreds of experiences one may arrive at a conclusion.

> *In the study of perfumes of which you spoke, one observes that some perfumes seem to be made up of several perfumes. Must one then study each sub-perfume separately?*

Yes, certainly. If one wants to study this is terribly complicated, for not only are there differences between flowers but even similar flowers must differ among themselves, which means that the study can never come to an end and one cannot reach anything final and complete.

There is, you know, the influence of climate, the influence of the hour—day and night—the influence of the time of the year, the influence of seasons...*

*

> *Scientists explain that flowers have perfume in order to attract insects. What do you think about that?*

It is men who see and find a reason for everything—but I doubt if the Supreme has any such preoccupation.*

The Offering of Roses

[This is the Timidity in the attachment for the Divine] I mean that the attachment is not complete and unreserved; there are parts of the being that question and hold back because they do not have a total trust...*

*

This is the Tenderness of the Divine for... for himself! The tenderness He has for his creation. 'Creation'... I don't like that word, as if it all were created for nothing! It is He himself, creating with all his tenderness. Some of these roses get quite big, they are so lovely!

*

> *Why do you generally give red roses to men, light-coloured roses to women and different colours to the little boys and girls?*

It is because red roses give an impression of force and light-coloured roses an impression of charm and sweetness.

> *Yesterday you told me that you give roses to people with a certain intention. May I ask with what intention you give me one red rose and one light-coloured one?*

XVIII

The human being transforms all its passions into love for the Divine and the Divine replies with His ineffable love. Roses as a whole, according to their form and colour, may be considered as 'Love for the Divine'. There is one rose which is 'Love from the Divine'.*

When I say 'Divine Love' I mean the vibration of love that is at the origin of all love and that fills the universe.

When I say 'Love from the Divine' I am speaking of the love that the Supreme directs upon a particular point—a person or a thing.*

Flowers on the Samadhi

Concerning the flowers on the Samadhi*, does Sri Aurobindo transmit a special message through them, apart from their significance?

I do not think so—that would depend on different cases. It could be rather that he would receive messages if people put them into the flowers. That is quite possible. It may happen that if people put flowers with an intention or a precise prayer, Sri Aurobindo receives the message and answers it and that one receives his answer if one is sufficiently sensitive.*

An Experience

A deep concentration seized on me, and I perceived that I was identifying myself with a single cherry-blossom, then through it with all cherry-blossoms, and, as I descended deeper in the consciousness, following a stream of bluish force, I became suddenly the cherry-tree itself, stretching towards the sky like so many arms its innumerable branches laden with their sacrifice of flowers. Then I heard distinctly this sentence:
"Thus hast thou made thyself one with the soul of the cherry-trees and so thou canst take note that it is the Divine who makes the offering of this flower-prayer to heaven."
When I had written it, all was effaced; but now the blood of the cherry-tree flows in my veins and with it flows an incomparable peace and force. What difference is there between the human body and the body of a tree? In truth, there is none: the consciousness which animates them is identically the same.
Then the cherry-tree whispered in my ear:
"It is in the cherry-blossom that lies the remedy for the disorders of the spring."

*

There are certain illnesses that people get particularly in spring—boils, impurities of the blood, etc.—which the Japanese cure with teas made from cherry-blossoms. I did not know this when I had the experience.

---

*The repository in the Ashram where the physical remains of both Sri Aurobindo and the Mother are placed.

The Mother (1950)

Life must blossom like a flower offering itself to the Divine.

Abelmoschus esculentus
> Okra, Gumbo, Lady's-finger
> light yellow rotate flower with dark
> maroon centre; seasonal vegetable

> ***Mentalised Power***
> *Power becomes utilisable.*

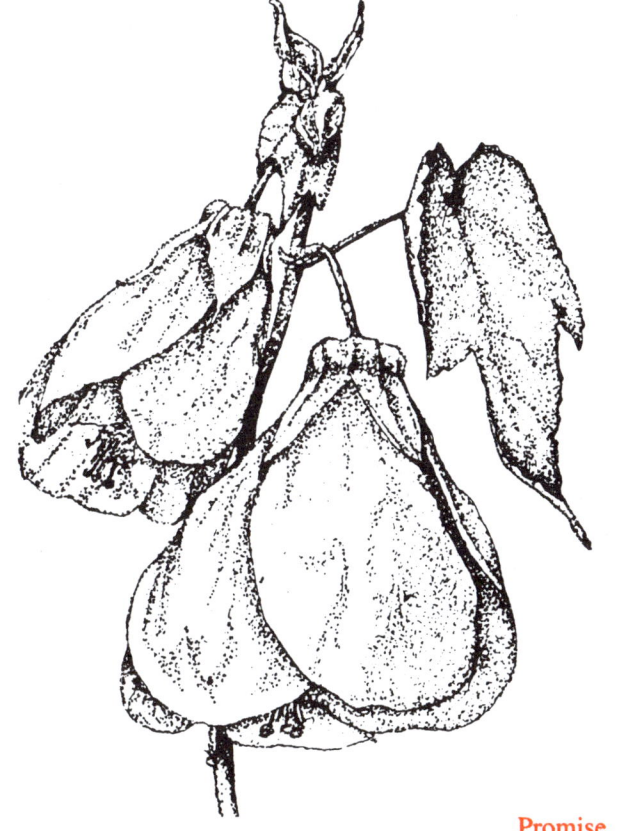

Promise

Abutilon hybridum
> Chinese lantern, Flowering maple
> several colours of pendulous bell-shaped
> flowers; shrub

> ***Promise***
> *The future is full of promise.*

Abutilon hybridum
> bright yellow flowers

> ***Mental Promise***
> *The assurance that the Supramental*
> *goal will be realised.*

Abutilon hybridum
> deep red-purple flowers with darker veins

> ***Vital Promise***
> *The vital is full of possibilities ready*
> *to develop.*

Work

Acacia auriculiformis
    Wattle
    fragrant golden-yellow catkins; tree

Work
Let us offer our work to the Divine,
this is the sure way of progressing.

Let us work as we pray, for indeed work is the body's best prayer to the Divine.

The essential character of Supermind is a Truth-Consciousness which knows by its own inherent right of nature, by its own light: it has not to arrive at knowledge but possesses it.

Supramental Knowledge

Acacia farnesiana
    Sweet acacia, Popinac, West Indian blackthorn
    small fragrant golden-yellow fluffy balls; shrub or thorny hedge

Supramental Knowledge
An infallible vision of all problems.

Acacia leucophloea
    terminal panicles of very small cream-white fluffy balls; tree

Detailed Knowledge
Manifold and minute, it forgets nothing.

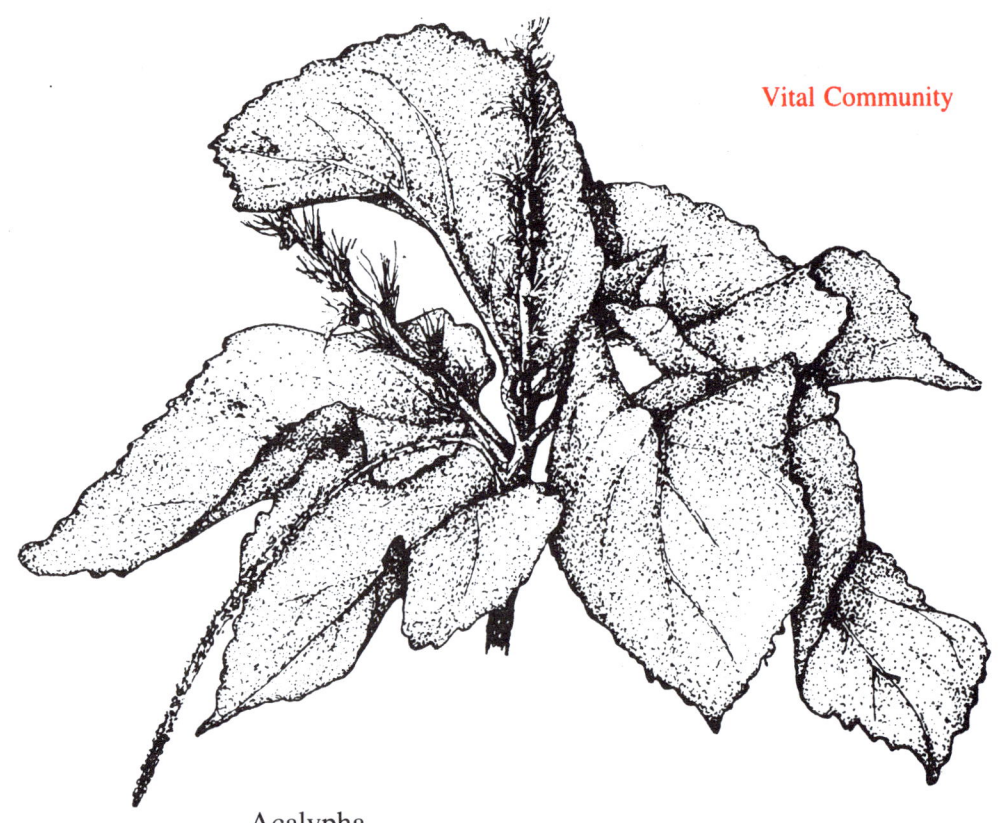

Vital Community

Acalypha
Copperleaf
prominent multi-coloured leaves, often
twisted and variously folded, with
prominent or inconspicuous catkins; shrub

Continuity
*Knowing how to persist in one's
effort.*

Acalypha wilkesiana 'Godseffiana'
green leaves with white border and short
light green catkins

Attempt towards Continuity
Vigorous and repeated but not lasting.

Acalypha hispida
Chenille plant, Red-hot cattail
very long velvety red catkins and green
leaves

Physical Continuity
*Prolongs itself indefinitely and never
comes to an end.*

Acalypha wilkesiana 'Macafeeana'
   Jacob's coat, Fire dragon
   large red leaves with russet patches and
   long sombre red catkins

Material Continuity
Powerful, enduring, solid.

Acalypha wilkesiana
   Jacob's coat
   partly curled brown-green leaves veined
   red and short sombre red catkins

Vital Continuity
Rich, abundant, persistent.

Acanthus ilicifolius (*Pl. 3*)
   Sea holly
   tall spikes of deep blue bilabiate flowers
   set in spiny bracts; countryside shrub

The Guardian
Vigilant and thorny, it knows how to protect what it has.

In the Yoga of Bhakti it is the emotional nature that is made the instrument. Its main principle is to adopt some human relation between man and the Divine Being by which through the ever intenser flowing of the heart's emotions towards him the human soul may at last be wedded to and grow one with him in a passion of divine Love.

Acanthus montanus
   Bear's-breech
   tall spikes of small lavender-rose bilabiate
   flowers tinged white, set in spiny bracts;
   low countryside shrub

Emotions Awake to the First Contact with the Divine
The Light begins to work in the emotive consciousness.

Acer
   Maple
   brilliant red autumn leaves; tree

Flame of Aspiration
A flame that illumines but never burns.

Achimenes grandiflora
> Japanese pansy
> light violet salverform flower with short corolla tube; tuberous herbaceous plant

Silence in the Vital
A powerful help for inner peace.

Acidanthera bicolor
> Abyssinian sword lily, Peacock flower
> mildly fragrant white flower with long corolla tube and six pointed petals, dark brown-maroon centre; bulbous plant

The Vital's Possibility of Perfection
The day the vital will be converted it will have much to give.

In truth, a cultivated and illumined vital can be as noble and heroic and disinterested as it is now spontaneously vulgar, egoistic and perverted when it is left to itself without education. It is enough for each one to know how to transform in himself the search for pleasure into an aspiration for the supramental plenitude. If the education of the vital is carried far enough, with perseverance and sincerity, there comes a time when, convinced of the greatness and beauty of the goal, the vital gives up petty and illusory sensorial satisfactions in order to win the divine delight.

Aegle marmelos
> Bael tree, Bengal quince
> small fragrant fleshy white star-shaped flower, trifoliate leaves and edible fruit; tree

Devotional Attitude
Modest and self-effacing, it gives remarkable fruit.

Aerva javanica
> tiny white woolly flowers in short branching spikes; large seasonal herbaceous plant

Aspiration for Integral Immortality
An organised, tenacious and methodical development of the consciousness.

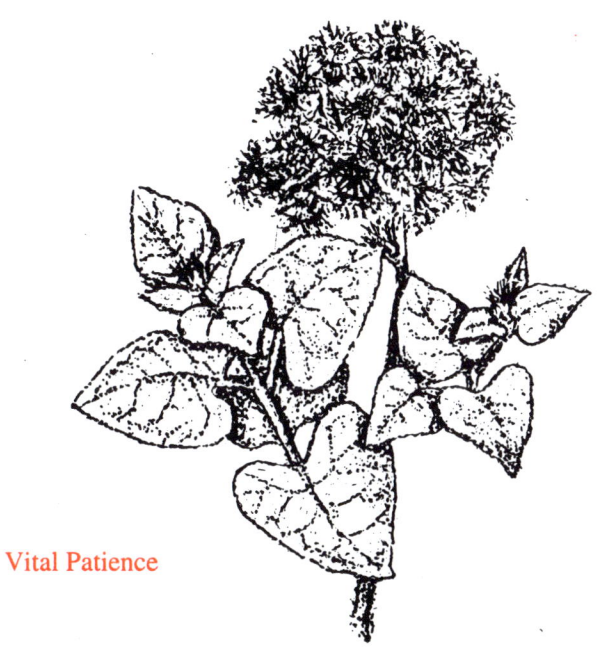
Vital Patience

Aganosma roxburghii (*Pl. 1*)
    airy clusters of fragrant white star-like salverform flowers; creeper

Rising Star
We must hope that it is the right one!

Aglaia odorata
    short spikes of fragrant yellow pinhead flowers; large shrub

Mental Suggestions of Organisation
Abundant and clustered but a little dull.

Ageratum houstonianum
    Flossflower, Pussy-foot
    clusters of minute lavender compositae flowers in soft brushlike heads; seasonal plant

Vital Patience
Indispensable for all progress.

Albizia lebbeck
    Frywood tree, Lebbeck tree
    fragrant white powderpuff flower with green centre; tree

Integral Wisdom
Obtained by union with the Divine.

Offering

When the resolution has been taken, when you have decided that the whole of your life shall be given to the Divine, you have still at every moment to remember it and carry it out in all the details of your existence. You must feel at every step that you belong to the Divine; you must have the constant experience that, in whatever you think or do, it is always the Divine Consciousness that is acting through you. You have no longer anything that you can call your own; you feel everything as coming from the Divine, and you have to offer it back to its source.

Alcea rosea
    Hollyhock
    various colours of tall erect spikes bearing single or double rotate flowers; seasonal plant

Offering
The only offering that truly enriches is the one that is made to the Divine.

Alcea
    all bicoloured flowers

Combined Offering of Two Parts of the Being
This indicates the efficacy and progress of the being.

Alcea
    white

Integral Offering
The surest road to realisation.

Alcea
    mauve-pink

Offering of the Emotions
Emotions put at the service of progress.

Alcea
    red

Offering of the Physical
Let the physical offer itself sincerely to the Divine and it will be transformed. This is proof of the resolution to liberate oneself from the ego.

Alcea
    light pink

Psychic Offering
It is the spontaneous attitude of the psychic in relation to the Divine.

Alcea
dark red

Offering of the Vital
The immediate result of conversion.

Alcea
white with mauve centre

Integral Offering of the Vital
An important stage towards transformation.

Offer yourself more and more,—all the consciousness, all that happens in it, all your work and action.

Alcea
red-violet

Offering of the Material Vital
Indispensable for conversion.

Alcea
very dark sombre red

Offering of the Most Material Vital
The first step towards transformation.

Alcea
dark purple, almost black

Offering of All Obscurities
Offer your obscurities sincerely to the Divine and you will be able to receive the Light.

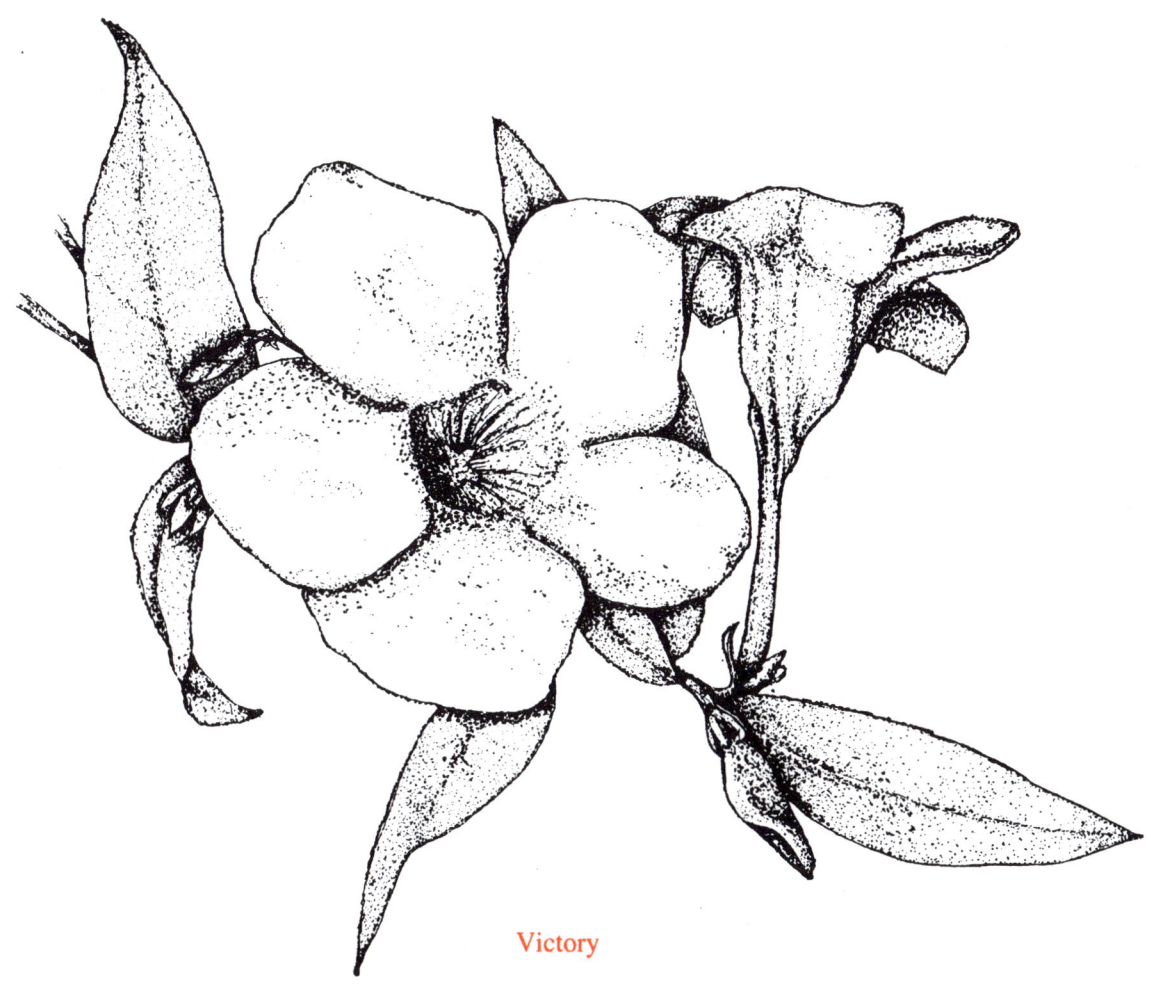

Victory

Allamanda cathartica
    medium to large golden-yellow
    funnel-shaped flower; heavy creeper

Victory
Will triumph over all obstacles!

Allamanda violacea
    Purple allamanda
    mauve-pink; spreading shrub

Victory in the Vital
In the vital even a little victory has great consequences.

More than one third of our existence is spent in sleeping, consequently, the time devoted to physical sleep well deserves our attention....

All the desires that have been repressed without being dissolved—and this dissociation can only be obtained after much sound and wide ranging analysis—seek satisfaction while the will is dormant.

And since desires are true dynamic centres of formation, they tend to organise, within and around us, the combination of circumstances that is most favourable to their satisfaction.

In this way the fruit of many efforts made by our conscious thought during the day can be destroyed in a few hours at night.

We must therefore learn to know our dreams, and first of all to distinguish between them, for they are very varied in nature and quality.

* * *

When at night we put a problem to ourselves, the problem goes to the higher regions of our being and in the morning we get the answer, the solution, because there, in the depths of our consciousness, we know things which we do not know in our external consciousness.

Aloe
Barbados aloe, True aloe
long stem bearing clusters of pendulous
light orange tubular flowers tinged
yellow and green; medicinal succulent

Dreams
*One can learn much by controlling
one's dreams*

Alpinia galanga
short spikes of white flowers with
prominent light yellow lip striped
maroon-red; rhizomatous plant

To Know what has to be Said
*Neither too many, nor too few
words—just what is needed.*

Alpinia speciosa (*Pl. 1*)
Shellflower, Porcelain ginger,
long racemes of light pink or white buds
tipped light red opening to show
prominent yellow lip streaked and spotted
red; large rhizomatous plant

Eloquence
*We know how to express ourselves in
a convincing way.*

Integral Immortality

Alternanthera
    Joseph's-coat
    small rounded heads of white papery flowers, dark maroon red leaves; erect groundcover

Integral Immortality
It is a promise! When will it be a material fact?

Amaranthus caudatus
    Love-lies-bleeding, Tassel flower
    terminal dense and branching sombre red spikes covered with tiny flowers, red stems and long reddish-green leaves; tall seasonal plant

Fearlessness in Action
Manifold, unfettered and fearless.

All truth and practice too strictly formulated becomes old and loses much, if not all, of its virtue; it must be constantly renovated by fresh streams of the spirit revivifying the dead or dying vehicle and changing it, if it is to acquire a new life. To be perpetually reborn is the condition of a material immortality.

Amaranthus 'Molten Fire'
    Amaranth
    maroon-red foliage with brilliant crimson upper leaves and clusters of tiny deep mauve flowers surrounding the stem; seasonal plant

Bravery
Fears nothing and knows how to hold tight against adversaries.

Anemone coronaria
>	Windflower, Lily-of-the-field
>	several colours of delicate rotate flowers;
>	low rhizomatous plant

> **Fragile Elegance**
> *Easily troubled, it needs to be treated with care.*

Anemopaegma chamberlaynii
>	small cream-white trumpet-shaped
>	flowers with light yellow corolla tube;
>	creeper

> **Voice of the Higher Mind**
> *In quest of Truth.*

Anemopaegma chamberlaynii (*Pl. 1*)
>	Yellow trumpet vine
>	large bright yellow trumpet-shaped
>	flower; heavy creeper

> **Joy of Victory**
> *It resembles victory without having victory's strength.*

Anethum graveolens
>	Dill
>	umbels of numerous tiny yellow flowers;
>	soft feathery leaves have pungent
>	fragrance; seasonal herb

> **Light in the Blood**
> *When the blood becomes receptive to the higher consciousness.*

If we are awake in the physical, we shall feel the light, power or Ananda flowing through the body, the limbs, nerves, blood, breath and, through the subtle body, effecting the most material cells making them conscious and blissful and we shall sense directly the Divine Power and Presence.

Divine Presence

Psychic Peace

Rising Star

Eloquence

Joy of Victory

Awakening of the Physical Mind

Greed for Money

Light

Beauty in Collective Simplicity

First Movement of the Riches towards the Divine

First Emergence of the Psychic in Matter   *The Divine Will Acting in the Subconscient*

Organisation of Action in Life

Never Tell a Lie   *The Guardian*

Will One with the Divine Will   *Aspiration*

Striving towards Wisdom   *Attentive Mind*

Peace in the Cells

Pl. 4

Observation — *Realisation of the Supramental Riches*

Matter under the Supramental Guidance — *Courage*

Radha's Consciousness

Logic in Thoughts

Spiritual Ascension

Intuitive Knowledge

Sweetness

Pl. 6

Mental Purity   *Fairy Freshness*

Accurate Perception

Opening of the Higher Vital to the Light   *No Quarrels*

Divine Love Governing the World

Divine Love Spreading over the World

Result of Harmonious Organisation

Spiritual Power of Healing

There is a sovereign royalty in taking no thought for oneself. To have needs is to assert a weakness; to claim something proves that we lack what we claim. To desire is to be impotent; it is to recognise our limitations and confess our incapacity to overcome them. If only from the point of view of a legitimate pride, man should be noble enough to renounce desire.

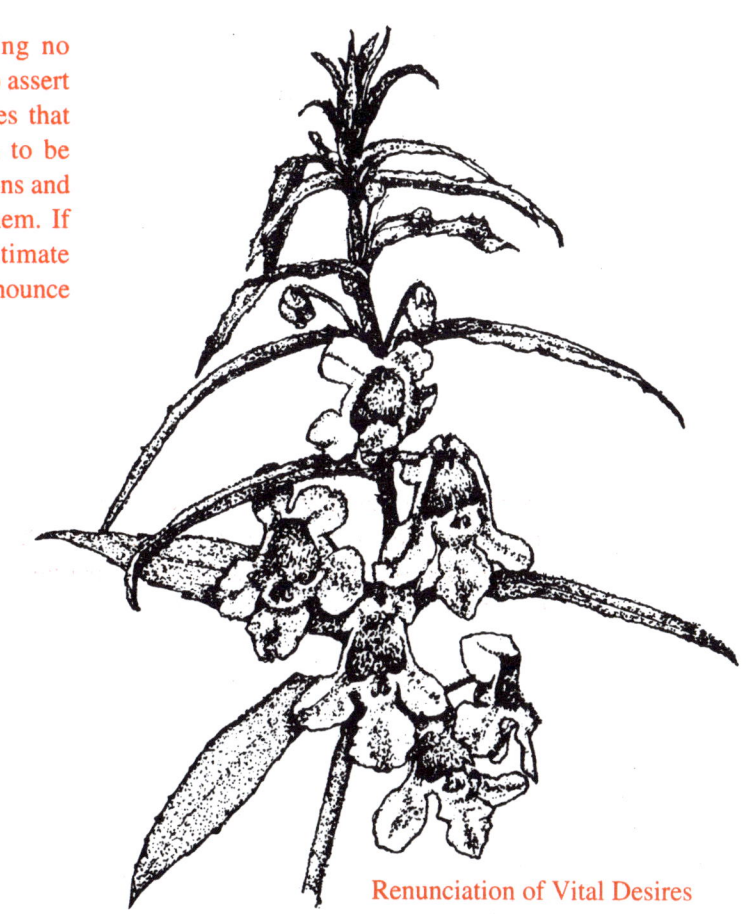

Renunciation of Vital Desires

Angelonia salicarifolia
> very small purple two-lipped cup-shaped flowers studding the erect stems, aromatic leaves when bruised; semi-herbaceous perennial

Renunciation of Vital Desires
It has understood the emptiness of desire.

Angelonia
> white with pale purple lines and dots

Renunciation of Emotional Desires
Indispensable for transformation.

Anemopaegma carrerense
> small cream-white trumpet-shaped flowers with light yellow corolla tube; creeper

Voice of the Higher Mind
In quest of Truth.

Angelonia
> white

Integral Renunciation of Vital Desires
An indispensable condition for true progress.

Anthocephalus cadamba (*Pl. 9*)
    Kadam tree
    striking mildly fragrant orange-yellow
    ball-shaped flowers with white stigmas;
    tree

Supramental Sun
*We aspire that its rays may enlighten
and transform us.*

There is a force of purity, not the purity of the moralist, but an essential purity of spirit, in the very substance of the being. When that comes, then sex waves either cannot approach or they pass without imparting any impulse, without touching anywhere.

Anthurium andreanum
    Flamingo lily
    firm waxy deep red spathe and prominent
    bright red spadix; rhizomatous foliage
    plant.

Mastery of Sex
Instead of being dominated by the sexual impulses, they must be put under the domination of the highest will.

Anthurium andreanum
    white

Purified Sex Centre
Is transformed into a force for progress.

Anthurium andreanum (*Pl. 11*)
    pink

Sex Centre Aspiring to Be Purified
The awakening of the consciousness to a higher life.

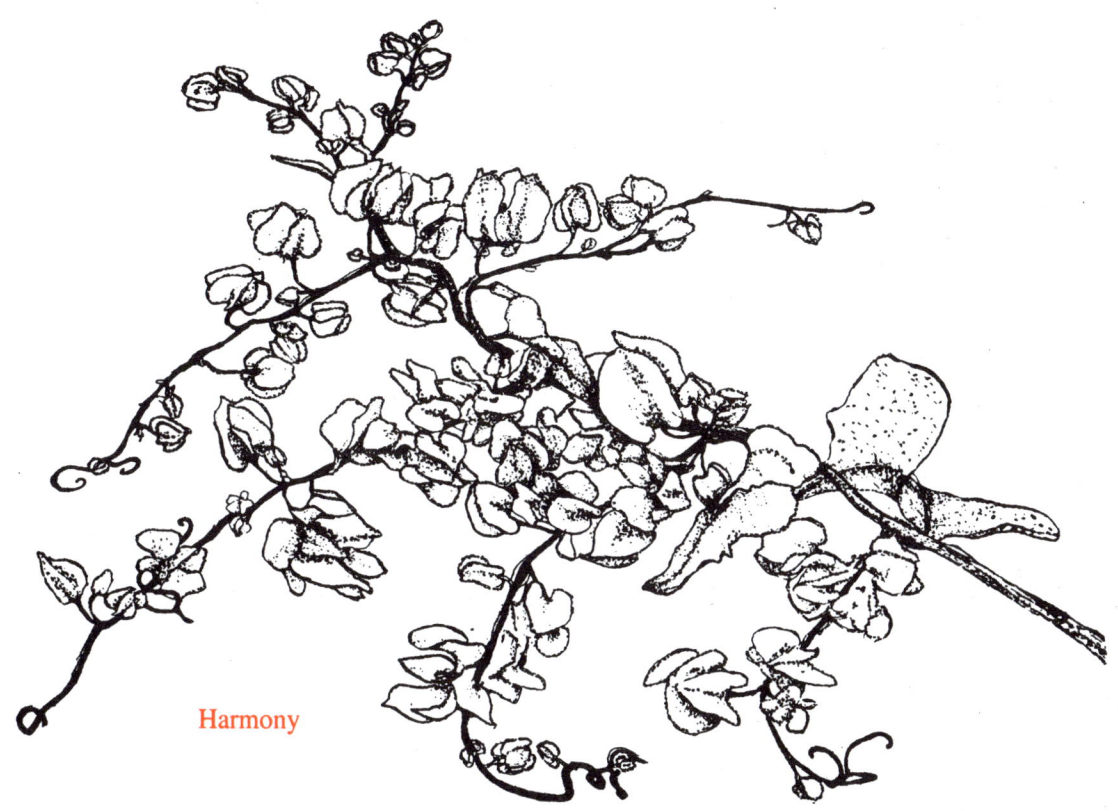

Harmony

Antigonon
    Coral vine, Corallita
    long trailing sprays with small delicate
    lantern-shaped flowers in several colours;
    creeper

Harmony
Let us strive that the day may come when this will be the means and the goal.

Antigonon
    deep pink

Harmony in the Material Vital
No disputes, no quarrels—the sweetness of a life without clashes.

Antigonon
    bright pink

Harmony in the Vital
To harmonise the vital is a psychological masterpiece; happy is the one who accomplishes it.

Antigonon 'Album'
    white

Integral Harmony
Harmony between things, harmony between persons, harmony of circumstances and above all, harmony of all aspirations directed towards the Supreme Truth.

Antirrhinum
: Snapdragon
several colours of long erect spikes of velvety two-lipped tubular flowers; seasonal plant

Power of Expression
It is the power to manifest that which is latent.

Antirrhinum
: all multi-coloured flowers

Power of Manifold Expression
The result of suppleness and plasticity.

Antirrhinum
: red

Power of Physical Expression
One of the benefits of conversion.

Antirrhinum
: purple to violet

Power of Vital Expression
Is useful only when the vital is converted.

Antirrhinum
: white with yellow throat

Power of Integral Expression
Nothing is too difficult for it to say.

Antirrhinum
: yellow

Power of Mental Expression
Has no value unless it is at the service of the Divine.

Antirrhinum
: pink

Power of Psychic Expression
The psychic obtains its power of expression when it governs the whole being.

Antirrhinum 'Butterfly hybrid'
: several colours of open-throated flowers

Progressive Expression
What you cannot say today, you will know how to say tomorrow!

Aphelandra tetragona
: short spikes of tubular pointed orange-red flowers; shrub

Sharp Tongue
Unhappily too frequent!

Arctotis
: Blue-eyed African daisy
several colours of delicate compositae flowers; seasonal plant

Cheerful Endeavour
The joy that one finds in the effort towards the Divine.

Areca catechu
: Betel-nut palm
branching spikes of tiny fragrant white flowers; palm tree

Steadfast Vitality
The vitality that depends on integral consecration.

Aristolochia elegans
: Calico flower
cream-white cup-shaped flower heavily blotched maroon with dark maroon centre, recurved and inflated corolla tube; creeper

Inspiration
Brings its manifold gifts to one who knows how to receive them.

Aristolochia ringens
: Pelican flower
greenish-yellow flower with dark purple veins, one petal hood-shaped and one long and trailing

Lasting Inspiration
Waits patiently to be received.

Oft inspiration with her lightning feet,
A sudden messenger from the all-seeing tops,
Traversed the soundless corridors of his mind
Bringing her rhythmic sense of hidden things.

Clear Mind

Artabotrys
   Ylang-Ylang
   very fragrant greenish-yellow solitary
   flowers with thick leaf-like petals; creeper

Clear Mind
The first step on the road to conversion.

Artabotrys
   clusters of small rounded fragrant yellow fruits

Reason
An excellent instrument when at the service of the Divine.

Asclepias curassavica
> Butterfly weed
> terminal umbels of small yellow flowers, each with prominent central yellow crown; low shrub

Response of the Mind to the Supramental Light
Represents an important step towards realisation.

Asclepias curassavica
> scarlet-red flowers

Response of the Physical Mind to the Supramental Light
The physical mind eager to understand and be transformed.

When a thought is expressed in speech, the vibration of the sound has a considerable power to bring the most material substance into contact with the thought, thus giving it a concrete and effective reality. That is why one must never speak ill of people or things or say things which go against the progress of the divine realisation in the world. This is an absolute general rule. And yet it has one exception. You should not criticise anything unless at the same time you have the conscious power and active will to dissolve or transform the movements or things you criticise. For this conscious power and active will have the capacity of infusing Matter with the possibility to react and refuse the bad vibration and ultimately to correct it so that it becomes impossible for it to go on expressing itself on the physical plane.

Asparagus densiflorus (*Pl. 13*)
> Sprenger asparagus
> tiny white fragrant (spiritual smell) starlike flowers in short spikes; rhizomatous plant with pendulous sprays of delicate foliage

Spiritual Speech
All-powerful in its simplicity.

Asparagus racemosus
> delicate snowy clusters of tiny fragrant starlike flowers; creeper with small leaf-like foliage (cladodes)

Beauty Arising from Consecration
Be sincere and absolute in your consecration to the Divine and your life will become harmonious and beautiful.

Sincerity means to lift all the movements of the being to the level of the highest consciousness and realisation already attained.

* * *

Sincerity in the vital is the most difficult to have and the most needful.

Simple Sincerity

Aster amellus
    Perennial aster
    clusters of single compositae flowers with yellow centre; mauve-pink with yellow centre, suckering plant

Emotional Sincerity
Does not try to travesty the emotions.

Aster amellus
    white with yellow centre

Simple Sincerity
The beginning of all progress.

Aster amellus
    lavender-blue with yellow centre

Sincerity in the Vital
The sure road to realisation.

It is not possible to enter utterly into the spiritual truth of the Eternal and Infinite if we have not the faith and courage to trust ourselves into the hands of the Lord of all things and the Friend of all creatures and leave utterly behind us our mental limits and measures.

Trust in the Divine

Asystasia dalzelliana
> short racemes of small pale violet salverform flowers with white lines; low herbaceous plant

Aspiration for Trust in the Divine
An intense need for that immutable peace given by the certitude of the Divine Grace.

Asystasia
> several colours of larger flowers; countryside herbaceous rambler

Trust in the Divine
Most indispensable for the impulsive vital.

Asystasia
> white

Integral Trust in the Divine
The trust that gives the true support to life.

Asystasia
> cream-yellow

Mental Trust in the Divine
Firm and definite, it does not argue.

Asystasia
white, marked mauve on throat

Trust of the Emotive Vital in the Divine
Smiling and sweet, it is sheltered from grief.

Asystasia
pale yellow, marked light mauve on throat

Trust in the Vital Mind for the Divine
Opens itself to the Divine Consciousness without trying to hide anything.

Asystasia
predominantly lavender shades

Vital Trust in the Divine
Full of courage and energy, it fears nothing.

Atalantia monophylla
clusters of small fragrant white star-shaped flowers; tree

Absence of Desire
Fragrant and luminous, it expresses at the same time peace and joy.

Averrhoa carambola
Carambola
compact clusters of small fragrant rose-pink bell-shaped flowers with red calyces; fruit tree

Organised Team-Work
Each in his place and all together.

We want an organisation which is the expression of a higher consciousness working to manifest the truth of the future.

Spiritual Atmosphere

Azadirachta indica
    Neem, Margosa
    airy clusters of tiny fragrant white
    star-shaped flowers; tree with medicinal
    value

Spiritual Atmosphere
Light, fluid, clear, transparent—and so clean!

A spiritual atmosphere is more important than outer conditions; if one can get that and also create one's own spiritual air to breathe in and live in it, that is the true condition of progress.

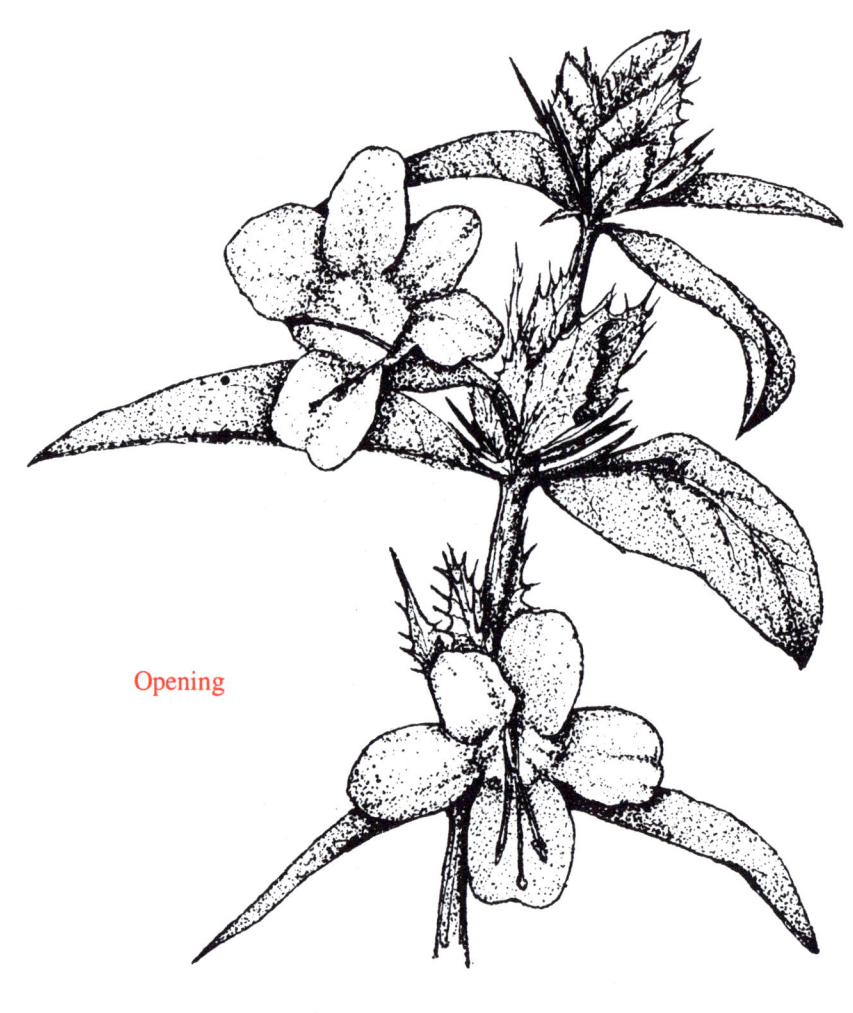

Opening

Barleria
    several colours of small trumpet-shaped flowers with prominent bracts; shrub

Opening
The help is constant on all levels; it is for us to know how to benefit from it.

Barleria
    white

Integral Opening of the Being towards the Divine
The first step of the ascent.

The opening is the same for all. It begins with an opening of mind and heart, then of the vital proper—when it reaches the lower vital and the physical the opening is complete. But with the opening there must be the full self-giving to what comes down, which is the condition of the complete change.

Barleria
white with lavender stripes

Emotional Opening
The progress of the emotions towards the Divine.

Barleria
pink

Opening of the Emotive Vital
One of the first steps on the way to transformation.

Barleria
yellow

Mental Opening
The first step of the mind towards transformation.

Baleria
lavender-blue

Elegance in the Emotions
Delicate and refined, does not permit itself any vulgarity.

The perfect supramental action will not follow any single principle or limited rule. . . . It will proceed by a spontaneous outflowing from the summits in the totality of an illumined and uplifted being, will and knowledge and not by the selected, calculated and standardised action which is all that the intellectual reason or ethical will can achieve.

Barringtonia asiatica (*Pl. 10*)
Mudilla
large fragrant white flower with
innumerable white stamens tinged pink;
tree

Supramental Action
An action that is not exclusive but total.

Bauhinia tomentosa
St. Thomas tree
pendulous light yellow elongated
cup-shaped flower; shrub

Gold
Should only be used in the service of the Divine.

Bauhinia acuminata
Dwarf white bauhinia
white open cup-shaped flower with
conspicuous golden pollen; shrub

Purified Gold
Placed at the service of the Divine it is purified.

Bauhinia purpurea
Butterfly tree, Orchid tree
light pink to red-violet rotate flowers with
long recurved stamens; tree

Stability in the Vital
One of the important results of conversion.

Beaumontia jerdoniana (*Pl. 11*)
Herald's trumpet
large mildly fragrant white open
bell-shaped flower; heavy creeper

Unselfishness
Deeply open so as not to refuse anything.

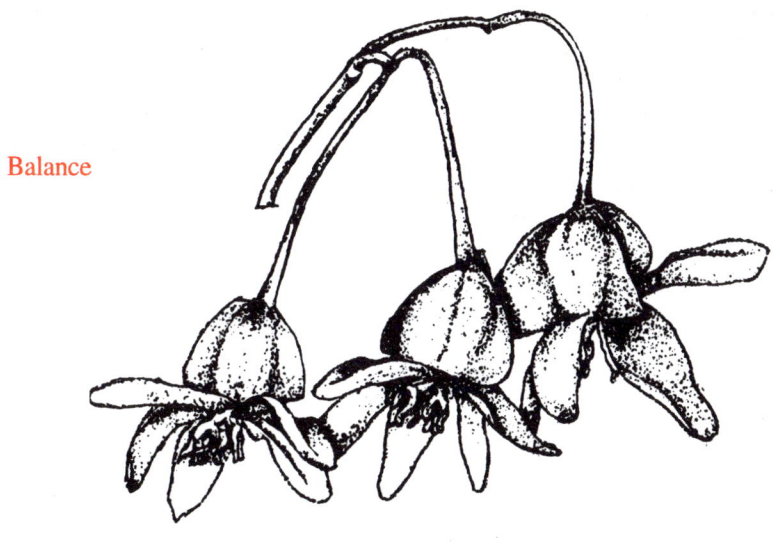

Balance

Begonia
several colours of small waxy flowers in delicately balanced cymes; succulent with variously coloured leaves

Balance
Each seeks one's own balance in order to stabilise oneself.

Begonia
white

Integral Balance
It multiplies so as not to be static.

Begonia
yellow

Mental Balance
Mind governed by reason.

Begonia
pink

Psychic Balance
Under the psychic influence all activities become balanced.

The maximum a human being can attain just now is an equilibrium which is not progressive. He may attain perhaps a static equilibrium but all that is static can be broken for lack of progress. . . .

Perfection will be attained in the individual, the collectivity, on the earth and in the universe, when, at every moment, the receptivity will be equal in quality and quantity to the Force which wants to manifest.

That is the supreme equilibrium.

Begonia
    large double flowers in several colours

Perfect Balance
One of the most important conditions of a growing peace.

Begonia
    white, large double

Perfect Integral Balance
One is ready for transformation.

Begonia
    yellow, large double

Perfect Mental Balance
Indispensable for facing the difficulties of life.

Begonia
    pink. large double

Perfect Psychic Balance
On the way to transformation.

Belamcanda chinensis
    Leopard flower
    scapes bearing orange rotate flowers with scarlet spots and erect stamens; bulbous plant

Attachment to the Divine
Wraps itself around the Divine and finds all its support in Him so as to be sure of never leaving Him.

Live constantly in the presence of the Divine; live in the feeling that it is this presence which moves you and is doing everything you do.

Thirst for Perfection

We thirst for perfection. Not this human perfection which is a perfection of the ego and bars the way to the divine perfection. But that one perfection which has the power to manifest upon earth the Eternal Truth.

Beleperone guttata, Justicia brandegena
    Mexican shrimp plant
    small white tubular labiate flowers borne
    beneath russet or greenish-yellow showy
    bracts; low rambling shrub

Thirst for Perfection
Constant and manifold aspiration.

Berrya cordifolia
: clusters of green to brown papery winged fruits; tree

Liberation in the Vital
Another result of conversion.

Bignonia purpurea
: clusters of rose-purple trumpet-shaped flowers; creeper

Vital Opening
The vital is ready to receive the Divine Influence.

Billbergia pyramidalis
: Summer torch
bright red inflorescence resembling a large candle formed of coloured bracts and narrow dark red to violet tubular flowers; perennial succulent

Control
Control over the lower impulses is the first step towards realisation.

When we begin to live the spiritual life, a reversal of consciousness takes place which is for us the proof that we have entered the spiritual life; well, another reversal of consciousness occurs when one enters the supramental world.

Besides, perhaps each time that a new world opens up, there will again be a new reversal of this kind. Thus even our spiritual life—which is such a total reversal in relation to ordinary life—is and appears to be, in relation to the supramental consciousness, the supramental realisation, something so totally different that the values of the two are almost opposite.

Bixa orellana (*Pl. 10*)
: Annatto, Lipstick tree
pink, lavender-pink or white rotate flowers with a centre of short golden stamens; tree

The New World
The result of transformation.

Bombax ceiba
: Red silk-cotton tree
fairly large deep pink to red cup-shaped flower with thick petals and innumerable stamens; tree

Solid Steadfastness in the Material Consciousness
The material consciousness has a firm and solid steadfastness.

Bougainvillea
: clusters of colourful showy bracts arranged in groups of three, each bract enclosing a very small cream-white flower; heavy thorny creeper

Protection
Let us give ourselves entirely and sincerely to the Divine and we shall enjoy His protection.

When we are in close contact with the Divine, a protection can come which helps or directly guides or moves us; it does not throw aside all difficulties, sufferings or dangers, but it carries us through them and out of them—except where for a special purpose there is need of the opposite.

Bougainvillea 'Trinidad'
: very pale lavender

Discreet Protection
Does its work discreetly without drawing attention.

Bougainvillea
: light lavender-pink

Emotional Protection
Surrender to the Divine is the best emotional protection.

Bougainvillea
: white

Integral Protection
That which can be given only by the Divine.

Bougainvillea 'Mary Palmer'
: two or more different coloured bracts, usually white and deep pink

Manifold Protection
A protection working not only on life as a whole but on each of its details.

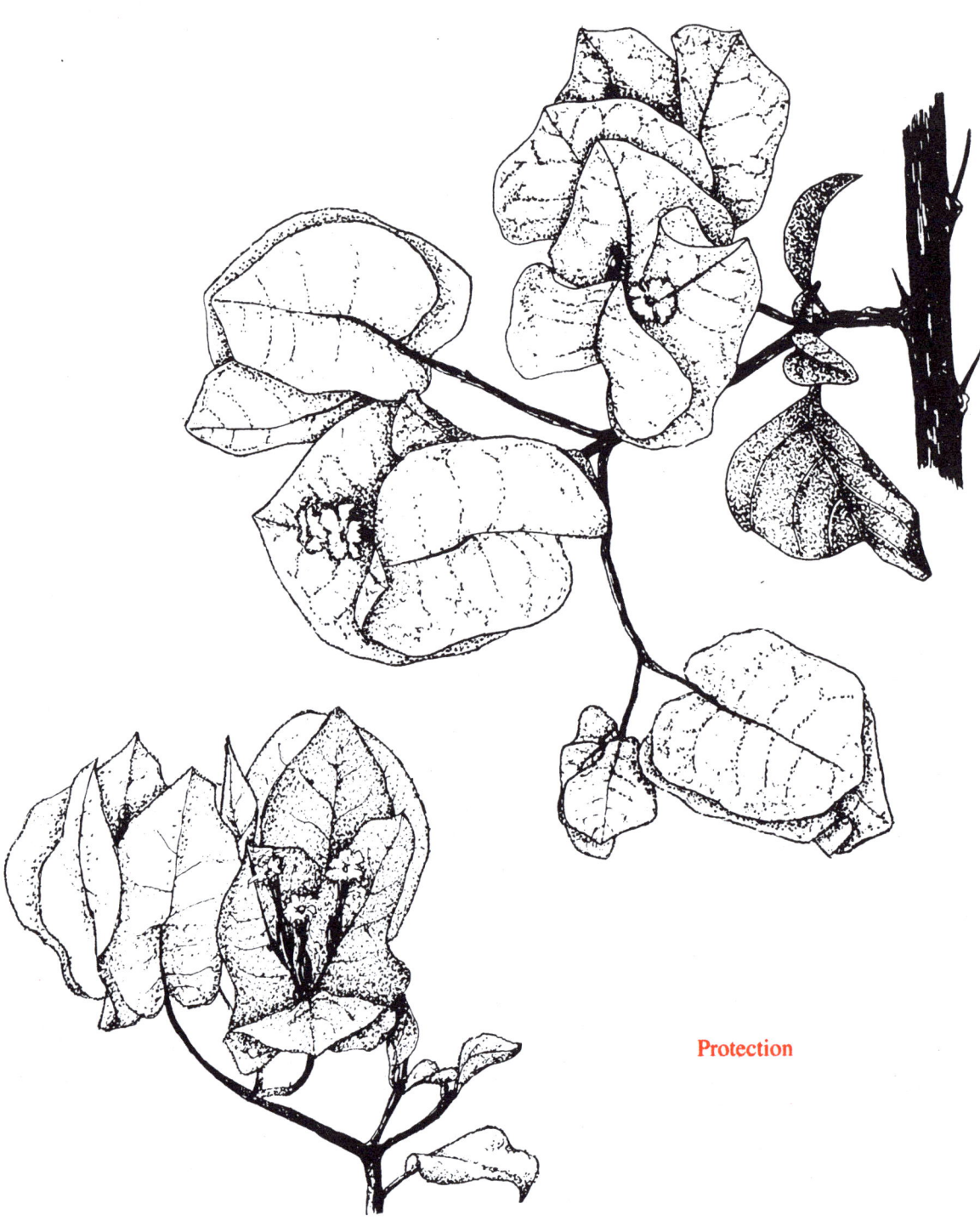

Protection

Bougainvillea
magenta red

Physical Protection
Is possible only with a total surrender to the Divine and the absence of all desire.

Bougainvillea
violet

Vital Protection
Surrender to the Divine is the best vital protection.

Bougainvillea
pink

Psychic Protection
The protection resulting from surrender to the Divine.

Bougainvillea 'Blondie'
subtle shadings of orange, gold and pink

Triple Protection
Protection in the mind, the vital and the physical.

Bougainvillea
shades of yellow and gold

Protection of the Gods
Luminous and clear-visioned.

Bougainvillea 'Mahara'
fully double with small magenta bracts

Attempt towards Protection
Irregular efforts are not always effective.

Brassaia actinophylla
Queensland umbrella tree
long spikes bearing groups of very small solid red ball-shaped flowers; shrub-like tree

Organised Material Energy
Well-arranged, compact and methodical, it is powerful by its organisation.

One's entire physical activity should be organised to help the body to grow in balance and strength and beauty.

The consent of all the being is necesary for the divine change, and it is the completeness and fullness of the constent that constitutes the integral surrender. But the consent of the lower vital must not be only a mental profession or a passing emotional adhesion; it must translate itself into an abiding attitude and a persistent and consistent action.

Consent of the Vital

Browallia
    Amethyst flower
    clusters of delicate light blue salverform flowers; seasonal plant

Consent of the Vital
Amiable, smiling, ever ready for action—with a great goodwill.

Browallia
    pale lilac, lined white

Enthusiastic Vital Consent
Here all the resources of its enthusiasm are put at the service of its adhesion.

Brownea coccinea (*Pl. 8*)
    Scarlet flame bean
    large striking ball-like inflorescence
    formed of numerous pendulous
    orange-red flowers; tree

Divine Love Governing the World
A beautiful and happy world for which we all aspire.

Brugmansia suaveolens
    pendulous large double white funnelform
    flowers; tree-like shrub

Perfect Tapasya
That which will reach its goal.

Brunfelsia americana
    Lady-of-the-night
    small clusters of very fragrant cream-white
    to pale yellow salverform flowers with
    long corolla tube; shrub

Resolution
Nothing can stop its development.

Brunfelsia australis
    Yesterday-today-and-tomorrow
    short fragrant salverform flower, each
    flower changing from purple to pale
    lavender to white

Refinement of Emotions
With progress even the emotions become refined.

Buddleja
    Butterfly bush
    several colours of dense terminal spikes
    bearing tiny fragrant salverform flowers;
    shrub

Refinement
Grossness is gradually eliminated from the being.

Butea monosperma
    Flame-of-the-forest
    dense racemes of medium-sized bright
    red-orange papilionaceous flowers; tree

Beginning of the Supramental Realisation
With its charming beauty it is the herald of victory.

Cactus
    all colours and forms of cactus flowers

Riches
It is the Divine to whom all riches belong; it is the Divine who lends them to living beings, and it is to Him that they must naturally return.

Caesalpinia coriaria (*Pl. 6*)
    Divi divi
    clusters of very small fragrant light
    yellow star-shaped flowers; tree

Intuitive Knowledge
Innumerable and vast for exploration, it is pure and fragrant.

Caladium
: Angel wings
mildly fragrant white spadix partly ensheathed by a greenish-white spathe; bulbous plant with large decorative arrowhead leaves

Transformed Sex Centre
Has no more desires and offers itself to the Divine.

Calandrinia grandiflora
: Rock purslane
small cymes of delicate magenta flowers; edible seasonal or perennial herbaceous plant

Material Power to Heal
Demands a great sincerity in one's goodwill.

The most material form [of endurance] is perseverance. Unless you are resolved to begin the same thing over again a thousand times if need be.... You know, people come to me in despair, "But I thought it was done and now I must begin again!" And if they are told, "But that's nothing, you will probably have to begin again a hundred times, two hundred times, a thousand times; you take one step forward and think you are secure, but there will always be something to bring back the same difficulty a little farther on. You think you have solved the problem, you must solve it yet once again; it will turn up again looking just a little different, but it will be the same problem."

Calendula officinalis
: Pot marigold
orange or yellow compositae flowers; low seasonal plant

Perseverance
The decision to go to the very end.

Calliandra falcata (*Pl. 4*)
: Powderpuff bush
various colours and sizes of powderpuff flowers; shrub

Striving towards Wisdom
A bit of wisdom is welcome.

Calliandra portoricensis
: large white flower

Striving towards Integral Wisdom
Like everything that belongs to creation, wisdom is progressive.

Calliandra marginata
: Large or small red flower

Wisdom in the Physical Mind
A first step towards the Supramental Manifestation upon earth.

Joy of Vegetal Nature in Answer to the New Light

The Force is here.
   Rejoice, O you who are waiting and hoping: the new manifestation is sure, the new manifestation is at hand.
The Force is here.
   All nature exults and sings in gladness, all nature is at a festival: *The Force is here.*

Callistemon
 Bottlebrush
 red bottlebrush flowers; tree

Joy of Vegetal Nature in Answer to the New Light
It dances with joy and laughs happily.

<blockquote>
Someone is in front of me and I am looking at him; I look into his eyes. And if this person is sincere or "transparent", through his eyes I go down and I see his soul—clearly. But—this is precisely the experience—when I look at somebody and see a little cloud, then I continue, I see a screen, and then sometimes it is a wall, and afterwards it is something quite black; and all this must be crossed, and holes bored in order to go through . . . of such a person I can immediately say that he is not sincere. But I can also say, figuratively, that he is not transparent.
</blockquote>

Callistephus chinensis
    China aster, Annual aster
    erect clusters of semi-double to double
    compositae flowers in many colours;
    seasonal plant

Transparency
Can come only as a result of perfect sincerity.

Callistephus
    semi-double, white with yellow centre

Illumined Transparency
An effect of the Divine Grace.

Callistephus
    double, white with yellow centre

Integral Transparency
The result of perfect goodwill and sincerity.

Callistephus
    semi-double, pink

Psychic Transparency
Manifests fully only when the psychic is perfectly developed.

Callistephus
fully double, pink

Supramentalised Psychic Activity
Luminous, manifold, balanced, it meets all needs.

Callistephus
fully double, violet

Supramentalised Vital Transparency
One of the results of conversion.

Callistephus
semi-double, red

Transparency in the Physical
The physical prepares itself for transformation.

Callistephus
semi-double, very light mauve

Transparency of the Emotive Vital
At once the condition and the result of the abolition of the ego.

Callistephus
semi-double, deep mauve to violet

Vital Transparency
Indispensable to conversion.

… like something which is not opaque or does not distort; something clear, transparent, sincere, which does not obstruct.

Transparency

Calluna vulgaris
> Heather, Scotch heather
> dense branching clusters of tiny fragrant rose-pink flowers; low countryside shrub

Blossoming of Nature
Abundant and solid, nothing can stop its growth.

Calonyction alba
> Moonflower
> large fragrant white salverform flower; creeper

Entire Self-Giving
Fully open, clear and pure.

Calophyllum inophyllum
> Alexandrian Laurel, Indian Laurel
> branching racemes of fragrant white rotate flowers with numerous yellow stamens; tree

Peace in the Physical
To want what God wills is its best condition.

Calotropis (*Pl. 5*)
> Mudar, Crown plant, Bowstring hemp
> pale lavender star-shaped flower with a sturdy crown at the centre; shrub

Courage
Bold, it faces all dangers.

Calotropis
> white flower

Integral Courage
Whatever the domain, whatever the danger, the attitude remains the same—calm and assured.

Camellia japonica
> medium to large formal sessile flowers in several colours; shrub

Static Beauty
Transfixed in an immutable beauty.

Campanula medium
> Canterbury bells
> open racemes of blue bell-shaped flowers; herbaceous perennial

Joy's Call
It is modest and rarely makes itself heard.

Cananga odorata (*Pl. 7*)
> Ylang Ylang
> very fragrant pale yellow flower with long twisted petals; tree

Accurate Perception
A perception that does not deform the Truth.

Canna indica (*Pl. 14*)
: Indian shot
racemes of small glowing red flowers with slender petals; rhizomatous plant

Friendship with the Divine
Delicate, attentive and faithful, always ready to respond to the smallest appeal.

Canna indica
: several colours of slightly larger flowers

Progressive Friendship with the Divine
As we progress and purify ourselves of our egoism, our friendship with the Divine becomes clearer and more conscious.

Canna
: cream-white with pink specks towards orange centre

Ananda in the Centres
This will be one of the benefits resulting from physical conversion.

Canna
: yellow, spotted or blotched red

Connection between the Light and the Physical
Awakens to the necessity of growth and blossoming.

Canna indica
: bright yellow flowers

Supramental Friendship with the Divine
Luminous and light, always smiling.

Canna
: racemes of large showy multi-coloured flowers with soft petals

Complexity of the Centres
Responds to several influences at a time.

Canna
: cream-white with red centre

Ananda in the Physical Body
Purified of all desire and all repulsion, with perfect equality and surrender, the physical body is ready to enjoy the Divine Ananda.

Canna
: bicoloured, orange and red

Connection between the Supermind and the Physical
On the way to transformation, it is generous and powerful.

Complexity of the Centres

Our hidden centres of celestial force
Open like flowers to a heavenly atmosphere;
Mind pauses thrilled with the supernal Ray,
And even the transient body then can feel
Ideal love and flawless hapiness
And laughter of the heart's sweetness and delight
Freed from the rude and tragic hold of Time,
And beauty and the rhythmic feet of the hours.

Canna
    deep rose-pink

Emotive Centre
Vibrant and sensitive, it needs to be controlled.

Canna
    predominantly orange shades

Future Supramental Centre
What is involved in Nature will evolve and become manifest.

Canna
    luminous yellow shades

Illumined Mind Centre
In the peace that comes from the perfect light.

Canna
    light yellow shades

Intuitive Mind Centre
The activity of correct perception.

Canna
    red

Physical Centre
Occupied mainly with material things, it likes to have an ordered life.

Canna
    pink

Psychic Centre
Luminous and calm, it is created to govern the human being.

Canna
    dark red

Vital Centre
Passionate and strong, it demands control.

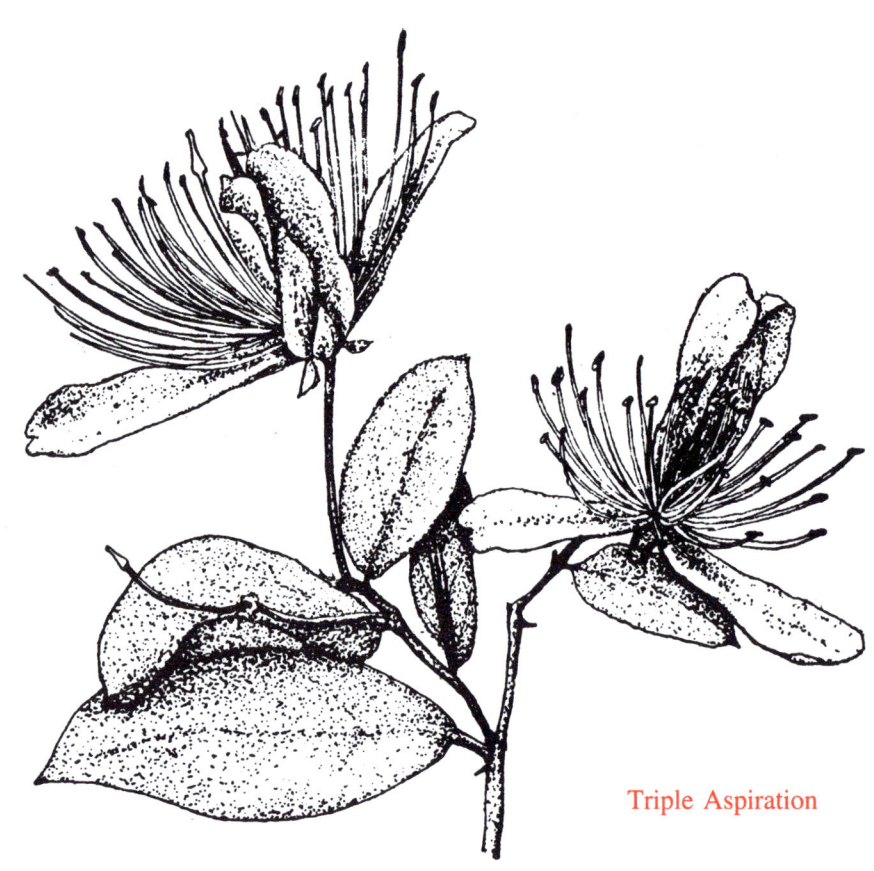

Triple Aspiration

Capparis brevispina
    Thorn straggler
    medium-sized white flowers with
    numerous stamens and a yellow patch on
    two petals; thorny rambler or shrub

Triple Aspiration
Recognising their Master, love, life,
and light respond to Sachchidananda.

O Thou, sole Reality, Light of our light and Life of our life, Love supreme, Saviour of the world, grant that more and more I may be perfectly awakened to the awareness of Thy constant presence.

> Intolerant of imperfection, she [Mahakali] deals roughly with all in man that is unwilling and she is severe to all that is obstinately ignorant and obscure; her wrath is immediate and dire against treachery and falsehood and malignity, ill-will is smitten at once by her scourge... If her anger is dreadful to the hostile and the vehemence of her pressure painful to the weak and timid, she is loved and worshipped by the great, the strong and the noble; for they feel that her blows beat what is rebellious in their material into strength and perfect truth.

Capsicum annuum
> Chilly pepper
> small white or purple star-shaped flowers
> and spicy fruits; seasonal condiment

A Whipping
A little brutal, but useful sometimes.

Carlina acaulis
> Carline thistle
> white or red compositae flower and everlasting silky seed pod; countryside thorny perennial

Incorruptible Faithfulness
Nothing can turn you away from the duty you have chosen.

Grant that we may be faithful to Thee utterly and for ever
We would be completely under Thy influence to the exclusion of every other.
Grant that we may never forget to own towards Thee a deep, an intense gratitude.

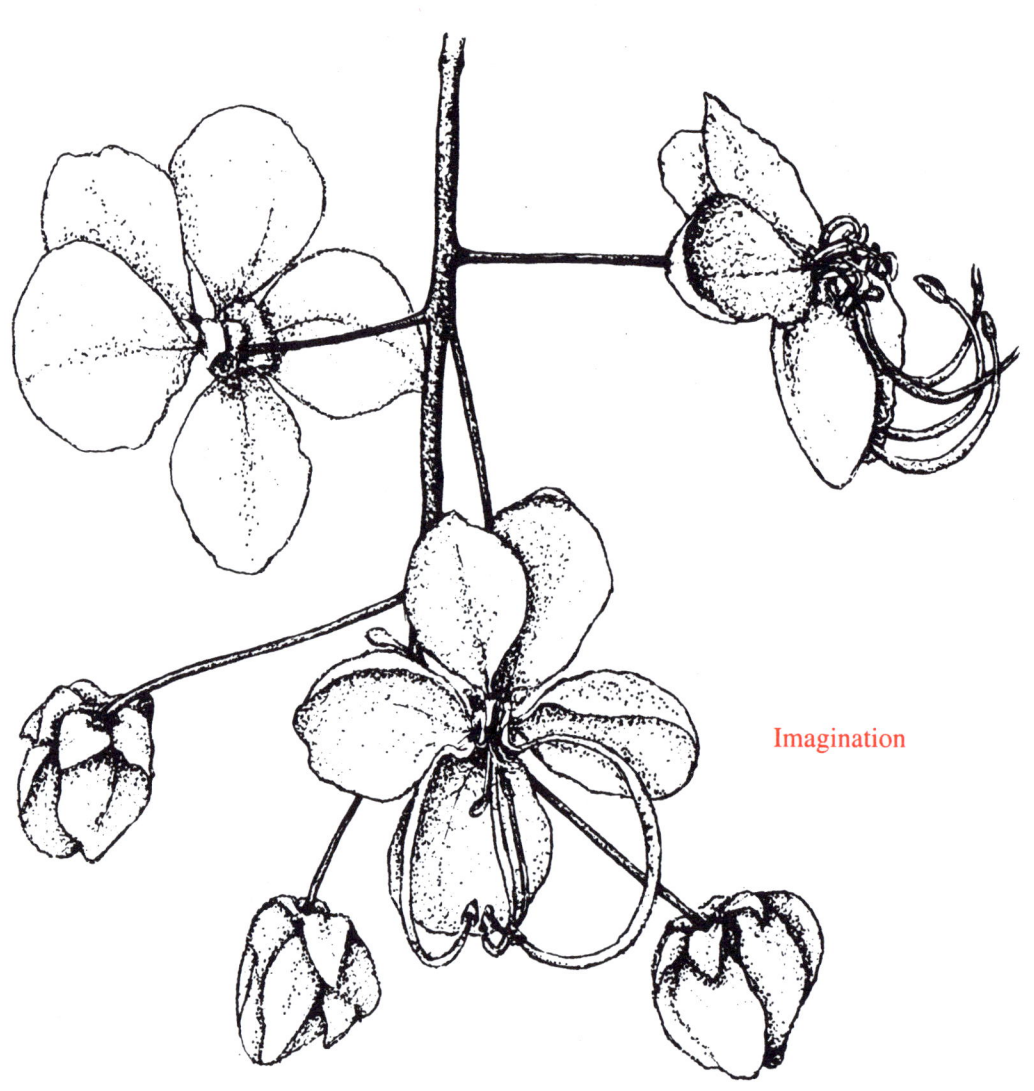

Imagination

Cassia alata
    Candlestick senna, Ringworm cassia candelabra spikes of ochre bracts and half-hidden yellow flowers; shrub

Idea
Essential for all organisers, on its quality depends the quality of the organisation.

Cassia fistula
    Golden shower tree, Indian laburnum long pendulous clusters of fragrant canary-yellow rotate flowers; tree

Imagination
Abundant and varied, may be charming, but must not be substituted for Truth.

Cassia javanica
>   Apple-blossom cassia, Java cassia
>   pendulous clusters of fragrant rose-pink flowers turning white
>
>   **Psychic Work**
>   *A work governed by harmony.*

Cassia roxburghii
>   Red cassia
>   clusters of terracotta to pink flowers
>
>   **Refinement of Sensations**
>   *Manifold, complex, perceiving the variety of details.*

Cassia (*Pl. 4*)
>   other yellow-flowered Cassias; tree or shrub
>
>   **Attentive Mind**
>   *The mind attains its full utility when it knows how to listen to the higher inspiration.*

A new humanity means for us the appearance, the development of a type or race of mental beings.... It would be possessed already of what could be called a mind of light, a mind capable of living in the truth, capable of being truth-conscious and manifesting in its life a direct in place of an indirect knowledge.

Castanospermum australe
>   Moreton bay chestnut
>   large sters of reddish-orange flowers; tree
>
>   **Mind of Light Acting in Matter**
>   *A powerful aid to progress.*

Catesbaea spinosa
>   Lily thorn
>   pendulous lemon-yellow funnel-shaped flower; shrub
>
>   **Certitude of Victory**
>   *It is not noisy, but it is sure.*

Catharanthus
 Madagascar periwinkle, Rose periwinkle several colours of starlike flowers with rounded petals and narrow corolla tube; countryside perennial

Progress
The reason why we are on earth.

Progress

Catharanthus
 light pink with red centre

Constant Progress in Matter
The result of an ardent aspiration.

Catharanthus
 light pink-violet, streaked white

Uninterrupted but Spasmodic Progress
Now here, now there, it seems very impulsive!

Catharanthus
 light pink-violet

Vital Progress
Organisation around the Divine Will and progressive surrender to this Will.

Catharanthus
 white

Integral Progress
Cannot be satisfied except by integrality, it is the best way of progressing quickly.

Catharanthus
white with red centre

Integral Progress in Matter
Matter awakens to consciousness.

Catharanthus
white with violet centre

Integral Progress in the Vital
The vital consents to be purified.

When the resolution has been taken, when you have decided that the whole of your life shall be given to the Divine, you have still at every moment to remember it and carry it out in all the details of your existence. You must feel at every step that you belong to the Divine; you must have the constant experience that, in whatever you think or do, it is always the Divine Consciousness that is acting through you. You have no longer anything that you can call your own; you feel everything as coming from the Divine, and you have to offer it back to its source.

Cattleya
Orchid
several colours of large showy exquisite orchids with delicately frilled lips; epiphyte

Attachment to the Divine
Wraps itself around the Divine and finds all its support in Him so as to be sure of never leaving Him.

Cattleya
lavender-pink fragrant flower with lime-green throat marked magenta

Beauty of the Attachment to the Divine
When the physical world will manifest the divine splendour, all will become marvellous.

Cattleya
large white flower

The Aim of Existence Is Realised
Exists only by and for the Divine.

Ceiba pentandra
Kapok tree, White silk-cotton tree
clusters of cream-white rotate flowers with velvety petals; tree

Material Enterprises
Many projects, many attempts, many constructions!

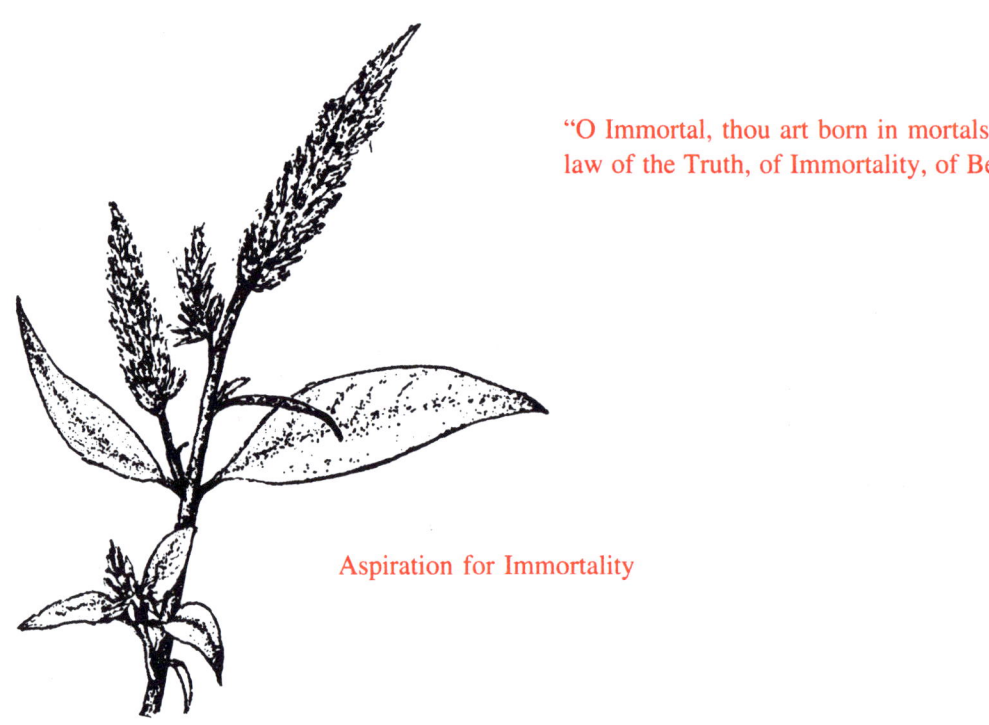

"O Immortal, thou art born in mortals in the law of the Truth, of Immortality, of Beauty."

Aspiration for Immortality

Celosia argentea
    long slender spikes of minute
    greenish-white papery flowers;
    seasonal countryside plant

Attempt towards Immortality
Persistent and co-ordinated.

Celosia plumosa
    Chinese woolflower
    several colours of long feathery spikes;
    seasonal plant

Aspiration for Immortality
Pure, soaring, trusting.

Celosia plumosa
    red

Physical Aspiration for Immortality
Intense aspiration, but ignorant of the means.

Celosia plumosa
    dark magenta

Vital Aspiration for Immortality
Clustered, intense, but short-lived.

Celosia cristata
: Cockscomb
several colours of dense rounded or flared velvety heads with intricate convolutions

Boldness
Do fearlessly what must be done, not dreading any difficulty.

Celosia cristata
: green

Spontaneous Boldness
One of the results of perfect trust in the Divine.

Celosia cristata
: yellow

Mental Boldness
Let your mind be capable of foreseeing the perfections of tomorrow.

Celosia cristata
: red

Physical Boldness
Does not know the impossible in its consecration to the Divine.

Celosia cristata
: dark magenta

Vital Boldness
Must surrender to reason.

Celosia plumosa
: Feathered amaranth
dense branching golden-yellow plumes

Abundant Expression
Has much to say and says it fully.

It is through flowers that Nature expresses herself most harmoniously.

Celosia plumosa
: golden-orange plumes

Joyful Expression
It amuses itself and entertains others.

Centaurea cyanus
   Bachelor's button, Cornflower
   several colours of soft rounded heads of
   compositae flowers; seasonal plant

Idealism
Delicate and harmonious, it gives elegance to life.

Always the Ideal beckoned from afar.
Awakened by the touch of the Unseen,
Deserting the boundary of things achieved,
Aspired the strong discoverer, tireless Thought,
Revealing at each step a luminous world.

Cereus peruviana
   Cactus night flower, Hedge cactus
   large many-petalled white cup-shaped
   flowers filled with innumerable stamens

Fortune
Very attractive, but beware, it pricks!

The true fortune is to spend inthe right way.
   You become truly rich when you dispose of your wealth in the best possible way.

* * *

Money is meant to increase the wealth, the prosperity and the productiveness of a group, a country or, better, of the whole earth. Money is a means, a force, a power, and not an end in itself. And like all forces and all powers, it is by movement and circulation that it grows and increases its power, not by accumulation and stagnation.

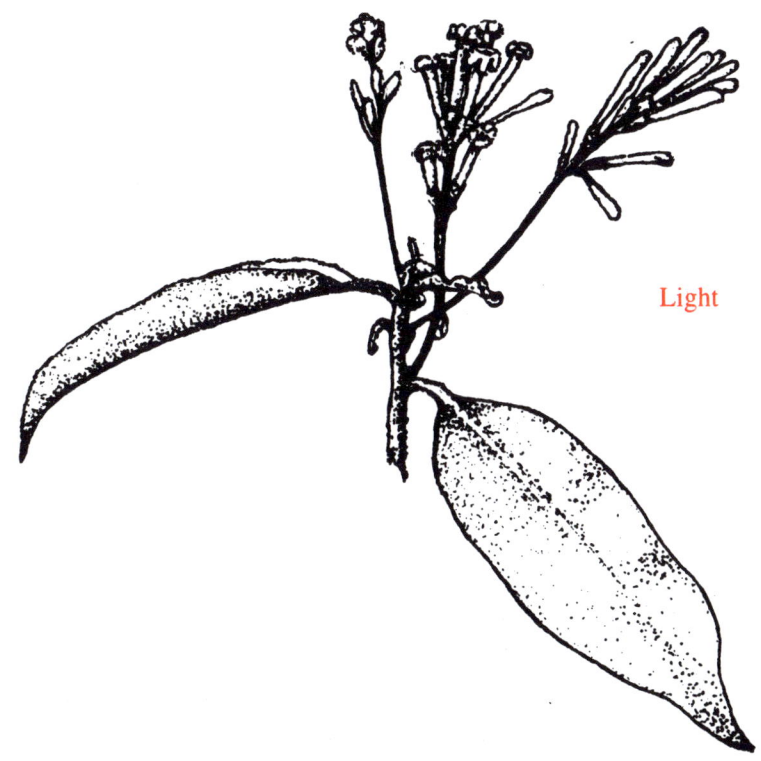

Light

Cestrum diurnum (*Pl. 2*)
    Queen-of-the-day
    branching clusters of small fragrant white tubular flowers; shrub

Light
Light and airy, it radiates.

Even if there is much darkness—and this world is full of it and the physical nature of man also—yet a ray of the true Light can prevail eventually against a tenfold darkness. Believe that and cleave to it always.

Cestrum elegans
    white to pale purple star-shaped flowers with elongated corolla tube; shrub

Light in the Vital
One of the first steps on the long road.

Cestrum nocturnum
    Queen-of-the-night
    intensely fragrant greenish-white to lemon yellow flowers; rambling shrub

Air
Light, subtle, almost invisible.

Cheiranthus cheiri
> Wallflower
> clusters of small very fragrant four-petalled autumn-coloured flowers; seasonal plant

> ***Optimism***
> *More helpful than its opposite!*

Chloris barbata
> Finger grass
> branching spikes of tiny reddish-brown graminae flowers; low perennial grass

> ***Repentance***
> *The first step towards correcting mistakes.*

True psychology is the knowledge of the soul, that is, the knowledge of the psychic being. And if one has the knowledge of the psychic being, one has at the same time the knowledge of all the true movements of the being, the inner laws of the being. This is true psychology.

Chlorophytum comosum 'Vittatum'
> Spider ivy, Ribbon plant
> small white star-shaped flowers on long branching scapes, decorative foliage; low spreading perennial

> ***Care***
> *To be careful in what one does.*

Chonemorpha fragrans (*Pl. 10*)
> soft fragrant cream-white salverform flower with a golden-yellow centre; heavy creeper

> ***Perfect Radiating Psychology***
> *Can be obtained only by acquiring divine vision.*

Chrysanthemum leucanthemum
   Ox-eye daisy
   medium-sized single white flower with
   yellow centre; countryside seasonal plant

Spontaneous Aspiration of Nature towards the Divine
*Wide open, spontaneous,
irrevocable in its spontaneous power.*

Life Energy

Chrysanthemum morifolium
   Florist's chrysanthemum
   several colours of medium to large
   double flowers; perennial suckering plant

Life Energy
Powerful and manifold, it meets all needs.

Chrysanthemum morifolium
   light mauve flowers

Life Energy in the Vital
Supple and resistant, it is tireless.

There are all kinds of old traditions, old Hindu traditions, old Chaldean traditions in which the Divine, in the form of the Creator... pronounces a word which has the power to create. So it is this... And it is the origin of the mantra. The mantra is the spoken word which has a creative power. An invocation is made and there is an answer to the invocation; or one makes a prayer and the prayer is granted. This is the Word, the Word which, in its sound... it is not only the idea, it is in the sound that there is a power of creation. It is the origin, you see, of the mantra.

In Indian mythology the creator God is Brahma, and I think that it was precisely his power which has been symbolised by this flower, "The Creative Word". And when one is in contact with it, the words spoken have a power of evocation or creation or formation or transformation; the words... sound always has a power; it has much more power than men think. It may be a good power and it may be a bad power. It creates vibrations which have an undeniable effect. It is not so much the idea as the sound; the idea too has its own power, but in its own domain—whereas the sound has a power in the material world.

Chrysanthemum x superbum
    Shasta daisy
    large single white flower; seasonal plant

The Creative Word
Belongs only to the Divine.

Chrysanthemum morifolium
    white flowers

Purified Dynamic Life Energy
Superb, indomitable, all powerful in its purity.

Chrysanthemum morifolium
    orange-yellow flowers

Supramentalised Life Energy
Manifold and supple, it has an immortal resistance.

Chrysanthemum 'Cascade' or 'Charm'
    several colours of tiny to small single or double compositae flowers; perennial plant

Specialised Detailed Energy
Nothing is too small to merit its attention.

This yoga demands a full ascension of the whole lower or ordinary consciousness to join the spiritual above it and a full descent of the spiritual (eventually of the supramental) into the mind, life and body to transform it. The total ascent is impossible so long as sex-desire blocks the way; the descent is dangerous so long as sex-desire is powerful in the vital. For at any moment an unexcised or latent sex-desire may be the cause of a mixture which throws back the true descent and uses the energy acquired for other purposes or turns all the action of the consciousness towards wrong experience, turbid and delusive. One must, therefore, clear this obstacle out of the way; otherwise there is either no safety or no free movement towards finality in the sadhana.

Citharexylum (*Pl. 6*)
Fiddlewood
slender pendulous racemes of very small fragrant white salverform flowers; tree

Spiritual Ascension
Fearless, regular, uninterrupted.

Citrus
Lemon tree
white flowers with fleshy petals; fruit tree

Chastity
A little proud and austere, it is very reserved.

Citrus maxima
Pummelo tree
fragrant white flowers

Continence
Control over oneself.

Glad Remembrance

Clarkia
Farewell-to-Spring, Godetia
several colours of erect spikes bearing flowers with soft delicate petals; seasonal plant

Glad Remembrance
In activity and in silence, in taking and in giving, always the glad remembrance of Thee!

My thought is filled with Thee, my heart is full, all my being is filled with Thy Presence, and peace grows ever deeper, giving rise to that happiness, so special, so unmixed, of a calm serenity, which seems vast as the universe, deep as the unfathomable depths which lead to Thee.

One cannot do the yoga if one does not take it seriously. For one must be very serious to have a constant aspiration and do tapasya. If one is not serious, for five minutes one has an aspiration and for ten hours one hasn't; for one day there is a great urge and for a month nothing, and so on. Well, one can't do yoga in these conditions. It must be a continuous, constant thing which does not flag. If one forgets or slackens, one cannot do yoga.

Should not one be born with a great aspiration?

No, aspiration is a thing to be developed, educated, like all activities of the being. One may be born with a very slight aspiration and develop it so much that it becomes very great. One may be born with a very small will and develop it and make it strong. It is a ridiculous idea to believe that things come to you like that, through a sort of grace, that if you are not given aspiration, you don't have it— this is not true.

Clematis triloba
    Virgin's bower
    full panicles of fragrant white star-shaped flowers; creeper

Sentinel (Sentry, origindalneme**)**
Always awake!

Cleome
    Spider flower
    erect racemes bearing pink or white flowers with long protruding stamens; seasonal plant

Soaring of Aspiration
Nothing is too high, nothing too far for its insatiable ardour!

Integral Even Basis in the Physical

Clerodendrum fragrans
    Glory bower, Kashmir bouquet
    compact clusters of fragrant white
    rose-like flowers with red calyces;
    spreading shrub

Integral Even Basis in the Physical
What you have, I have; what you can do, I can do; what you express, I express—we are all alike!

To be equal souled to all things, unmoved by joy and sorrow, the pleasant and the unpleasant, success or failure, to look with an equal eye on high and low, friend and enemy, the virtuous and the sinner, to see in all beings the manifold manifestation of the One.

Clerodendrum indicum (*Pl. 3*)
>Tube flower, Turk's turban
>dense clusters of delicate white flowers with long corolla tubes; shrub

>***The Divine Will Acting in the Subconscient***
>*The rare moments when the Divine asserts Himself visibly.*

Clerodendrum minahassae
>erect clusters of small fragrant cream-white salverform flowers; shrub

>***The Divine Will Acting in the Inconscient***
>*Is all powerful even when we are not aware of it.*

Clerodendrum inerme
>small white salverform flowers with violet or white elongated stamens; shrub or hedge

>***Faultless Planning of Work***
>*Can only be obtained by the Divine Consciousness.*

Clerodendrum wallichii
>small clusters of sturdy white flowers with long slender corolla tubes, short recurved petals and erect reddish-violet stamens; shrub

>***Prevision***
>*The power of projecting one's consciousness into the future.*

Clerodendrum paniculatum
>Pagoda flower
>large erect terminal inflorescence with innumerable small orange flowers; shrub

>***Grouping***
>*Indispensable for collective action.*

Clerodendrum subserratum
>erect terminal panicles of white flowers with long tubes and prominent calyces turning red when mature; countryside shrub

>***Belief***
>*Simple and candid, it does not argue.*

Clerodendrum speciosissimum
    few-flowered panicles of soft light orange salverform flowers with recurved petals; shrub

Right Attitude
Simple and open, it is without complications.

Aspiration for the Right Attitude

Clerodendrum speciosum
    Java glory bean, Pagoda flower
    large flattened cymes of red or crimson flowers with greenish-pink or white calyces; creeper

Aspiration for the Right Attitude
Energetic, willing, determined.

Clerodendrum splendens
    erect clusters of dark orange-red salverform flowers with recurved petals; creeper

Right Attitude Established
There is a moment when the right attitude comes spontaneously and without effort.

Clerodendrum ugandense
   small groups of blue flowers with recurved stamens; low shrub

Rest
The true repose is that of a perfect surrender to the Divine.

Rest

The minute one stops going forward, one falls back. The moment one is satisfied and no longer aspires, one begins to die. Life is movement, it is effort, it is a march forward, the scaling of a mountain, the climb towards new revelations, towards future realisations. Nothing is more dangerous than wanting to rest. It is in action, in effort, in the march forward that repose must be found, the true repose of complete trust in the divine Grace, of the absence of desires, of victory over egoism.

Radha's Prayer

O Thou whom at first sight I knew for the Lord of my being and my God, receive my offering.

Thine are all my thoughts, all my emotions, all the sentiments of my heart, all my sensations, all the movements of my life, each cell of my body, each drop of my blood. I am absolutely and altogether Thine, Thine without reserve. What Thou wilt of me, that I shall be. Whether Thou choosest for me life or death, happiness or sorrow, pleasure or suffering, all that comes to me from Thee will be welcome. Each one of Thy gifts will be always for me a gift divine bringing with it the supreme Felicity.

Clitoria ternatea
> Mussel-shell creeper
> papilionaceous flower with one cup-shaped petal, pale blue with white centre; countryside creeper

Krishna's Light in the Senses
A first step towards transformation.

Clitoria ternatea
> white single flowers

Purified Senses
Can only be obtained by total surrender to the Truth.

Clitoria ternatea (*Pl. 6*)
> ultramarine, single or double flowers

Radha's Consciousness
Symbolises perfect attachment to the Divine.

Clitoria ternatea
> light mauve single flowers

Radha's Consciousness in the Vital
Perfect attachment to the Divine replaces all vital attractions and passions.

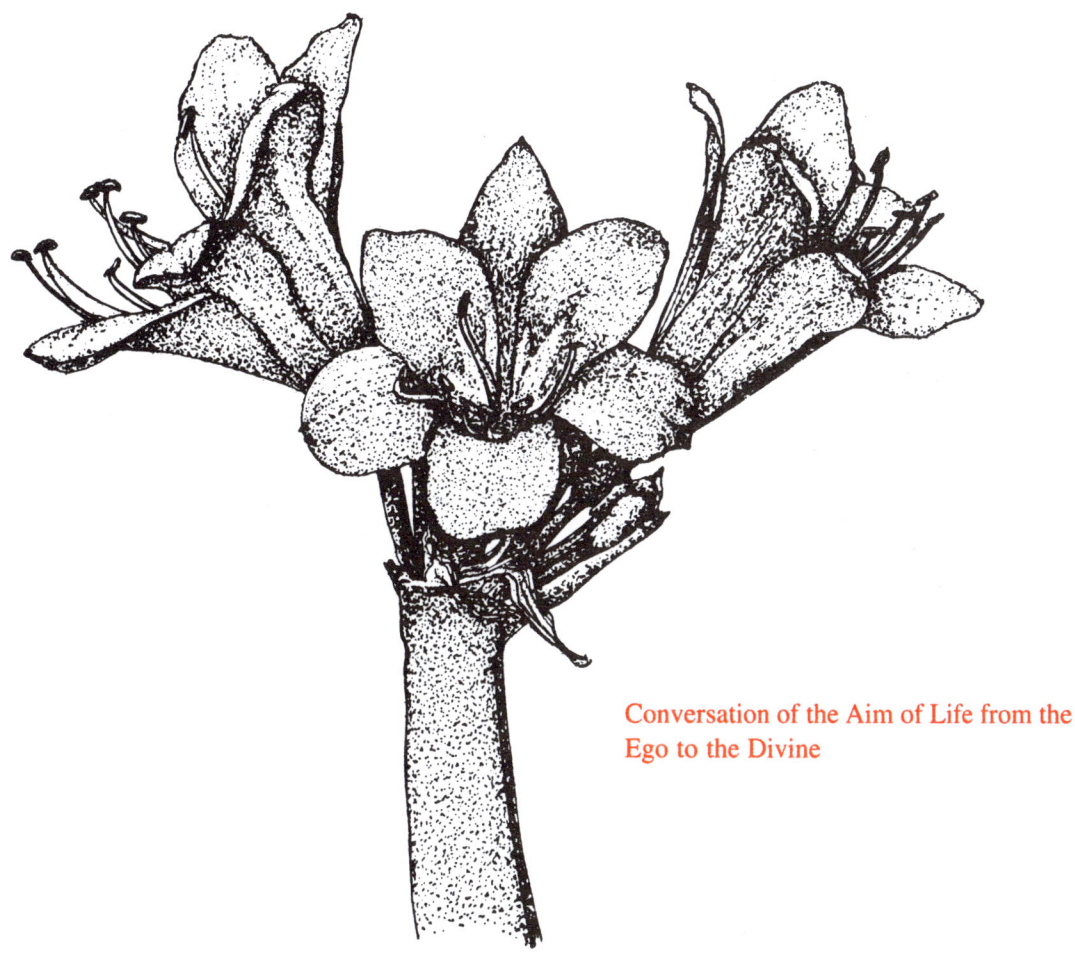

Conversation of the Aim of Life from the Ego to the Divine

Clivia miniata
    Kaffir lily
    umbels of apricot to bright orange
    trumpet-shaped flowers borne on a short
    scape; bulbous plant

Conversion of the Aim of Life from the Ego to the Divine
Instead of seeking one's own satisfaction, to have the service of the Divine as the aim of life.

To give everything one is or has to the Divine and regard nothing as one's own, to obey only the Divine will and no other, to live for the Divine and not for the ego.

What the supramental will do the mind cannot foresee or lay down. The mind is ignorance seeking for the Truth, the supramental by its very definition is the Truth-Consciousness, Truth in possession of itself and fulfilling itself by its own power. In a supramental world imperfection and disharmony are bound to disappear. But what we propose just now is not to make the earth a supramental world but to bring down the supramental as a power and established consciousness in the midst of the rest—to let it work there and fulfil itself as Mind descended into Life and Matter and has worked as a Power there to fulfil itself in the midst of the rest. This will be enough to change the world and to change Nature by breaking down her present limits.

Cochlospermum religiosa (*Pl. 10*)
    Yellow silk-cotton tree
    golden-yellow open cup-shaped flowers
    with numerous stamens; small tree

Success in Supramental Work
The result of a patient labour and a perfect consecration.

Cocos nucifera
    Coconut palm
    long branching spikes of small cream
    flowers with stiff petals; palm tree

Multitude
Gives itself freely and satisfies innumerable needs.

Power to Reject Adverse Suggestions

Codiaeum
    Croton
    variously coloured foliage and spikes of very small mildly fragrant ball-like flowers; shrub

Power to Reject Adverse Suggestions
The power that comes from conscious union with the Divine.

If the attack takes the form of adverse suggestions try quietly to push them away, as you would some material object. The quieter you are, the stronger you become. . . .

The only way to fail in your battle with the hostile forces is not to have a true confidence in the divine help.

Coffea
: Coffee plant
small clusters of very fragrant white star-shaped flowers; tree

Perfect Path
For each one it is the path that leads fastest to the Divine.

One may say that the perfection of the integral Yoga will come when each man is able to follow his own path of Yoga, pursuing the development of his own nature in its upsurging towards that which transcends the nature. For freedom is the final law and the last consummation.

Coleus
: variously coloured leaves; herbaceous seasonal plant

Strength in the Vital
Likes to show its beauty and its power.

Coleus
: slender spikes of tiny lavender-blue flowers

Spiritual Awakening of the Vital
It soars towards the heights in the hope of reaching them.

Combretum coccineum
: branching spikes with small brick-red star-shaped flowers and prominent stamens; shrub or climber

True Action in the Material Vital
Graceful and simple in its spontaneity.

Combretum gloriosum (*Pl. 3*)
: branching spikes of yellow to light red bottlebrush flowers; shrub

Organisation of Action in Life
Clustered, compact, its action is irresistible.

Charity

Commelina
  Dayflower
  prominent light blue flower emerging from a folded bract; perennial herbaceous plant

Charity
Simple and sweet, attentive to the needs of all.

Commelina
  smaller light or deep blue flowers; countryside groundcover

First Conscious Reception of the Light in Nature
The origin of the will to progress: Nature has an instinctive thirst for light.

Coniferae
    Conifers
    trees bearing evergreen needles

Perpetual Vitality
A vitality that is not affected by external influences.

Cordia sebestena
    Geiger tree
    terminal clusters of orange or apricot-yellow salverform flowers; tree

Adoration
Manifold, smiling, regular, it offers itself untiringly.

Cordyline terminalis
    Good-luck plant, Ti
    colourful pink to dark red foliage and occasional branching terminal racemes of small whitish pink tubular flowers; shrub

Return
The salvation of those who have wandered away.

Convallaria majalis
    Lily of the valley
    short scapes bearing small fragrant nodding white bell-shaped flowers; bulbous plant

Power of Purity
Purity is the best of powers.

Flowers are the spontaneous expression of Nature's adoration.

Coreopsis (*Pl. 11*)
    Tickweed
    erect airy clusters of small single, semi-double and double compositae flowers in several autumn colours; seasonal plant

Cheerfulness in Work done for the Divine
Work for the Divine and you will feel an ineffable joy filling your being.

Coriandrum sativum
    Coriander, Chinese parsley
    compound umbels of tiny white flowers, aromatic leaves; low seasonal condiment

Delicacy
Charming to refined tastes.

The transformation of the sex-centre and its energy is needed for the physical siddhi; for this is the support in the body of all the mental, vital and physical forces of the nature. It has to be changed into a mass and a movement of intimate Light, creative Power, pure divine Ananda. It is only the bringing down of the supramental Light, Power and Bliss into the centre that can change it.

Cosmos
    several colours of single or semi-double compositae flowers with delicately scalloped petals; seasonal plant

Supramental Influence in the Sex Centre
It is the assurance of the coming conquest of desires.

Cosmos
    white flowers

Tranquillity of the Sex Centre When under the Influence of the Supramental Light
The Supramental influence liberates man from all that binds him to the animal.

Costus speciosus
    Spiral ginger
    rounded spike of compact bracts bearing a mildly fragrant funnel-shaped flower in various colour combinations; rhizomatous plant

Revelation
True revelation is the revelation of the Divine.

Costus
    white flowers

Integral Revelation
Half-way to transformation.

Couroupita guianensis
    Cannonball tree
    pendulous racemes of large very fragrant light to deep red rotate flowers with a central recurved hood; tree

Prosperity
Stays consistently only with those who offer it to the Divine.

Couroupita guianensis
    lighter coloured flowers with rosy-white hood

Unselfish Prosperity
Those who receive it abundantly give all they have as they receive it.

We can say that youth is constant growth and perpetual progress—and the growth of capacities, possibilities, of the field of action and range of consciousness, and progress in the working out of details. . . .

Crataegus
Hawthorn
dense clusters of small rosy-white starlike flowers; shrub or small tree

Spring Purity
The charm and freshness of youth!

Crataeva nurvala
Caper tree
clusters of fragrant cream-white to yellow flowers with numerous long stamens; tree

Working of the Enlightened Mind
It is very powerful in leading the being to the Divine and can be very useful for progress.

Crinum
Spider lily
umbels of medium to large fragrant white flowers with narrow or broad petals; bulbous plant

Disinterested Work Done for the Divine
The surest means of progressing.

Crinum
very large fragrant white and violet-pink flowers

Disinterested Work Done for the Divine in the Vital
Calm and powerful, it reaches its goal.

Crinum
pendulous fragrant white funnel-shaped flowers banded light pink

Joy of Integral Peace
Calm and tranquil, a smile which does not disappoint.

Supramental Influence in the Subconscient

So long as there is not the supramental change down to the subconscient, complete and full, the lower nature has always a hold on some part of the being.

Crossandra
   bracted spikes of orange to reddish-orange half-salverform flowers; shrub

Supramental Influence in the Subconscient
Under its modest appearance it is a great force for transformation.

Crossandra
   light to deep yellow flowers

Supramental Light in the Subconscient
The essential condition for transformation.

The action of the subconscient is irrational, mechanical, repetitive. It does not listen to reason or the mental will. It is only by bringing the higher Light and Force into it that it can change.

* * *

The subconscient is a dark and ignorant region, so that it is natural that the obscurer movements of the Nature should have more power there. It is so indeed with all the lower parts of the nature from the lower vital downwards. But it does send up good things also though more rarely. It has in the course of the sadhana to be illumined and made a support of the higher consciousness in the physical nature instead of a basis of the instinctive lower movements.

* * *

The subconscient is to be penetrated by the light and made a sort of bed-rock of truth, a store of right impressions, right physical responses to the Truth.

Crossandra
pink flowers

Psychic Light in the Subconscient
The preliminary condition for progress.

Thirst to Understand

Crossostephium
    Chinese lavender
    short racemes of very small yellow
     compositae heads, aromatic leaves;
    perennial groundcover

Thirst to Understand
Very useful for transformation.

By the understanding we mean that which at once perceives, judges and discriminates, the true reason of the human being not subservient to the senses, to desire or to the blind force of habit, but working in its own right for mastery, for knowledge.

It is the thinking mind that works out ideas—the externalising mental or physical mind gives them form in words. . . . The gift of verbal expression is comparatively rare.

* * *

The power of expression comes by getting into touch with the inner source from which these things come. A calm and silent mind is a great help for the free flow of the power.

Crotalaria juncea
    Sun hemp
    long erect racemes of bright yellow
    papilionaceous flowers; seasonal plant or
    perennial shrub

Formative Faculty in the Mind
It is a natural and very spontaneous gift.

Crotalaria varrucosa
    light purple or blue flowers; low
    countryside shrub

Formative Faculty in the Vital
Spontaneous but not always happy, it needs to be disciplined.

Cucurbita maxlma
    Gourd, Marrow, Squash, Pumpkin
    large yellow funnel-shaped flower;
    rambling vegetable plant

Abundance
Nature gives us much at a time generously and we have the joy of abundance.

Good and well-wishing, flowers answer abundantly all the creative fantasies of Nature.

Vegetal Goodwill towards the
Supramental Forces

Cuphea micropetala
    Cigar flower
    long spikes of narrow erect tubular
    flowers, light yellow with scarlet base;
    small shrub

***Vegetal Goodwill towards the
Supramental Forces***
Each one does what he can.

O Nature, material Mother,
Thou hast said that thou wilt collaborate
and there is no limit to the splendour of this
collaboration.

Like a flame that burns in silence, like a perfume that rises straight upward without wavering, my love goes to Thee; and like the child who does not reason and has no care, I trust myself to Thee that Thy Will may be done, that Thy Light may manifest, Thy Peace radiate, Thy Love cover the world. When Thou willest I shall be in Thee, Thyself, and there shall be no more any distinction; I await that blessed hour without impatience of any kind, letting myself flow irresistibly toward it as a peaceful stream flows toward the boundless ocean.

Thy Peace is in me, and in that Peace I see Thee alone present in everything, with the calm of Eternity.

Curculigo orchioides
> small yellow star-shaped flowers appearing from the ground; countryside rhizomatous plant

Attraction for the Light
In its attraction it tries to imitate the stars!

Curcuma pallida
> Turmeric, Zedoary
> sturdy spikes of small yellow tubular flowers set in large bracts; rhizomatous condiment

Peace
To will what Thou willest, always and in all circumstances, is the only way of enjoying an unshakable peace.

Cyclamen
> Alpine violet
> fragrant white, pink to deep mauve flowers resembling shooting stars; low tuberous plant

Scented Marvel
One of the innumerable generosities of Nature.

A fragrance wandered in a coloured haze
As if the scent and hue of all sweet flowers
Had mingled to copy heaven's atmosphere.

To grow in the spirit is the greatest help one can give to others, for then something flows out naturally to those around that helps them.

Cymbopogon citratus
    Lemongrass
    long slender lemon-scented leaves and
    long spikes bearing tiny graminae
    flowers; tall perennial economic grass

Help
You bring help to those who know how to use it!

Cymbopogon nardus
    Citronella
    long slender scented leaves and
    long spikes bearing tiny graminae
    flowers; tall perennial economic grass

Help
You bring help to those who know how to use it!

Cynoglossum amabile
    Chinese forget-me-not
    loose racemes of small deep sky-blue
    flowers; seasonal plant

Subconscient Remembrance
Must be purified of all that is useless.

Cytisus scoparius
    Scotch broom
    short spikes of yellow papilionaceous
    flowers on long branches; countryside
    shrub

Inventions
Have no use except when they are controlled by the Divine.

Dahlia
    several colours of medium to fairly large double compositae flowers, tuberous plant

Dignity
Affirms its worth, but asks for nothing.

Dahlia
    blood-red

Dignity in the Physical
Above all bargaining.

Dahlia
    orange-yellow

Supramentalised Mental Dignity
Tolerates no pettiness in its thought turned towards the Truth.

Dahlia
    mauve-pink

Dignity of the Emotions
Not to permit one's emotions to contradict the inner Divinity.

Dahlia
    pink

Psychic Dignity
Refuses to accept anything that lowers or debases.

Dahlia
    several colours of small semi-double or double flowers

Pride
A great obstacle to progress.

Dahlia
    several colours of small single flowers with flat petals and hard centre; tuberous plant

Vanity
One of the most frequent forms of falsehood.

Just imagine, there are plants which are vain! I am speaking of plants one grows for oneself. If one pays them compliments by words or by feelings, if one admires them, well, they hold up their head—with vanity!

Aristocracy

Dahlia
  several colours of very large, often variegated flowers

Aristocracy
Incapable of baseness and pettiness, it asserts itself with dignity and authority.

Dahlia
  very large magenta or royal red flowers

Nobility
The incapacity for any pettiness either of sentiments or action.

Dahlia
  very large pure white flowers

Superhumanity
The aim of our aspirations.

Datura
Angel's trumpet
large mildly fragrant white
trumpet-shaped flowers; countryside shrub

Tapasya
A discipline aiming at the realisation of the Divine.

Datura
double white flower

Integral Tapasya
The entire being lives only to know and serve the Divine.

Datura
single or double yellow flower

Mental Tapasya
The process leading to the goal.

Datura
single, double or triple violet flower

Vital Tapasya
The vital undergoes a vigorous discipline in order to transform itself.

When the will and energy are concentrated and used to control the mind, vital and physical and change them or to bring down the higher consciousness or for any other yogic purpose or high purpose, that is called Tapasya.

* * *

All life is only a lavish and manifold opportunity given us to discover, realise, express the Divine.

Delonix elata
cream-white rotate flowers fading to ochre yellow with very long stamens; tree

Mental Fantasy
Wild, dishevelled, it usually lacks co-ordination.

Delonix regia (*Pl. 14*)
Flamboyant, Gul Mohur
clusters of striking orange-red to deep red flowers, one petal white to cream or yellow and marked orange-red; tree

Realisation
The goal of our efforts.

Without care for time, without fear for space, surging out purified from the flames of the ordeal, we shall fly without stop towards the realisation of our goal, the supramental victory.

Soaring

Delphinium
    Larkspur
    dense erect racemes of small graceful single or double flowers with long or short spur, sky-blue and other colours; seasonal plant

Soaring
Take your flight towards the heights!

Dendrobium moschatum
    Orchid
    pendulous clusters of fragrant buff-yellow
    orchids; epiphyte

    Mental Attachment to the Divine
    Beautiful in form and in expression.

Supreme Lord, Eternal Truth
Let us obey Thee alone and
live according to Truth.

Obedience

Dianthus caryophyllus
    Carnation, Clove pink
    several colours of scented double flowers;
    erect seasonal plant

    Collaboration
    Ever ready to help and knowing how
    to do it.

Dianthus chinensis
    Chinese pink
    several colours of single rotate flowers;
    seasonal plant

    Obedience
    To learn to obey is good; to obey only
    the Divine is better.

Dianthus chinensis
> Chinese pink
> double flowers

Perfect Obedience
Without reserve or hesitation, joyous obedience in every sphere to the command of the Divine.

Dianthus barbatus
> Sweet William
> clusters of small fragrant single rotate flowers in several colours; low seasonal plant

Detailed Obedience
The obedience to the Divine Will must be total.

The Spirit's tops and Nature's base shall draw
Near to the secret of their separate truth
And know each other as one deity.
The Spirit shall look out through Matter's gaze
And Matter shall reveal the Spirit's face.
Then man and superman shall be at one
And all the earth become a single life.

Dicentra spectabilis
> Bleeding-heart
> long hanging racemes of rose-pink heart-shaped flowers; perennial herbaceous plant

Sentimental Remembrance
Only those circumstances which helped us in our seeking for the Divine must be the object of this remembrance.

Dodonaea viscosa
> Hopseed bush
> clusters of greenish-brown to pink papery-winged fruits; countryside shrub

Psychic Awakening in Matter
Matter opens itself to the spiritual life.

Conquest over the Greed for Food

Dombeya
    umbels of small mildly fragrant white or pink cup-shaped flowers; shrub

Conquest over the Greed for Food
A promise of good health.

Greed for food has to be overcome, but it has not to be given too much thought. The proper attitude to food is a certain equality. Food is for the maintenance of the body and one should take enough for that—what the body needs; if one gives less the body feels the need and hankers; if you give more, then that is indulging the vital.

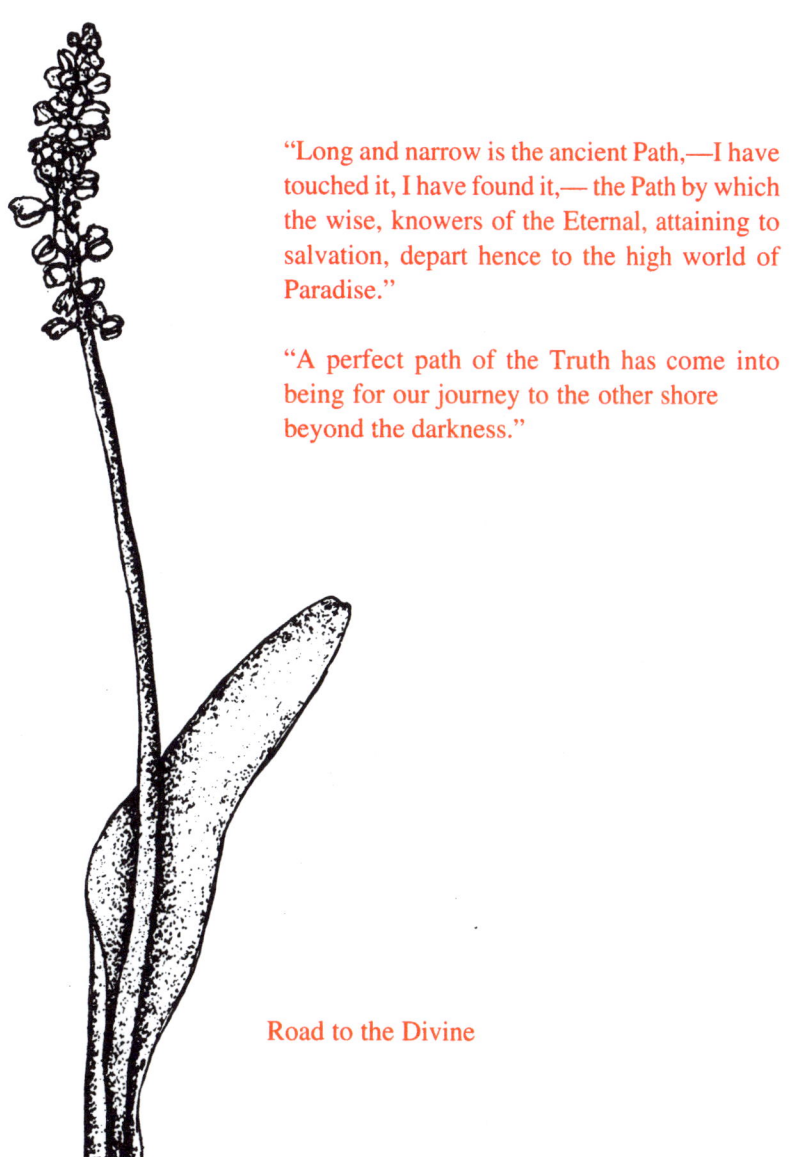

"Long and narrow is the ancient Path,—I have touched it, I have found it,— the Path by which the wise, knowers of the Eternal, attaining to salvation, depart hence to the high world of Paradise."

"A perfect path of the Truth has come into being for our journey to the other shore beyond the darkness."

Road to the Divine

Doxantha unguis-cati (*Pl. 16*)
    Cat's claw
    luminous golden-yellow salverform flowers, delicately scented; clinging creeper

Supramental Influence
Innumerable and rapid in its action.

Drimiopsis kirkii
    clusters of very small white rounded flowers on a long smooth scape; bulbous plant with decorative foliage

Road to the Divine
Always long, at times apparently dry, but always abundant in its results!

The purification of the vital takes a long time because until all the parts are free, none is quite free and because they use a multitude of movements which have to be changed or enlightened,—and moreover there is a great habit of persistence and resistance in the habitual movements of the nature. One therefore easily thinks that one has made no progress,—but all sincere and sustained effort of purification has its result and after a time the progress made will become evident.

Aspiration for the Vital Purity

Duranta repens
    Skyflower, Golden-dewdrop
    delicate pendulous racemes of small sweetly scented light violet-blue flowers; shrub

Aspiration for Vital Purity
Delicate, modest, insistent.

Duranta repens 'Alba'
    white flowers

Vital Purity
It begins with the abolition of desire.

Ecbolium
    dull greenish-blue flowers; low countryside perenniel

Krishna's Influence in the Subconscient
The best way to be above all contingencies.

Echinopsis multiplex
> Easter-lily cactus
> large fragrant white to light pink funnel-shaped flower with innumerable petals; small rounded cactus

> ***Richness of Feelings***
> *Sincere and concentrated, without deception.*

Eichhornia crassipes (*Pl. 12*)
> Water hyacinth
> dense spikes of lilac-blue flowers, each flower having one petal resembling a peacock feather; floating water plant, often growing wild

> ***Krishna's Play in the Vital***
> *All is charming in His midst.*

Emilia javanica
> Tassel flower, Flora's paintbrush
> loose corymbs of soft scarlet tassel-like heads; seasonal plant

> ***Prudence***
> *Very useful for weakness since weakness needs prudence; strength does not need it.*

Emilia javanica 'Lutea'
> golden-yellow

> ***Enlightened Prudence***
> *Carefully examines its path before advancing.*

Enterolobium saman
> Monkey-pod, Rain-tree
> delicate pink soft powder-puff flower with white centre; large tree

> ***Wisdom***
> *Can only be acquired through union with the Divine Consciousness.*

Attachment of the Cells to the Divine

Epidendrum obrienanum
    Butterfly orchid, Scarlet orchid
    clusters of small red orchids; epiphyte

Attachment of the Cells to the Divine
*They know how to expect everything
from Him and to count only on Him.*

Episcea cupreata
    Flame violet
    variously coloured foliage and small
    salverform flowers, coral-pink or other
    colours; herbaceous groundcover or
    hanging-basket plant

Will Manifesting in Life
Precise and concentrated.

Episcea reptans
    bright red flowers

Vital Will Manifesting in Life
*It is often the cause of the greatest
disorders!*

Attachment of the Material Vital
to the Divine

Eranthemum hypocrateriforme
    pairs of small light purple-red salverform flower; low shrub

Attachment of the Material Vital to the Divine
An attachment that wants to feel the power of contact.

Eranthemum pulchellum
    short bracteated spikes bearing sky-blue salverform flowers with elongated carolla tube; spreading shrub

Aspiration for Silence in the Mind
Too noisy to be effective.

Eranthemum pulchellum
    violet-blue flowers

Aspiration for Silence in the Physical Mind
Does what it can, but cannot do much.

Eranthemum wattii
    small dark blue flowers and variegated bracts; countryside shrub

Krishna's Light in the Subconscient
Soon there will be no subconscient.

There is the possibility of the material being transfiguring itself through the acceptation of a higher law than its own which is yet its own because it is always there latent and potential in its own secrecies.

* * *

Evolution comes by the unceasing pressure of the supra-material planes on the material compelling it to deliver out of itself their principles and powers which might conceivably otherwise have slept imprisoned in the rigidity of the material formula.

Erythrina indica
    Indian coral tree
    one-sided dense racemes of dark red
    sabre-shaped flowers; tree

Beginning of Realisation in Matter
Matter responds to the Divine's influence.

Erythrina variegata 'Alba'
    white veined light pink

Psychic Governing Matter
The psychic influence compels the physical to turn towards the Divine.

Erythrina variegata
    bright orange

Matter Prepares Itself to Receive the Supramental
Matter tries to liberate itself from old habits in order to prepare for the New Creation.

The ego is what makes one conscious of being separate from others. If there were no ego, you would not perceive that you are a person separate from others. You would have the impression that you are a small part of a whole, a very small part of a very great whole....

When you begin to be aware that everything is yourself, and that this is only a very small point in the midst of thousands and thousands of other points of the same person that you are everywhere, when you feel that you are yourself in everything and that there is no separation, then you know that you are on the way towards having no more ego.

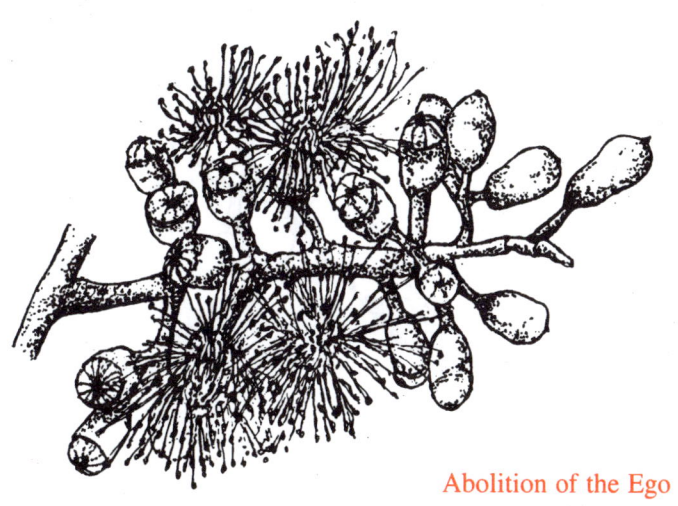

Abolition of the Ego

Eucalyptus
   Gum tree
   clusters of white or pink rounded brushlike flowers; tree

Abolition of the Ego
One exists only by the Divine and for the Divine.

Human nature is shot through in all its stuff with the thread of ego; even when one tries to get away from it, it is in front or could be behind all the thoughts and actions like a shadow. To see that is the first step, to discern the falsity and absurdity of the ego movements is the second, to discourage and refuse it at each step is the third,—but it goes entirely only when one sees, experiences and lives the One in everything and equally everywhere.

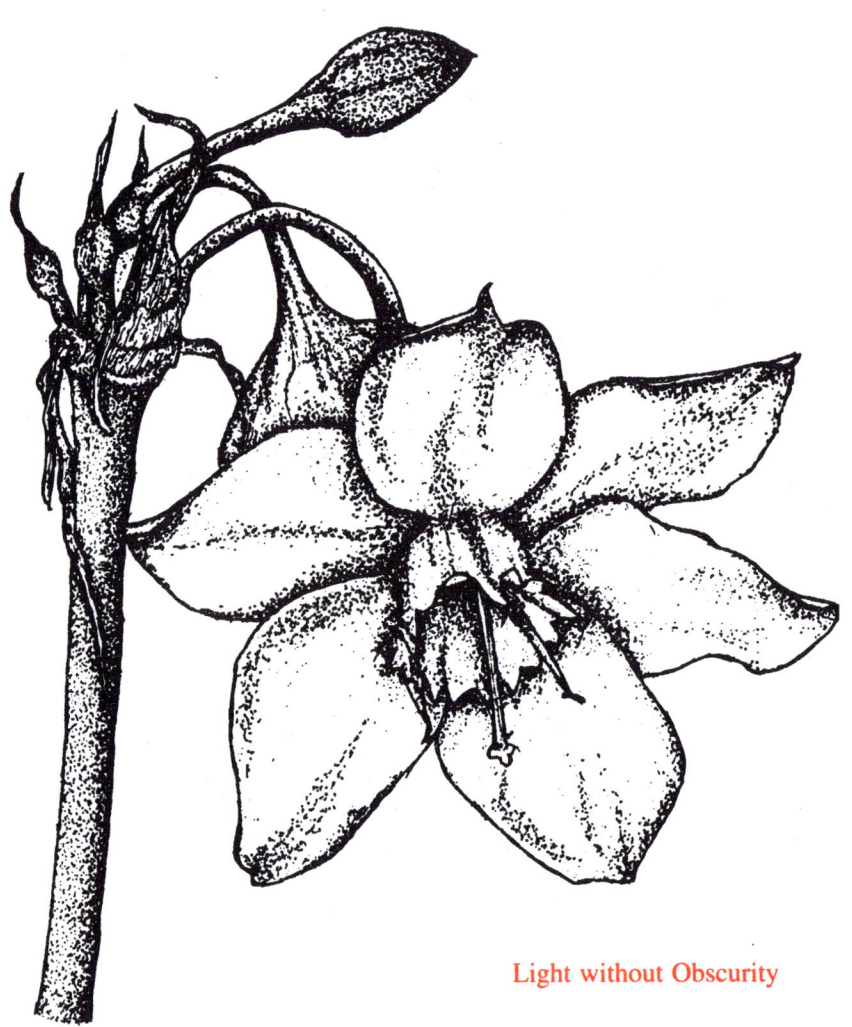

Light without Obscurity

Eucharis grandiflora
    Amazon lily, Cup-and-saucer lily
    umbels of fragrant pure white flowers with
    a central cup emerging from spreading
    petals; bulbous plant

Light without Obscurity
All-powerful in its simplicity.

Eulophia
    Orchid
    long erect racemes of small light green
    orchids veined maroon or dark red; ground
    orchid

Exclusive Turning of All Movements towards the Divine
The sure means of security.

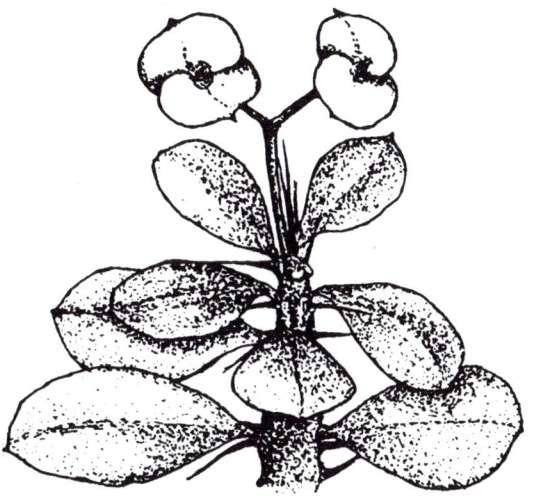

Concentration

Euphorbia milii
    Crown-of-thorns
    small clusters or pairs of red buttonlike
    flowers; low shrub

Concentration
Does not aim at effect, but is simple and persistent.

By concentration on anything whatsoever we are able to know that thing, to make it deliver up its concealed secrets. . . .

By concentration again the whole will can be gathered up for the acquisition of that which is still ungrasped. . . .

By concentration of our whole being on one status of itself, we can become whatever we choose.

Euphorbia cyathophora
    Painted leaf, Mexican fire plant
    small red floral bracts surrounding
    clusters of small greenish-yellow flowers;
    herbaceous countryside seasonal plant

Opening of the Vital to the Divine Love
Little by little it is no longer the ego that governs but the Divine.

Euphorbia pulcherrima
    Poinsettia, Christmas flower
    large white, cream, pink or red floral
    bracts; shrub

Opening of the Vital to the Divine Love
Little by little it is no longer the ego that governs but the Divine.

Eurycles sylvestris
   Brisbane lily
   umbels of small milk-white funnel-shaped flowers; bulbous plant

Silver
White and manifold, it aspires for spirituality.

Evolvulus alsinoides
   sky-blue buttonlike flowers; countryside groundcover

First Sign of Krishna's Light in Matter
It announces the coming transformation.

To know is good,
to live is better,
to be, that is perfect

Fittonia vershaffeltii
   Mosaic plant, Silver-net plant
   decorative foliage with upright bracteated spikes bearing very small pale yellow, orange or red flowers; succulent groundcover

Application
Modest, but harmonious.

Foeniculum vulgare
   Fennel
   wide umbels of innumerable tiny yellow flowers and soft feathery leaves with pungent fragrance; seasonal herb

Light in the Blood
When the blood becomes receptive to the higher consciousness.

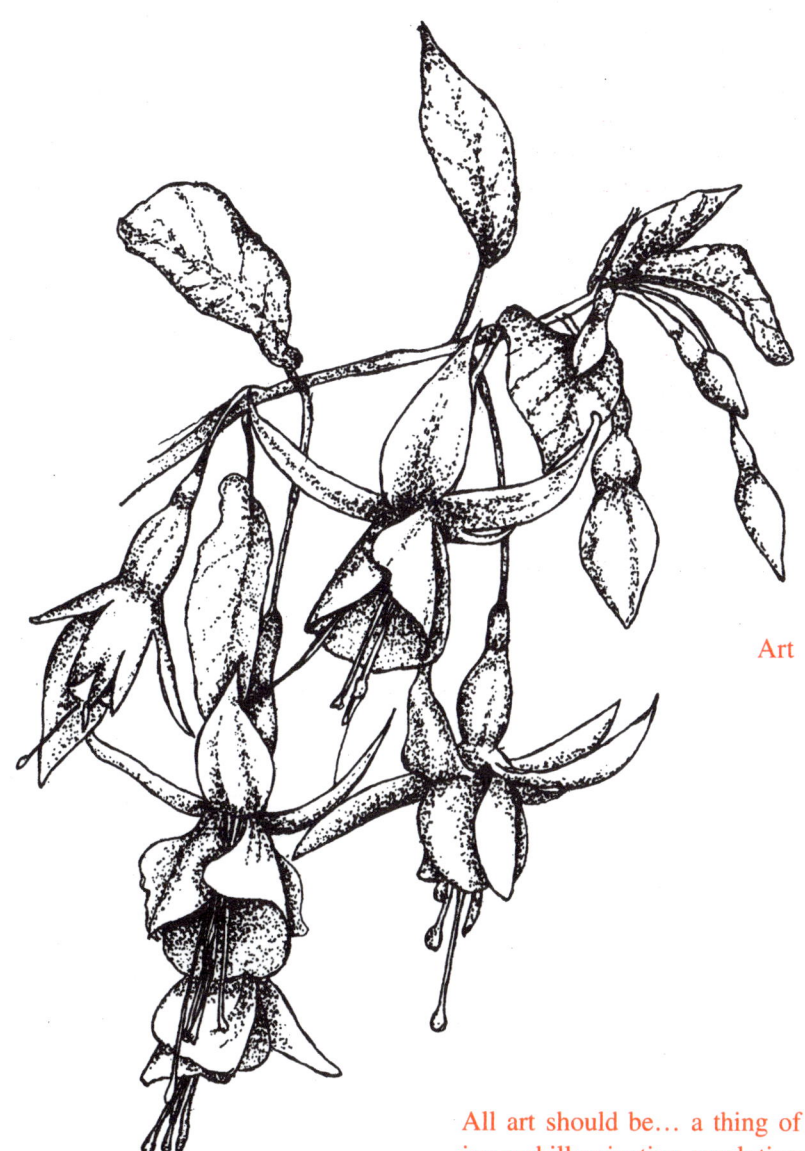

Art

Fuchsia
    Lady's-eardrops
    beautiful pendulous small lanternlike
    flowers in many shades; shrub

Art
Living only to express beauty.

All art should be… a thing of harmony and joy and illumination, a solution and release of the soul from its vital unrest and questioning and struggle.… In the greatest art and poetry there should be something of the calm of the impersonal basing and elevating the effort and struggle of the personality, something of the largeness of the universal releasing and harmonising the troubled concentrations of the individual existence, something of the sense of the transcendent raising the inferior, ignorant and uncertain powers of life towards a greater strength and light and Ananda.

Do you know what the flower which we have called "Successful Future" signifies when given to you? It signifies the hope—nay, even the promise—that you will participate in the descent of the supramental world. For that descent will be the successful consummation of our work, a descent of which the full glory has not yet been or else the whole face of life would have been different. By slow degrees the Supramental is exerting its influence; now one part of the being and now another feels the embrace or the touch of its divinity; but when it comes down in all its self-existent power, a supreme radical change will seize the whole nature.

Successful Future

Gaillardia pulchella
> Blanket-flower
> autumn colours of single or double compositae flowers with trumpet-shaped florets; seasonal plant

Successful Future
Full of promise and joyous surprises.

Gaillardia pulchella 'picta'
> flat florets in several autumn colours

Cheerfulness
A joyous smile of Nature.

Gaillardia pulchella 'picta'
> yellow florets

Mental Cheerfulness
It knows how to take delight in everything.

Galanthus nivalis
  Snowdrop
  dainty nodding white bell-shaped flowers edged green; low bulbous plant

Promise of Renewal
May ugliness disappear from the world!

Gardenia jasminoides
  Cape jasmine
  highly fragrant single white salverform flower; shrub

Radiating Purity
It charms and fascinates making all Nature fragrant.

Galphimia glauca
  light erect racemes of small yellow star-shaped flowers; low shrub

Honesty in the Physical Mind
The preliminary indispensable condition for transformation.

Gardenia jasminoides (*Pl. 15*)
  double flowers

Perfect Radiating Purity
Nothing escapes its action.

Gazania
  erect compositae flowers in autumn colours with a dark band towards the centre; low seasonal plant

Seeking for Clarity
Likes to say clearly what has to be said.

Genista
  Broom
  erect racemes of yellow papilionaceous flowers; countryside shrub

Inventions
Have no use except when they are controlled by the Divine.

Gerbera jamesonii
  Transvaal daisy
  single or double erect compositae funnel-shaped flowers with long slender petals, in a variety of pastel colours; rhizomatous plant

Frankness
Says candidly what it has to say without caring for the result.

To be receptive is to feel the urge to give and the joy of giving to the Divine's Work all one has, all one is, all one does.

* * *

If one is inwardly open, if one is receptive, one receives right down into the subtle physical all that is necessary for one's integral progress. And in the order of things, the outer contact should come only as a crowning and an aid so that the body—the material physical consciousness and the body—may be able to follow the movement of the inner being.

* * *

Flowers are very receptive and they are happy when they are loved.

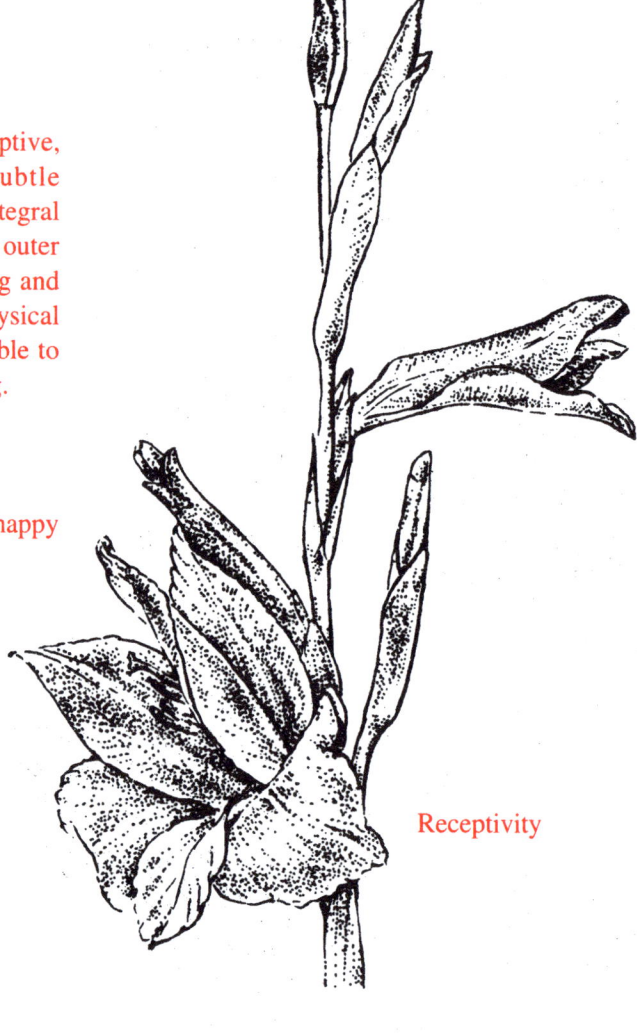

Receptivity

Gladiolus hortulanus
   Sword lily
   all colours of long graceful scapes of
   elegant flared or ruffled tubular flowers;
   bulbous plant

Receptivity
*Conscious of the Divine Will and
surrendered to it.*

Gladiolus
   carmine pink or light mauve

Emotional Receptivity
Emotions wanting to be divinised.

Gladiolus
white

Integral Receptivity
The whole being is aware of the Divine Will and obeys it.

Gladiolus
multi-coloured

Manifold Receptivity
Nothing resists the Light.

Gladiolus
yellow

Mental Receptivity
Always ready to learn.

Gladiolus
predominantly bright red

Physical Receptivity
That which one should have only towards the Divine.

Gladiolus
dark red or deep violet

Vital Receptivity
Happens only when the vital understands that it must be transformed; it blossoms in aspiration for the Divine.

Gladiolus
pink and rose-pink

Psychic Receptivity
The psychic responds joyously to the ascending force.

Gladiolus
bicoloured, pink and orange

Receptivity of the Supramentalised Psychic
This happens to the psychic that continues to progress.

Gladiolus
orange

Supramentalised Receptivity
The receptivity of tomorrow.

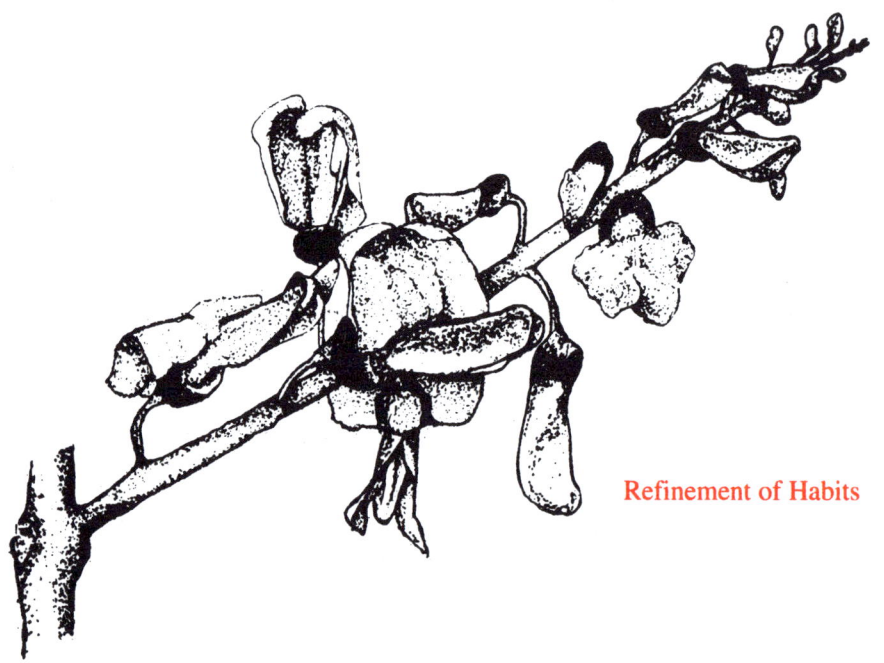

Refinement of Habits

Gliricidia sepium
> Madre, Nicaraguan cocoa-shade
> dense pendulous clusters of pink and white papilionaceous flowers; tree

Refinement of Habits
Ordered, neat and regular in their organisation.

Gloriosa superba (*Pl. 7*)
> Climbing lily, Flame lily, Glory lily
> lilylike flowers with long stamens and slender red and yellow twisted recurved petals; tuberous plant

No Quarrels
A very important condition to fulfil in order to facilitate the advent of the Supermind.

Quarrels and clashes are a proof of the absence of the yogic poise and those who seriously wish to do yoga must learn to grow out of these things. It is easy enough not to clash when there is no cause for strife or dispute or quarrel; it is when there is cause and the other side is impossible and unreasonable that one gets the opportunity of rising above one's vital nature.

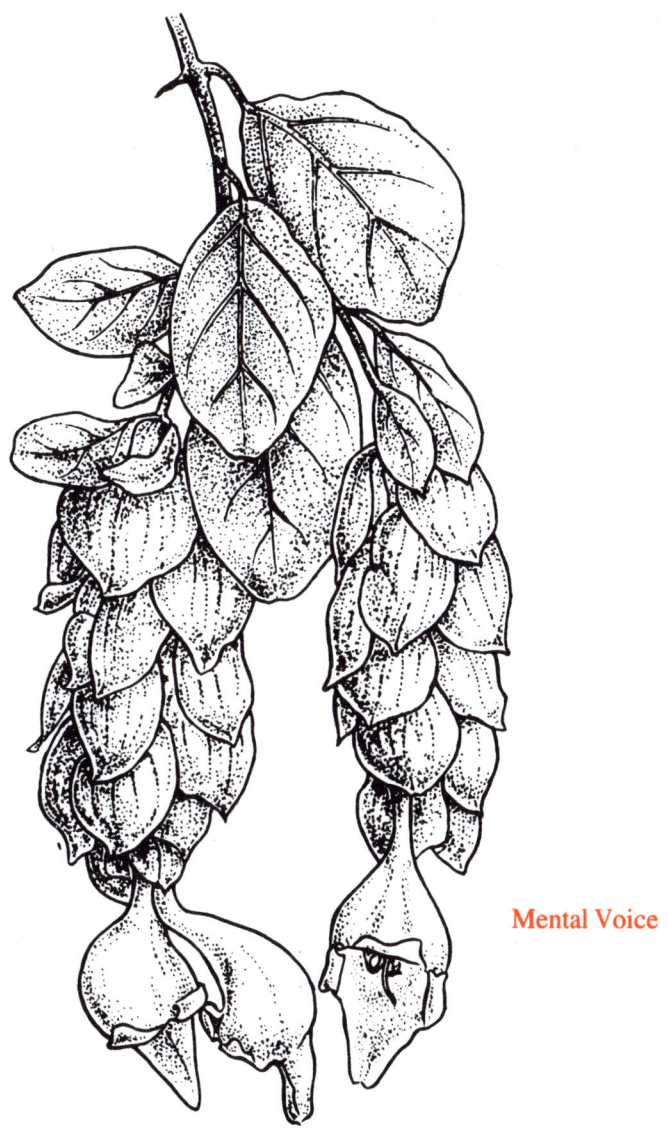

Mental Voice

Gloxinia perennis
> short racemes of small velvety light mauve bell-shaped flowers; decorative foliage plant

Blossoming of the Emotional Being
It broadens and opens so as to receive better.

Gmelina
> pendulous racemes of yellow open-mouthed flowers, with or without large russet bracts; large shrub or countryside shrub

Mental Voice
The mind must learn to express only what is dictated by the Divine.

Gomphrena globosa
: Globe amaranth
various colours of small rounded heads of everlasting flowers; low seasonal plant

Immortality
Forms are in perpetual transformation; identify yourself with the Immortal Consciousness and you will become It.

Immortality is not the survival of the mental personality after death, though that also is true, but the waking possession of the unborn and deathless Self of which body is only an instrument and a shadow.

Gomphrena
: violet

Vital Immortality
Exists in its own field, but is conditioned by surrender to the Divine.

Gomphrena
: light purple

Conscious Vital Immortality
The immortality of an organised and conscious vital being.

Gomphrena
: white

Integral Immortality
It is a promise. When will it be a material fact?

Gomphrena
: orange

Supramental Immortality
It is an established fact, but few human beings have experienced it.

He who acquires for himself alone, acquires ill though he may call it heaven and virtue.

Gossypium
> Cotton plant
> yellow or cream-white funnelshaped flower set in green bracts; seasonal plant

Material Abundance
Nature always shows us what true abundance is—it is overwhelming!

Gossypium arboreum
> Tree cotton
> dark red; tree

Success in the Most Material Vital
Has value only when it is offered to the Divine.

Graptophyllum
> Caricature plant
> variegated leaves and short racemes of dark red tubular labiate flowers; shrub

Vital Impulses
They look like nothing at all but they assert themselves and are stubborn!

Guettarda speciosa
> small cymes of fragrant white salverform flowers; tree

Peace in the Nerves
Indispensable for good health.

Gypsophila elegans
> Baby's breath
> graceful airy sprays of delicate tiny white flowers; seasonal plant

Modesty of Beauty
It blossoms without attracting attention.

> The manifestation of the Supramental upon earth is no more a promise but a living fact, a reality.
> It is at work here, and one day will come when the most blind, the most unconscious, even the most unwilling shall be obliged to recognise it.

Haemanthus multiflorus
    Blood lily
    short scape bearing a large striking ball of small glowing pinkish-red flowers with gold-tipped stamens; low bulbous plant

Supramental Manifestation
It will be welcome.

Haematoxylum campechianum (*Pl. 7*)
    Bloodwood tree, Logwood
    clusters of small mildly fragrant light yellow star-shaped flowers; shrub or small tree

Fairy Freshness
Charming, it refreshes the eyes.

Hamelia patens (*Pl. 5*)
    Firebush, Scarlet bush
    cymes of small tubular bright orange flowers; shrub or hedge

Matter under the Supramental Guidance
The condition required for its transformation.

Hedera
    Ivy
    dark glossy evergreen leaves with prominent lobes; clinging creeper

Lasting Attachment
Modest, without glamour, but persistent.

Sachchidananda

Hedychium
Butterfly lily, Garland lily, several sizes and colours of fragrant delicate butterfly-like flowers set in bracteated spikes; rhizomatous plant

Sachchidananda
Strong and pure, it stands erect in its creative power.

That which has thrown itself out into forms is a triune Existence-Consciousness-Bliss, Sachchidananda.... All things that exist are what they are as terms of that existence, terms of that conscious force, terms of that delight of being.

Helianthus
: Sunflower
: single yellow sunflowers of several sizes and shades; seasonal plant

Consciousness Turned towards the Light
It thirsts for Light and cannot live without it.

Helianthus
: orange-yellow flowers

Consciousness Turned towards the Supramental Light
It thirsts for Truth and will find its satisfaction only in the Truth.

Helianthus
: large flowers, sienna ray florets streaked gold and yellow with a golden aura radiating from the centre

Body-Consciousness Undergoing the Supramental Transformation
Solid and resolute, it faces all difficulties.

Helianthus
: large double yellow chrysanthemum-type sunflower

Intensity of the Consciousness in the Full Supramental Light
It is radiant and radiates in order to illumine the world.

Helianthus
: large red-brown sunflower with golden-yellow glow at base and back of ray florets

Supramental Artistic Genius
It blossoms in the Light and makes it manifest.

Helichrysum bracteatum
: Everlasting, Strawflower
: several colours of compositae flowers with strawlike petals and golden-yellow centre; seasonal plant

Supramental Immortality Upon Earth
This remains to be realised.

Bird of Paradise

Heliconia
Lobster-claw
branching spikes of striking red boat-shaped bracts and inconspicuous flowers; rhizomatous plant

Bird of Paradise
A bird that never flies away!

Heliotropium
Cherry-pie, Heliotrope
compact one-sided spikes of tiny or very small fragrant purple flowers; seasonal or perennial plant

Vital Consecration
Delightfully modest and fragrant, it smiles at life without wanting to draw attention.

Aesthetic Power

The highest aim of the aesthetic being is to find the Divine through beauty; the highest Art is that which by an inspired use of significant and interpretative form unseals the doors of the Spirit.

Hibiscus
  large or small single reddish-pink flower with dark red centre and smooth petals, each petal splashed white on one lower edge; shrub

Aesthetic Power
Beauty is a great power.

Hibiscus
: medium-sized double light or dark salmon-pink flower often with fine red veins and red centre

Agni
The flame of purification which must precede all contact with the invisible worlds.

Hibiscus
: small to medium single cream white or cream-yellow flower with pure white centre

Ananda
Calm, tranquil, equal, smiling and very gentle in its truly simple austerity.

Hibiscus *Hawaiian*
: medium to large single crimson-pink flower with smooth or crinkled petals shading to pale pink or white on the edges, deep red or reddish pink centre

Beauty of the New Creation
The New Creation strives to better manifest the Divine.

Hibiscus
: medium single salmon pink flower often changing to apricot yellow similar or dark shade at centre

Beauty of Supramental Youth
Exquisitively freshed and powerful, with an uncontested beauty.

Hibiscus
: Lavender-grey with the ring of magenta and a bright red centre, edge of petals dull white, smooth or crinkled petals; varieties with other gaudy colours

All-powerful Charm of an Alluring Beauty
It is a beauty used to turn one away from the Divine.

Hibiscus
: single, small to medium cream-yellow flower with red or magenta centre

Ananda in the Physical
It is welcome, even if it manifests rarely.

Hibiscus *Hawaiian*
: large single salmon-pink flower with pink centre and pale pink aura or medium single light apricot-orange flower with small light red centre

Beauty of Supramental Love
It invites us to live at its height.

Hibiscus *Hawaiian*
: medium to large single orange flowers with smooth or ruffled petals, centres of various colours other than white

Beauty of Tomorrow
The beauty that will express Divine Power.

Hibiscus *Hawaiian* (Pl. 15)
>large single orange flower with white centre and pale pink aura, smooth or crinkle petals

Beauty of Tomorrow Manifesting the Divine
A beauty that exists only for the Divine and by the Divine.

Hibiscus *Hawaiian*
>large semi-double flower with rounded outer petals and tufted centre; shades of yellow, blended with fire-red and orange towards the centre

Blossoming of the New Creation
The more we concentrate on the goal the more it grows and becomes precise.

Hibiscus *Hawaiian*
>large single pink or deep pink flowers with crinkled or smooth petals, centres varying from pink through dark pink

Charm of the New Creation
The New Creation is attractive for all those who want to progress.

Hibiscus *Hawaiian*
>medium-sized yellow cup-shaped flower splashed orange with crinkled petals and light yellow centre

Concentration of the New Creation
Concentration on a precise goal helps development.

Hibiscus
>large double flower, light pink shading to deeper pink with red centre, with or without pale cream border on outer edge of petals

Consciousness One with the Divine Consciousness
Smiling and happy, it no longer knows any shadows.

Hibiscus 'Dream'
>medium to large double flower, mauve shading to grey-lavender or light mauve

Controlled Power
True power is always quiet. *

*extract from a message

No matter how great your faith and trust in the Divine Grace, no matter how great your capacity to see it at work in all circumstances, at every moment, at every point in life, you will never succeed in understanding the marvellous immensity of Its Action, and the precision, the exactitude with which this Action is accomplished; you will never be able to grasp to what extent the Grace does everything, is behind everything, organises everything, conducts everything, so that the march forward to the divine realisation may be as swift, as complete, as total and harmonious as possible, considering the circumstances of the world.

As soon as you are in contact with It, there is not a second in time, not a point in space, which does not show you dazzlingly this perpetual work of the Grace, this constant intervention of the Grace.

And once you have seen this, you feel you are never equal to it, for you should never forget it, never have any fears, any anguish, any regrets, any recoils... or even suffering. If one were in union with the Grace, if one saw It everywhere, one would begin living a life of exultation, of all-power, of infinite happiness.

And that would be the best possible collaboration in the divine Work.

Hibiscus mutabilis
Changeable rose, Confederate rose
large double flower with soft delicate
petals, opening pure white, gradually
turning pink

The Divine Grace
*Thy goodness is infinite; we bow
before Thee in gratitude!*

What is lacking is a spiritual knowledge and spiritual power, a power over self, a power born of inner unification with others, a power over the surrounding or invading world-forces, a full-visioned and fully equipped power of effectuation of knowledge; it is these capacities missing or defective in us that belong to the very substance of gnostic being, for they are inherent in the light and dynamis of the gnostic nature.

Hibiscus rosa-sinensis
    medium-sized light in dark red single erect or pendulous flowers, separated recurved petals and often with crenate border

Dynamic Power
Indispensable for progress.

Hibiscus
    medium to large single orange-pink cup-shaped flower with light orange or apricot border and large deep pink centre

Effective Power of the Supermind
All-powerful, it imposes itself on all in the certitude of its knowledge.

Hibiscus 'Viceroy'
    small single light or deep magenta flower with separated petals

Individual Power
Limited in capacity and action.

Hibiscus
    small to medium single coral-pink flower with cream border, luminous pink veins and intense red centre

Enlightened Individual Power
Limited in its action but of a very high capacity.

Hibiscus hirtus
> very small delicate single white flower; small shrub

Eternal Smile
A boon only the Divine can give.

Hibiscus hirtus
> very small salmon-orange flower

Eternal Youth
A gift that the Divine gives us when we unite ourselves with Him.

The eternal smile means the self-existent joy and gladness of the Spirit.

* * *

To know how to be reborn into a new life at every moment is the secret of eternal youth.

* * *

There is one kind of faith demanded as indispensable by the integral Yoga and that may be described as faith in God and the Shakti, faith in the presence and power of the Divine in us and the world.

Hibiscus albo-variegata (*Pl. 9*)
> medium-sized double flower, variegated red and white

Faith
You flame up and triumph!

Hibiscus Hawaiian
> large single flower with long smooth yellow petals veined orange-red, deep red or bright pink centre and lighter pink aura

Firmness of the New Creation
The New Creation wants to be firm in its manifestation.

Flame

"O seeing Flame,
   thou carriest man of the crooked ways
     into the abiding truth and the knowledge."

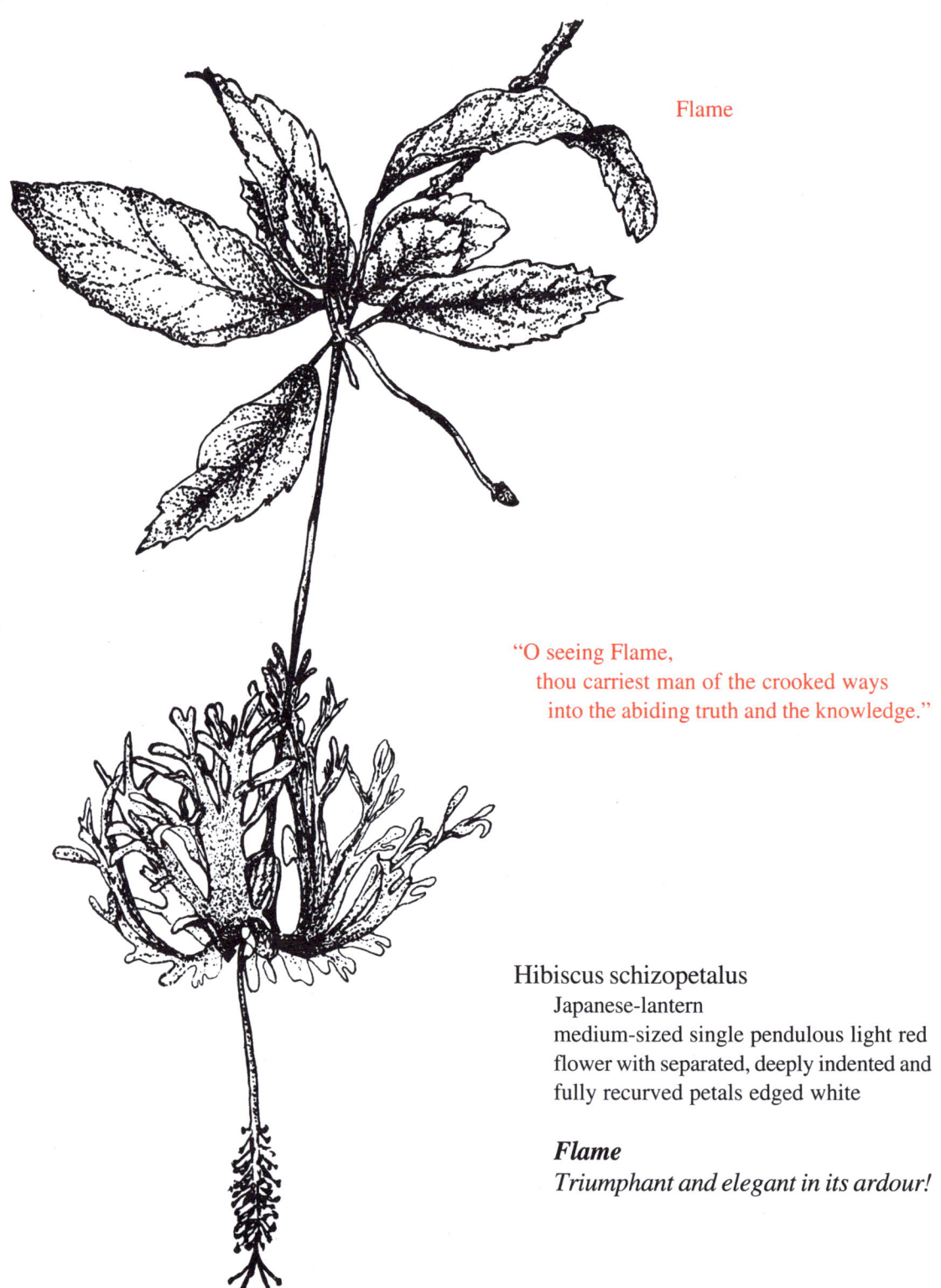

Hibiscus schizopetalus
   Japanese-lantern
   medium-sized single pendulous light red
   flower with separated, deeply indented and
   fully recurved petals edged white

Flame
Triumphant and elegant in its ardour!

Hibiscus Hawaian, 'Cromwell'
large single cream or very pale
yellow flower with smooth or crinkled
petals and a light pink or white centre

Godhead
*Pure and perfect, it puts out its force
in the world.*

Hibiscus Hawaiian
medium-sized single light lavender pink
or blushing pink cup-shaped flower with
heavily crinkled petals and intense red or
magenta centre; edge of petals pink, nearly
white

Ideal of the New Creation
*The ideal must be progressive in
order to be realised in the future.*

Hibiscus
medium to large single white flower with
slender or rounded separated milk-white
petals

Light of the Purified Power
*Of irresistible simplicity in its power
solely consecrated to the Divine.*

Hibiscus 'Splash'
medium to large single bi-coloured or
variegated flower with crinkled petals,
usually orange-red splashed with gold and
white

Manifold Power of the New Creation
*The New Creation will be rich in
possibilities.*

Hibiscus Hawaiian
medium to large single lemon-yellow
flowers with centres varying from light
red to scarlet

Mentalised Power
Power rendered utilisable.

Power of Consciousness

Hibiscus *Hawaiian*
    medium-sized single bright cardinal-red flower with firm petals, with or without dark red centre

Power of Action
The power resulting from true surrender to the Divine.

Hibiscus
    all shades of red small to large double flowers

Power of Consciousness
All the powers of controlling and dominating the lower movements of inconscient nature.

The liberated individual being, united with the Divine in self and spirit, becomes in his natural being a self-perfecting instrument for the perfect outflowering of the Divine in humanity.

Hibiscus Hawaiian
: large single bright ochre-yellow or golden flower with smooth or crinkled petals

Power in the Converted Mind
When the mind turns towards the Divine it becomes a powerful instrument.

Hibiscus 'Sebactini'
: medium or large single light grey to deep lavender flower with smooth or crinkled petals and deep magenta or dark pink centre

Power of Effort
Efforts well-directed break down all obstacles.

Hibiscus 'Comet'
: medium or large sturdy single deep magenta flower with rounded petals

Power of the Future
To be capable of working for the future.

Hibiscus
: medium to large single light or bright yellow flowers with smooth petals; pink, red or light orange centre

Power of Harmony
Simple, noble, dignified, powerful and charming.

Hibiscus syriacus
: Rose-of-Sharon, Shrub althaea medium-sized single deep lavender cup-shaped flower changing to blue, magenta centre and white anthers and stigma

Power in the Higher Vital
Power that wants to be at the service of the Divine.

Hibiscus
: medium or large single white flower with long or rounded separated petals and bright red or vermilion centre

Power of Integral Purity
The power to accept only the Divine's influence.

Hibiscus Hawaiian
: large single bright orange-red flower often with orange border and deep red centre

Power of Perseverance
The perseverance that overcomes all obstacles.

The power needed in yoga is the power to go through effort, difficulty or trouble without getting fatigued, depressed, discouraged or impatient and without breaking off the effort or giving up one's aim or resolution.

Hibiscus Hawaiian
: large single light to deep pink flower, centre white often with lavender-pink aura

Power of Progress
Progress is the sign of the Divine's influence in creation.

Hibiscus 'Sweetheart'
: small single cream-white flower with mauve-pink veins and deep pink centre, separated petals and orange stigma

Power to Progress
Precious because of its rarity, it must be cultivated with care.

Hibiscus
    medium to large double flowers with delicate petals, light to dark pink

Power of the Psychic Consciousness
The psychic power organises the activities of the nature to make it progress.

Hibiscus Hawaiian
    large single deep magenta flower with firm crinkled or smooth petals, dark red centre

Power in Service of the Future
Without haste, but sure of its success.

In a gnostic life, a life of superreason and supernature, a self-aware spiritual unity of being and a spiritual conscious community and interchange of nature would be the deep and ample root of understanding: this greater life would have evolved new and superior means and powers of uniting consciousness inwardly with consciousness; intimacy of consciousness communicating inwardly and directly with consciousness, thought with thought, vision with vision, sense with sense, life with life, body-awareness with body-awareness, would be its natural basic instrumentation. All these new powers taking up the old outward instruments and using them as a subordinate means with a far greater power and to more purpose would be put to the sevice of the self-expression of the Spirit in a profound oneness of being and life.

Hibiscus Hawaiian
    medium-sized or large single golden-yellow flower with tinge orange, soft crinkled petals, deep magenta centre and silver-white aura

Power of Spiritual Beauty
Spiritual beauty has a contagious power.

Hibiscus Hawaiian
: large single cream-white flower with crinkled petals and magenta pinwheel centre, with or without white aura

Power of Success
The power of those who know how to continue their effort.

Hibiscus
: medium to large double golden-yellow or light orange-yellow flower with red to deep orange centre

Power of the Supramental Consciousness
Organising and active, irresistible in its influence.

Hibiscus Hawaiian
: medium-sized single cup-shaped yellow flower with heavily crinkled petals and large reddish-orange firelike centre

Progress of the New Creation
Each must find the activity favourable to one's own progress.

Hibiscus
: all pink medium or large single flowers with or without separated petals

Psychic Power in Existence
Manifold, imperious, irresistible in its comprehensive sweetness.

Hibiscus Hawaiian
: large single bright orange-red flower with firm crinkled petals, light gold on back of petals, reddish pink centre

Puissance of Realisation
With realisation all obstacles will be overcome.

Hibiscus Hawaiian
: large single lemon-yellow or luminous yellow flower with crinkled or smooth petals white or light pink centre with white aura

Realisation of the New Creation
It is for this that we must prepare ourselves.

Hibiscus
> medium to large single golden-orange or deep apricot flowers with separated petals often fading to yellow, large red or deep crimson centre

> ***Supramental Beauty in the Physical***
> *Its promise is charming!*

Hibiscus 'Daffodil'
> medium to large double bright yellow or golden-yellow flower

> ***Supramental Consciousness***
> Gloriously awake and powerful—luminous, sure of itself and infallible in its movements!

The one rule of the gnostic life would be the self-expression of the Spirit, the will of the Divine Being; that will, that self-expression could manifest through extreme simplicity or through extreme complexity and opulence or in their natural balance, — for beauty and plenitude, a hidden sweetness and laughter in things, a sunshine and gladness of life are also powers and expressions of the Spirit.

Hibiscus Hawaiian (*Pl. 12*)
> large single light golden-yellow or apricot-yellow flower with crinkled petals and white or light pink pinwheel centre, with or without light pink aura

> ***Sweetness of the Power Surrendered to the Divine***
> *Sweetness itself becomes powerful when it is at the service of the Divine.*

Hibiscus Hawaiian
> medium to large single deep pink flower with firm smooth petals, and reddish-pink centre

> ***Usefulness of the New Creation***
> *A creation which aims at teaching men to surpass themselves.*

Hibiscus Hawaiian
large single golden-ochre to mustard
flower with crinkled petals, vermilion
or magenta centre with or without
silver-white aura

Victorious Beauty
When it has resolved the ugliness of life!

One must feel within oneself the touch, the approach of something positively beautiful and true, and willingly drop all the rest so that nothing may burden the journey to this new beauty and truth.

Hibiscus mutabilis 'rosa'
Changeable rose, Confederate rose
large double light to medium pink flower
with delicate petals; large shrub

Victorious Love
Sure of itself, fearless, generous and smiling.

O victorious power of divine Love, Thou art the sovereign Master of this universe, Thou art its creator and its saviour, Thou hast permitted it to emerge from chaos, and now Thou leadest it to its eternal goal.

The will to enjoy is proper to the vital being but not the choice or the reaching after the enjoyment which must be determined and acquired by higher functions; therefore the vital being must be trained to accept whatever gain or enjoyment comes to it in the right functioning of the life in obedience to the working of the divine Will and to rid itself of craving and attachment.

Hibiscus
    medium to large double cream-white or light yellow flower

Will in Course of Uniting with the Divine Will
On the way to perfection.

Hibiscus syriacus (*Pl. 4*)
    Rose-of-Sharon, Shrub althaea
    small to medium-sized double white flower

Will One with the Divine Will
The condition for surmounting all obstacles.

How can we know what the divine Will is?

One does not know it, one feels it. And in order to feel it one must will with such an intensity, such sincerity, that every obstacle disappears. As long as you have a preference, a desire, an attraction, a liking, all these veil the Truth from you. Hence, the first thing to do is to try to master, govern, correct all the movements of your consciousness and eliminate those which cannot be changed until all becomes a perfect and permanent expression of the Truth.

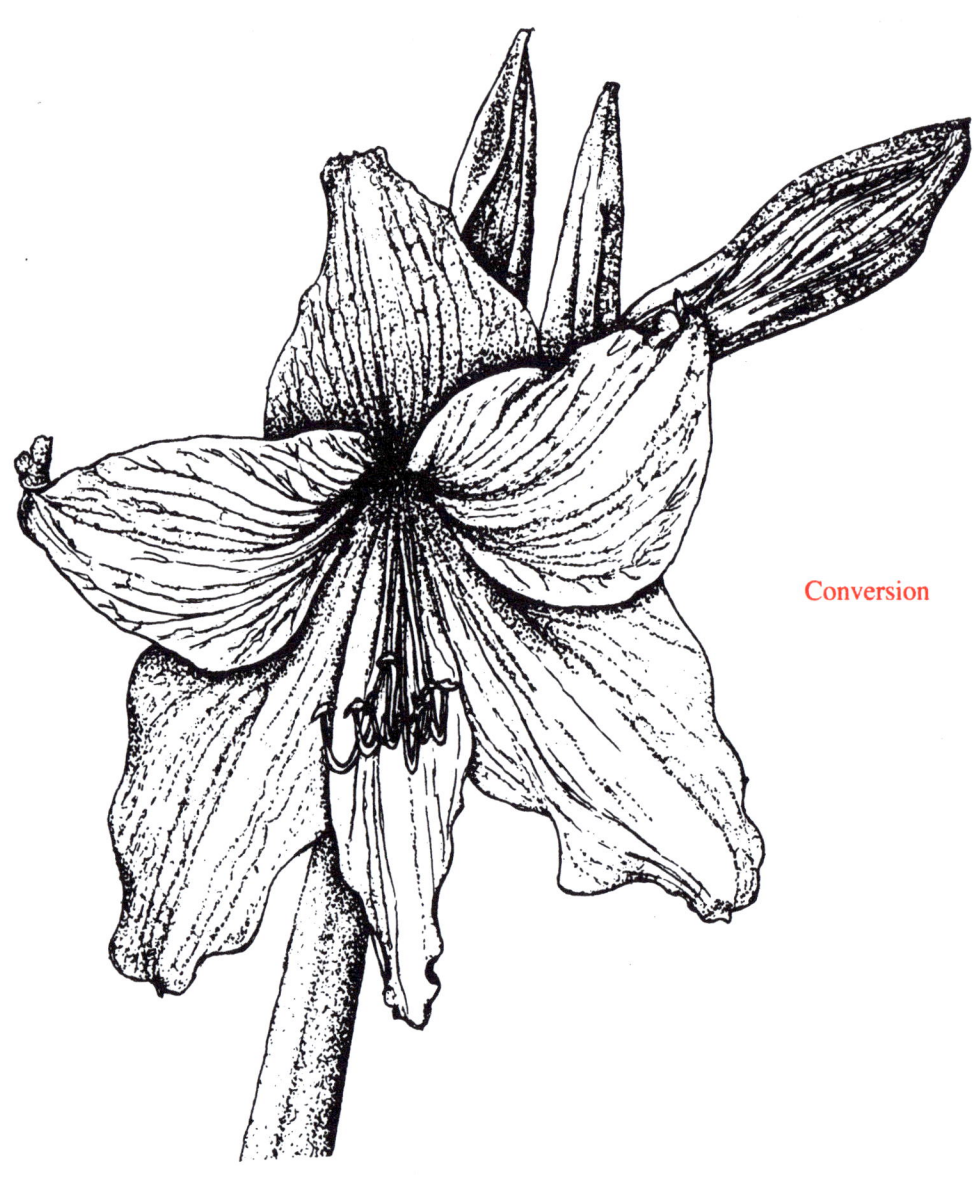

Conversion

Hippeastrum
    Amaryllis
    long sturdy scapes bearing umbels of large trumpet-shaped flowers in several colours; bulbous plant

Conversion
The starting point of realisation.

Hippeastrum
yellow trumpet-shaped flowers borne on a long a short scape; bulbous plant

Conversion of the Mind
The mind has freed itself from its arrogance and knows it is only an instrument.

Hippeastrum
light pink with carmine-pink lines and a white streak through the middle of each petal

Conversion of the Emotional Being
It blossoms in harmonious receptivity.

Hippeastrum
medium-sized bright red flower

Conversion of the Physical
Compact and stable, without fluctuations.

Hippeastrum
medium-sized salmon-orange flower

Conversion of the Physical Mind
Ready to understand everything and to grow continuously.

Hippeastrum
medium-sized dark red or violet flower

Conversion of the Vital
Enthusiastic and spontaneous, it gives itself unstintingly.

Hippeastrum
large white fragrant flower

Integral Conversion
A harmonious blossoming above all conflicts and struggles.

Hippeastrum
white specked pink, curly-edged petals

Integral Conversion with the Help of the Psychic
Sweetness mingles with resolution.

Hippeastrum 'Dutch hybrid'
large flower with thick fleshy petals, red

Total Conversion
The whole being has given itself in all its movements.

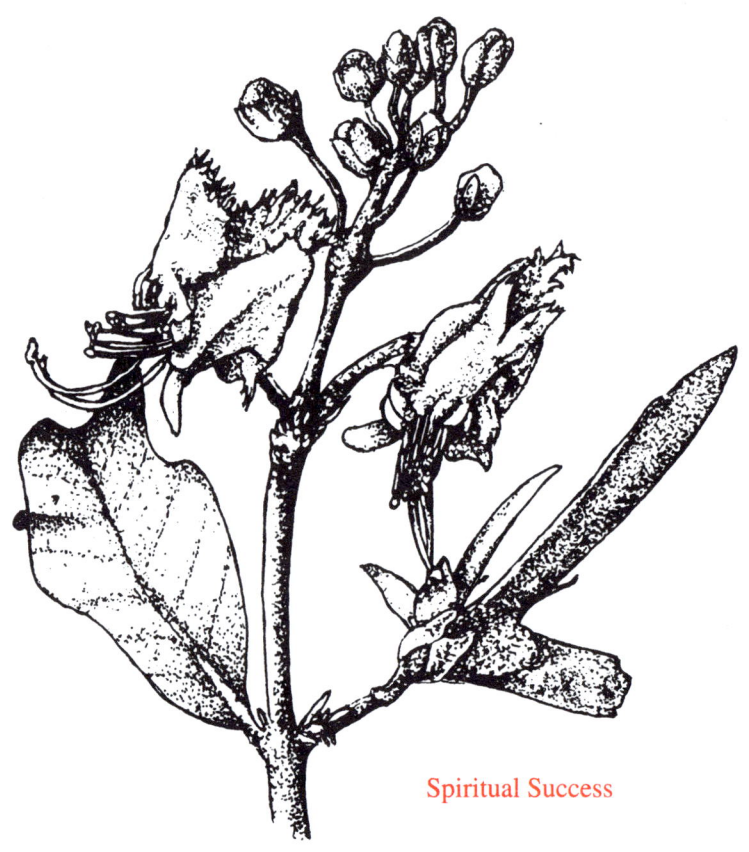

Spiritual Success

Hiptage benghalensis
   clusters of small fragrant white flowers, recurved and frilled petals, one splotched yellow; heavy creeper

Spiritual Success
Spiritual success is conscious union with the Divine.

Hollarrhena antidysenterica (*Pl. 1*)
   Conessi bark, Easter tree
   loose cymes of small fragrant cream-white salverform flowers with recurved petals; tree

Psychic Peace
It is spontaneous and does not make a fuss.

Curiosity

Holmskioldia
Chinese-hat plant, Parasol flower
few-flowered clusters of small striking parasol-like flowers in various colours; shrub

Curiosity
If we want to be exceptional, may it be our capacities that make us so!

Every child has an insatiable intellectual curiosity and turn for metaphysical enquiry. Use it to draw him on slowly to an understanding of the world and himself.

Holmskioldia
lemon-yellow

Mental Curiosity
Must be earnestly controlled so as not to be dangerous.

Holmskioldia
orange-red

Physical Curiosity
Its value depends on its purpose.

> For all problems of existence are essentially problems of harmony. They arise from the perception of an unsolved discord and the instinct of an undiscovered agreement or unity. . . . For essentially, all Nature seeks a harmony, life and matter in their own sphere as much as mind in the arrangement of its perceptions.

Hoya carnosa
> Wax flower
> full umbels of small pale pink waxy star-shaped flowers; creeper

Power of Collective Aspiration
A harmonious collective aspiration can change the course of circumstances.

Hyacinthus orientalis
> Hyacinth
> short scapes bearing densely clustered fragrant bell-shaped flowers with flared petals, several colours; bulbous plant

Pride of Beauty
Likes to show itself and be admired.

Hydrangea
> large rounded heads of small four-petalled flowers ranging in colour from white through pink to blue; shrub

Collective Harmony
Collective harmony is the work undertaken by the Divine Consciousness; it alone has the power to realise it.

Hymenocallis
> Crown-beauty, Spider lily
> umbels of fragrant white flowers; each flower with slender recurved petals and elongated stamens emerging from a central cup; bulbous plant

Alchemy
Plastic and supple, ready to take any form.

Equanimity

The more a person is quiet in front of all occurrences, equal in all circumstances, and keeps a perfect mastery of himself and remains peaceful in the presence of whatever happens, the more he has progressed towards the goal.

Iberis
    Candytuft
    heads of small white, pink to blue
    irregular rotate flowers; low seasonal plant

Equanimity
Immutable peace and calm.

Ilex
    Holly
    red berries set in shiny glossy evergreen
    spiny leaves; shrub

Courageous Goodwill
Is solid and resistant, fearing neither inclemency nor the cold.

Impatiens balsamina
: Balsam, Snapweed
several colours of single or double flowers with delicately recurved petals and a long spur; low seasonal plant

Generosity
Giving and self-giving without bargain.

Impatiens balsamina
: rose-purple

Generosity in the Vital
Gives itself unstintingly.

Impatiens balsamina
: pink

Psychic Generosity
Gives for the joy of giving.

Impatiens balsamina
: red

Generosity in the Physical
Likes abundance and gives abundantly.

Impatiens balsamina
: all multi-coloured shades except pink-red

Manifold Generosity
All in Nature is spontaneously generous.

Impatiens balsamina
: pink-red

Psycho-physical Generosity
Generosity of thought and act.

Impatiens walleriana
: Busy Lizzie, Perennial balsam
several colours of small single rotate flowers with flat petals and a long spur; low herbaceous plant

Works of Love
The best condition for work.

Iochroma cyaneum
: pendulous clusters of deep violet tubular flowers; low shrub

Seeking the Light in the Lower Vital
Does more work, makes less noise!

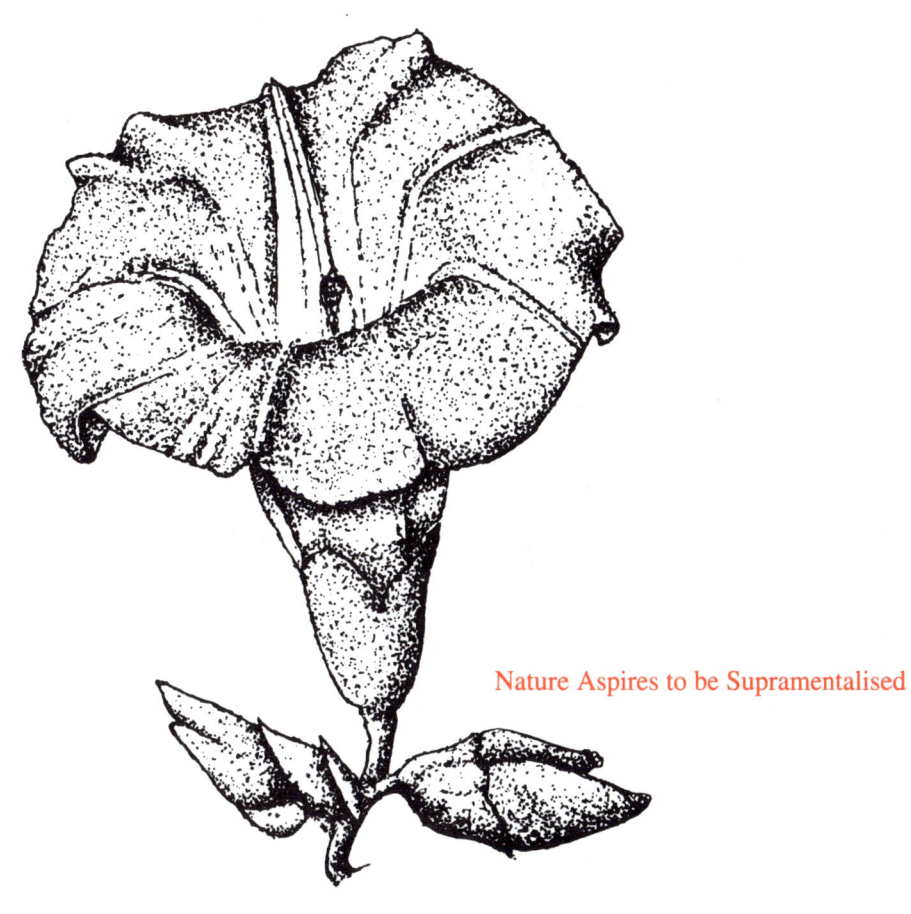

Nature Aspires to be Supramentalised

The plants offer their beauty to the Supreme.

Ipomoea
    delicate funnel-shaped flowers in many colours; cultivated or countryside creeper

Nature Makes an Offering of Her Beauty
It is a spontaneous and effortless offering.

Ipomoea beveriensis 'Candy king'
    large striking scarlet flower with large yellow centre streaked scarlet; perennial creeper

Nature Aspires to Be Supramentalised
The first vegetal response to the action of the Supramental forces.

In the world of forms a violation of Beauty is as great a fault as a violation of Truth in the world of ideas. For Beauty is the worship Nature offers to the supreme Master of the universe; Beauty is the divine language in forms. And a consciousness of the Divine which is not translated externally by an understanding and expression of Beauty would be an incomplete consciousness.

But true Beauty is as difficult to discover, to understand and above all to live as any other expression of the Divine; this discovery and expression exacts as much impersonality and renunciation of egoism as that of Truth or Bliss. Pure Beauty is universal and one must be universal to see and recognise it.

Ipomoea acuminata
    Morning glory, Blue dawn flower
    large violet-blue flower fading to mauve;
    perennial creeper

Artistic Taste
Pleased with beautiful things, it is itself beautiful.

Ipomoea tricolor
    Blue dawn flower
    large light blue flower; seasonal creeper

Artistic Sensibility
A powerful aid to fight ugliness.

Ipomoea tricolor 'Scarlet O'Hara'
    large bright magenta flower

Joy of Beauty
Beauty is the joyous offering of Nature.

Ipomoea tricolor 'Heavenly blue'
    medium to large translucent sky-blue flower

Pure Sense of Beauty
Can be acquired only through a great purification.

Ipomoea tricolor 'Cornell'
    medium to large rose-pink flower with white centre and border

Spontaneous Beauty
Delicate and magnificent, it has an incomparable charm.

Ipomoea cairica
    Railway creeper
    small light mauve to purple flower; perennial creeper

Detachment from All That Is Not the Divine
A single occupation, a single aim, a single joy—the Divine!

Ipomoea carnea (*Pl. 12*)
    large pale lavender-pink to light mauve flower with deeper mauve throat; shrub or heavy creeper

Gratitude
It is you who open all the closed doors and allow the saving Grace to enter.

Ipomoea horsfalliae
    small magenta star-shaped flower with waxy petals; heavy perennial creeper

Heroic Thought
To the conquest of the unknown without fear of difficulty and incomprehension!

Ipomoea tricolor 'Pearly Gates'
    large radiant translucent white flower with cream-yellow throat

Integral Unconditional Offering
The joy of offering oneself without asking for anything in return.

Aristocracy of Beauty

Iris
    Fleur-de-lis
    tall scapes bearing large flowers in
    various colours with three crested and three
    recurved petals; bulbous plant

    Aristocracy of Beauty
    So perfect a form as to compel
    admiration!

Divine Purity

Purity means freedom from soil or mixture. The divine Purity is that in which there is no mixture of the turbid ignorant movements of the lower nature.

Isotoma longiflora
   pure white star-shaped flower with long corolla tube

Divine Purity
Happy just to be, in all simplicity!

When I speak of aspiration in the physical I mean that the very consciousness in you which hankers after material comfort and well-being should of itself, without being compelled by the higher parts of your nature, ask exclusively for the Divine's Love. Usually you have to show it the Light by means of your higher parts; surely this has to be done persistently, otherwise the physical would never learn and it would take Nature's common round of ages before it learns by itself. Indeed the round of Nature is intended to show it all possible sorts of satisfactions and by exhausting them convince it that none of them can really satisfy it and that what it is at bottom seeking is a divine satisfaction. In Yoga we hasten this slow process of Nature and insist on the physical consciousness seeing the truth and learning to recognise and want it.

Ixora
    small or full corymbs of dark red flowers with narrow corolla tube and pointed petals; shrub

Aspiration in the Physical
Manifold, simple and joyous.

Ixora singaporensis
    smaller orange to brick-red flowers with less pointed petals

Aspiration in the Physical for the Supramental Light
Clustered, persistent, it is obstinately organised and methodical.

Ixora
    yellow flowers

Mental Aspiration
Its expression is clear, precise and very reasonable!

Ixora chinensis
    tiny to small mildly fragrant pink flowers

Psychic Aspiration
Constant, regular, organised, at the same time gentle and patient—it resists all opposition, overcomes all difficulties.

Ixora thwaitesii (*Pl. 4*)
    very fragrant white flowers; small tree

Peace in the Cells
The indispensable condition for the body's progress.

Ixora arborea
    Torch tree
    branching clusters of very fragrant tiny white flowers; countryside shrub or tree

Straightforwardness
Shows itself as it is, without compromise.

Jacaranda
    Green ebony
    large panicles of lavender-blue tubular flowers with flared petals; tree

Attempt at Vital Goodwill
An attempt is a small thing, but it can be a promise for the future.

Jacquemontia pentantha
    small light blue rotate flower; creeper

Hope
Paves life's path.

Hope

Purity

Purity is perfect sincerity and one cannot have it unless the being is entirely consecrated to the Divine.

* * *

On earth, true purity is to think as the Divine thinks, to will as the Divine wills, to feel as the Divine feels.

Jasminum
: Jasmine
fragrant single white star-like salverform flowers; shrub or creeper

Purity
True purity is fragrant!

Jasminum
: fully double white flowers

Integral Purity
The whole being is purified of the ego.

Jasminum
: small semi-double white flowers

Psychic Purity
The natural condition of the psychic.

Jasminum
: Italian Jasmine, Yellow Jasmine
sparse clusters of mildly fragrant yellow flowers

Correct Self-Evaluation
Simple and modest, it does not try to assert itself.

Flowers lift towards the sky their fragrant prayer and aspiration.

* * *

By communing with flowers we can see that the vegetal kingdom has her own way of aspiring towards the Divine.

Jatropha integerrima
> Peregrina, Spicy jatropha
> terminal cymes of small pink or red rotate flowers; shrub

Awakening and First Response of Nature to the Supramental Manifestation
Interested, she opens herself and tries to understand.

Jatropha multifida (*Pl. 3*)
> Coral plant, Physic nut
> sparse cymes of very small deep pink flowers and palmate leaves with deeply cut lobes; shrub

First Emergence of the Psychic in Matter
A messenger of beauty!

Jatropha podagarica
> Guatemala Rhubarb
> flat cymes of very small bright orange-red flowers and round or violin-shaped leaves; low shrub with swollen base

First Response of the Subconscient to the Supramental Action
The open door to realisation!

Justicia aurea
> dense terminal bracteated spikes of yellow tubular labiate flowers; shrub

Aspiration of the Mind for the Supramental Guidance
The mind feels that its complexity is powerless and asks for a greater light to illumine it.

Justicia oblongata
> short one-sided racemes of pink tubular labiate flowers; low shrub

Psychic Influence in the Emotions
Indispensable for beginning the sadhana.

Fundamentally, without this kind of inner will of the psychic being, I believe human beings would be quite dismal, dull, they would have an altogether animal life. Every gleam of aspiration is always the expression of a psychic influence. Without the presence of the psychic, without the psychic influence, there would never be any sense of progress or any will for progress.

Would there be a sense of beauty?

Yes. Perhaps not the highest sense of beauty, but in the vital one finds a complete sense of beauty and harmony. The beauty which is fundamental, profound, universal, constant belongs only to the psychic, but the sense of the beauty of form, of appearance, of colour, the educated, refined vital fully possesses.

Kaempferia pulchra
> small delicate lavender flower with white throat appearing between beautifully marked leaves; tuberous ornamental

Refined Taste
Lovable and delicate, always avoids the mistakes of bad taste.

Kaempferia rotunda
> Tropical crocus, Resurrection lily fragrant delicate pale lavender flowers with deeper coloured inner petals veined purple, coming directly from the ground before the leaves appear; tuberous ornamental

Vital Honesty
Not to allow our sensations and desires to falsify our judgment or determine our actions.

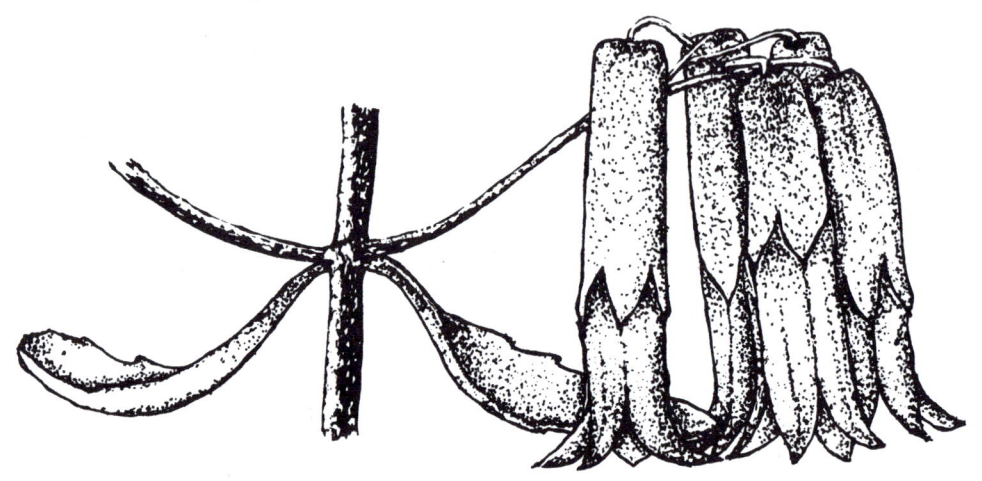
Light in the Fairyland

Kalanchoe pinnata
Air plant, Floppers, Life plant
clusters of pendulous bell-shaped calyces
and deep pink to maroon corollas; low
succulent or countryside herbaceous plant

Light in Fairyland
Fairies are ready to allow themselves to be guided by the Divine.

Kigelia pinnata
Sausage tree
pendulous racemes of mildly fragrant dark
red open funnel-shaped flowers with thick
crinkled petals; tree

First Response of the Inconscient to the Divine Force
The first step towards transformation.

Kleinhovia hospita
terminal airy panicles of very small
delicate light pink flowers and papery
green-brown fruits; tree

Joy in Fairyland
Light, smiling and effortless, it invites us to share its joy!

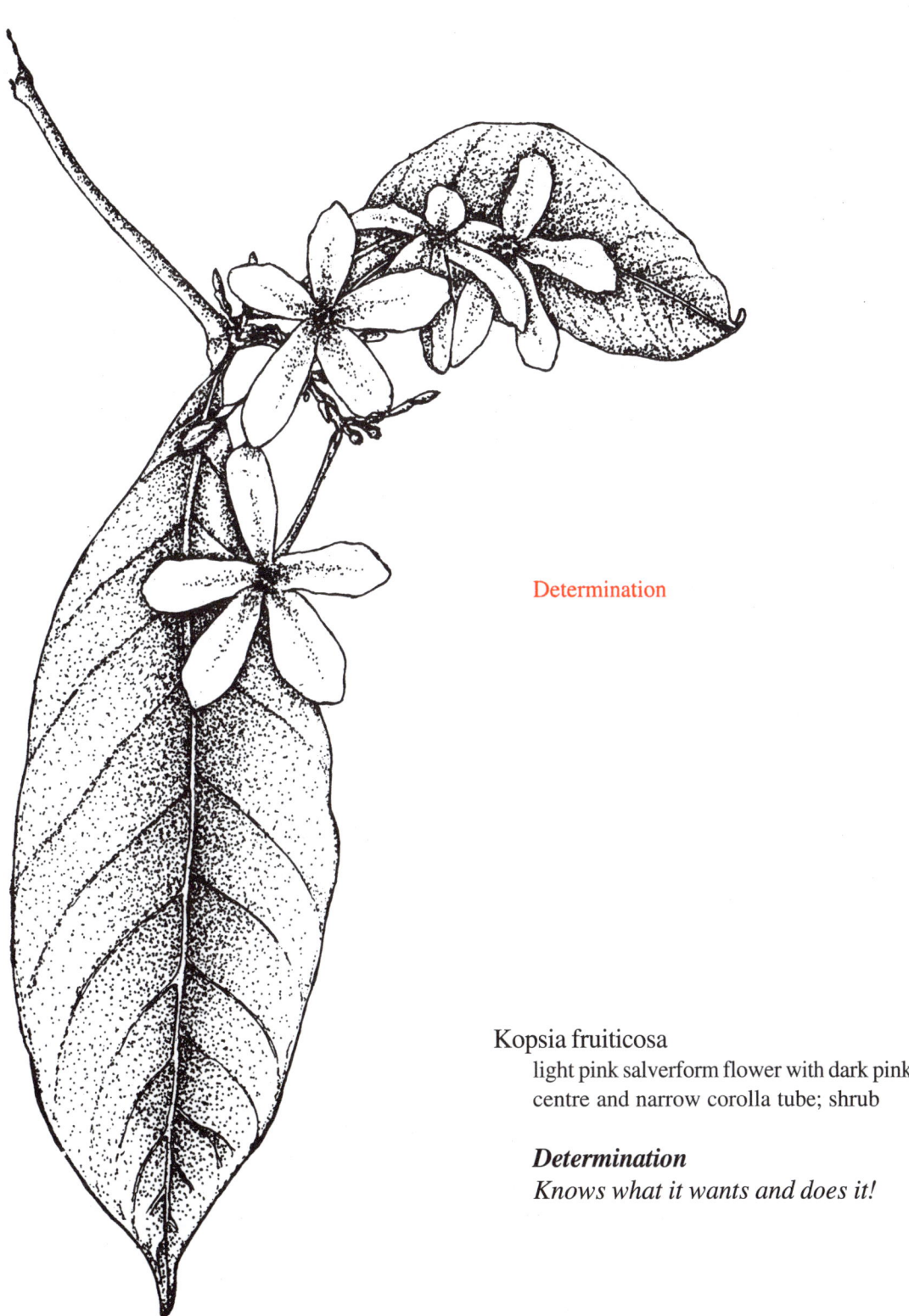

Determination

Kopsia fruiticosa
light pink salverform flower with dark pink centre and narrow corolla tube; shrub

Determination
Knows what it wants and does it!

An inner fullness has come in like the coming in of light in dark caves. It fills, it illumines, it vibrates the multiple strings of life; it has found the contact with the forgotten achievements of the past to enable me to start the new ones of the future on the basis of the changing formations of the present. The currents of life well up to meet the descending rays of light from the upper heavens for transmutation of the base and the dark into the luminous and the true, for transmutation of the ugly and the wrong into the beautiful and the right.

Laburnum anagyroides
    Golden-chain tree
    cascading racemes of silky golden-yellow papilionaceous flowers; tree

Descent of the Light
It flows towards the earth in a harmonious movement!

Lagenaria siceraria
    Bottle gourd, White-flowered gourd
    large white funnel-shaped flower; seasonal climbing cucurbit

Emotional Abundance
Good feelings expressing themselves unstintingly.

A divine force shall flow through tissue and cell
And take the charge of breath and speech and act
And all the thoughts shall be a glow of suns
And every feeling a celestial thrill.

Lagerstroemia
>Crape myrtle
>rounded panicles of rotate flowers with delicate deeply crinkled and lacy petals, several colours; shrub or small tree

Intimacy with the Divine
Complete surrender to the Divine and total receptivity to His influence are the conditions of this intimacy.

Lagerstroemia
>white

Integral Intimacy with the Divine
The entire being no longer vibrates except with the Divine's touch.

Lagerstroemia
>deep cerise

Intimacy with the Divine in the Physical
Possible only for one who lives exclusively for the Divine and by the Divine.

Lagerstroemia
>pink

Intimacy with the Divine in the Psychic
The natural state of the fully developed psychic.

Lagerstroemia
>light to deep mauve

Intimacy with the Divine in the Vital
Only a pure, calm and desireless vital can hope to have access to this marvellous state.

Lagerstroemia speciosa
>Pride of India, Queen's flower
>larger pink or purple flowers with flat petals; tree

Intimacy with Universal Nature
This intimacy is only possible for those who are vast and who are without preference or repulsion.

In sadhana vital intimacy would ordinarily signify inner intimacy with the Divine on the vital plane.

The Prayer of the Cells of the Body

Now that, by the effect of the Grace, we are slowly emerging out of inconscience and waking to a conscious life, an ardent prayer rises in us for more light, more consciousness,

"O Supreme Lord of the universe, we implore Thee, give us the strength and beauty, the harmonious perfection needed to be Thy divine instruments upon earth."

Lantana
> Shrub verbena
> compact heads of very small salverform flowers in many hues and colour combinations; rambling countryside shrub with aromatic leaves

Supramental Influence in the Cells
Unexpected variety in colours and qualities.

Lantana
> yellow

Light in the Cells
The first step towards purity in the cells.

Lantana
> white

Purity in the Cells
Can only be obtained through the conquest of desires; it is the true condition for good health.

Lantana
> mauve to violet

Emotional Beauty in the Cells
Seeking and emanating all the emotions of beauty.

Lathyrus odoratus
> Sweet Pea
> racemes of fragrant papilionaceous
> flowers in a range of pastel colours;
> seasonal creeper

Gentleness (Kindness)
Always gracious and loves to please.

Lawsonia inermis
> Henna, Mignonette tree
> intensely fragrant compact clusters of very
> small cream-yellow or red flowers; large
> shrub or hedge

Energy Turned towards the Divine
The power of realisation offers itself in the service of the Divine.

Leonotis nepetifolia
> Lion's tail
> ascending column of separate spiny round
> heads studded with small velvety orange
> labiate flowers; seasonal countryside plant

Ascension
Step by step one climbs towards consciousness.

Spiritual beauty illumining human sight
Lines with its passion and mystery Matter's mask
And squanders eternity on a beat of Time.

* * *

To find highest beauty is to find God; to reveal, to embody, to create, as we say, highest beauty is to bring out of our souls the living image and power of God.

Leontopodium alpinum
> Edelweiss
> many-pointed white starlike flowers with
> a woolly texture and tufted yellow centre;
> low mountain plant

Spiritual Beauty
Immaculate whiteness, sweetness and purity, you seem to come from another world!

Leucaena
: White popinac, Subabu
small mildly fragrant cream-white fluffy balls; shrub or small tree

Knowledge
It is conversant with all sides of a question whatever it may be.

Leucas aspera
: rounded heads of green calyces with small white labiate flowers; low seasonal countryside plant

True Worship
Total and constant, without demand or claim.

Lilium candidum
: Annunciation lily, Easter lily, Madonna lily
pearl-white trumpet-shaped flowers on a long scape; bulbous plant

Purity Arising from Perfect Consecration
Perfect purity can be realised by living only for the Divine and by the Divine.

Linaria maroccana
: Baby snapdragon, Fairy flax
erect spikes of small labiate flowers with long spurs in several pastel colours; seasonal plant

Expressive Silence
Certain silences are revealing and more expressive than words.

The plants are very psychic, but they can express it only by silence and beauty.

Sri Aurobindo came upon earth to announce the manifestation of the supramental world. And not only did he announce this manifestation but he also embodied in part the supramental force and gave us the example what we must do to prepare ourselves for this manifestation. The best thing we can do is to study all he has told us, strive to follow his example and prepare ourselves for the new manifestation.

Remembrance of Sri Aurobindo

Lobelia erinus
> Lobelia
> small blue half-salverform flowers; low seasonal or perennial plant

Remembrance of Sri Aurobindo
Let us strive to realise the ideal of life that Sri Aurobindo has shown us.

Lobularia maritima
> Sweet alyssum
> compact rounded clusters of tiny fragrant white or mauve flowers; low seasonal or perennial plant

Goodwill
Modest in appearance it does not make a noise and is always ready to be useful.

Constant Remembrance of the Divine

Lonicera japonica
    Japanese honeysuckle
    small clusters of fragrant cream-white
    tubular flowers with recurved petals;
    creeper

Constant Remembrance of the Divine
Spontaneous and joyful, it is the ideal condition.

This, in short, is the demand made on us, that we should turn our whole life into a conscious sacrifice. Every moment and every movement of our being is to be resolved into a continuous and a devoted self-giving to the Eternal. All our actions, not less the smallest and most ordinary and trifling than the greatest and most uncommon and noble, must be performed as consecrated acts.

Loranthus
: short racemes of long yellow or orange tubular flowers with small green petals; parasitic plant

Mental Spirit of Imitation
What you cannot find out for yourself, you copy!

Luffa acutangula
: Ridge gourd, Sing-kwa, Sponge-gourd
mildly fragrant yellow rotate flower; seasonal climbing cucurbit

Kind Mind
The mind prepares itself for conversion.

Lupinus
: Lupin
showy erect spikes of small papilionaceous flowers in ascending tiers, several pastel colours; seasonal or perennial plant

Steps to the Supreme
We will take as many steps as are needed, but we will arrive!

Lycoris africana
: Golden spider lily
long scapes bearing umbels of bright golden-yellow trumpet-shaped flowers with slightly twisted and recurved petals; bulbous plant

Conversion of the Higher Mind
Receives its inspirations from the Divine Consciousness.

Magnolia grandiflora
: large fragrant ivory-white cup-shaped flower with firm rounded petals; tree

Perfect Vigilance
Its observation neglects nothing.

Malpighia coccigera
: Miniature holly, Singapore holly
small delicate light pink to white rotate flowers studding the branches; small shrub

Sensitivity
One result of the refinement of the being.

Malpighia glabra
: Acerola, Barbados cherry
dark to light pink rotate flower; small fruit tree

Sensitivity
One result of the refinement of the being.

Divine Solicitude

Malvaviscus arboreus
    Turk's-cap
    medium-sized red tubular flower with twisted petals; shrub

Divine Solicitude
Always active, even when we do not perceive it.

O Lord, Thou art my refuge and my blessing, my strength, my health, my hope and my courage. Thou art supreme Peace, unalloyed Joy, perfect Serenity.

Malvaviscus arboreus
    pink

Divine Solicitude Rightly Understood
Let us understand and receive with gratitude this Divine Solicitude, so often misunderstood.

Malvaviscus drummondii
    small red candlelike flower

Divine Help
Modest in appearance, powerful in action!

All knowledge is ultimately the knowledge of God, through himself, through Nature, through her works. Mankind has first to seek this knowledge through the external life; for until its mentality is sufficiently developed, spiritual knowledge is not really possible, and in proportion as it is developed, the possibilities of spiritual knowledge become richer and fuller.

Mangifera indica
> Mango tree
> large panicles of compact racemes
> bearing tiny fragrant cream flowers
> changing to light red; tree

Nature's Hope for Realisation
Nature knows that one day she will realise.

Mangifera
> fruit

Divine Knowledge
Succulent, nourishing, strength-giving!

Martynia annua
> Tiger-claw plant
> delicate velvety white and pink tubular
> flower with red-purple on petals and
> yellow on throat; seasonal countryside
> plant

Regularity
Indispensable for all serious accomplishment.

Birth of True Mental Sincerity

Melampodium paludosum
    small yellow compositae flowers densely covering the plant; seasonal

Birth of True Mental Sincerity
With its birth the mind will understand that it is only a means and not an end in itself.

To be perfectly sincere it is indispensable not to have any preference, any desire, any attraction, any dislike, any sympathy or antipathy, any attachment, any repulsion. One must have a total, integral vision of things, in which everything is in its place and one has the same attitude towards all things: the attitude of true vision.

Distinction of the Vital

Melia azedarach
   Chinaberry, Indian lilac, Persian lilac panicles of small fragrant light mauve star-shaped flowers with recurved petals and purple centres; tree

Distinction of the Vital
Light and graceful, with refined elegance.

It is by educating the vital, by making it more refined, more sensitive, more subtle and, one should almost say, more elegant, in the best sense of the word, that one can overcome its violence and brutality, which are in fact a form of crudity and ignorance, of lack of taste.

In truth, a cultivated and illumined vital can be as noble and heroic and disinterested as it is now spontaneously vulgar, egoistic and perverted when it is left to itself without education.

Memecylon tinctorium (*Pl. 13*)
    Ironwood
    tiny mildly fragrant brilliant deep blue flowers in clusters studding the branches; country side shrub

Miracle
Marvellous, strange, unexpected!

Merremia quinquefolia
    clusters of small white funnelform flowers; seasonal creeper

Detailed Gratitude
The gratitude that awakens in us all the details of the Divine Grace.

There is nothing which gives you a joy equal to that of gratitude. One hears a bird sing, sees a lovely flower, looks at a little child, observes an act of generosity, reads a beautiful sentence, looks at the setting sun, no matter what, suddenly this comes upon you, this kind of emotion—indeed so deep, so intense—that the world manifests the Divine; that there is something behind the world which is the Divine.

Merremia tuberosa
    Yellow morning-glory
    medium-sized bright yellow flower; heavy creeper

Mental Gratitude
The gratefulness of the mind for what makes it progress.

Merremia tuberosa
    Hawaiian wood rose
    dark brown rattlebox fruit with light brown persistent calyx

Call of the Divine Grace
Not noisy but persistent and very perceptible to those who know how to listen.

Michelia champaca
    Champak
    highly fragrant cream-yellow or light orange flower with separate slender pointed petals; tree

Supramentalised Psychological Perfection
A psychological perfection aspiring to be divinised.

Michelia champaca 'alba' (*Pl. 13*)
    spicy fragrant cream-white flower

Divine Smile
We can contemplate the smiles of the Divine when we have conquered our ego.

Supramentalised Psychological Perfection

Have you noticed this flower? It has twelve petals in three rows of four. We have called it "Supramental psychological perfection".

I had never noticed that it had three rows: a small row like this, another one a little larger, and a third one larger still. They are in gradations of four: four petals, four petals, four petals.

Well, if one indeed wants to see in the forms of Nature a symbolic expression, one can see a centre which is the supreme Truth, and a triple manifestation — because four indicates manifestation — in three superimposed worlds: the outermost — these are the largest petals, the lightest in colour — that is a physical world, then a vital world and a mental world, and then at the centre, the supramental Truth.

And you can discover all kinds of other analogies.

Transformation

Do you know the flower I have called "Transformation"? Yes. You know it has four petals; well, these four petals are arranged like a cross: one at the top which represents the transcendent, two on each side: the universal, and one on the bottom: the individual. . . .

The transcendent is one and two (or dual) at the same time. This flower is almost perfect in its form. This was the original meaning of the cross also, but that was not as perfect as the flower, for it was one, two, and three. It was not so good — the flower is perfect.

Millingtonia hortensis
    Indian cork tree
    loose panicles of fragrant white flowers with long corolla tubes; tree

Transformation
The goal of creation.

Mimosa pudica
    Sensitive plant, Touch-me-not
    small lavender-pink fluffy ball-like flower with sensitive leaves which fold when touched; low rambler

Vital Sensitivity
Is excessive if not controlled.

Mimusops elengi
    Medlar, Spanish cherry
    very fragrant small cream-white star-shaped flowers; tree

Patience
Indispensable for all realisation.

Mimusops elengi
    Spanish cherry, Medlar
    small oblong orange fruits

Accomplishment
Accomplishment is undoubtedly the fruit of patience.

God has all time before him and does not need to be always in a hurry. He is sure of his aim and success and cares not if he break his work a hundred times to bring it nearer perfection. Patience is our first great necessary lesson, but not the dull slowness to move of the timid, the sceptical, the weary, the slothful, the unambitious or the weakling; a patience full of a calm and gathering strength which watches and prepares itself for the hour of swift great strokes, few but enough to change destiny.

Thirst to Learn

Mina lobata
    Spanish flag
    erect racemes of prominent orange-red
    buds blossoming into small
    cream-yellow candlelike flowers;
    seasonal creeper

Thirst to Learn
One of the qualities that facilitates integral progress.

The true wisdom is to be ready to learn from whatever source knowledge can come.

We can learn things from a flower, an animal, a child, if we are eager to know always more, because there is only One Teacher in the world—the Supreme Lord, and He manifests through everything.

Mirabilis jalapa
> Beauty-of-the-night, Four-o'clock, Marvel of Peru
> several colours of plain or variegated fragrant salverform flowers; low perennial herbaceous plant with tuberous root

Solace
The blessings the Divine grants us.

Mirabilis jalapa
> white

Integral Solace
One can receive it only from the Divine.

Mirabilis jalapa
> yellow

Solace in the Mind
A silent peace.

Peace … carries with it a sense of settled and harmonious rest and deliverance.

Mirabilis jalapa
> carmine red

Solace in the Vital
Modest but effective.

Momordica charantia (*Pl. 6*)
> Balsam-pear, Bitter gourd, Karela, La-kwa
> small fragrant yellow rotate flower; seasonal climbing cucurbit

Sweetness
Adds its smiling touch to life without making a fuss.

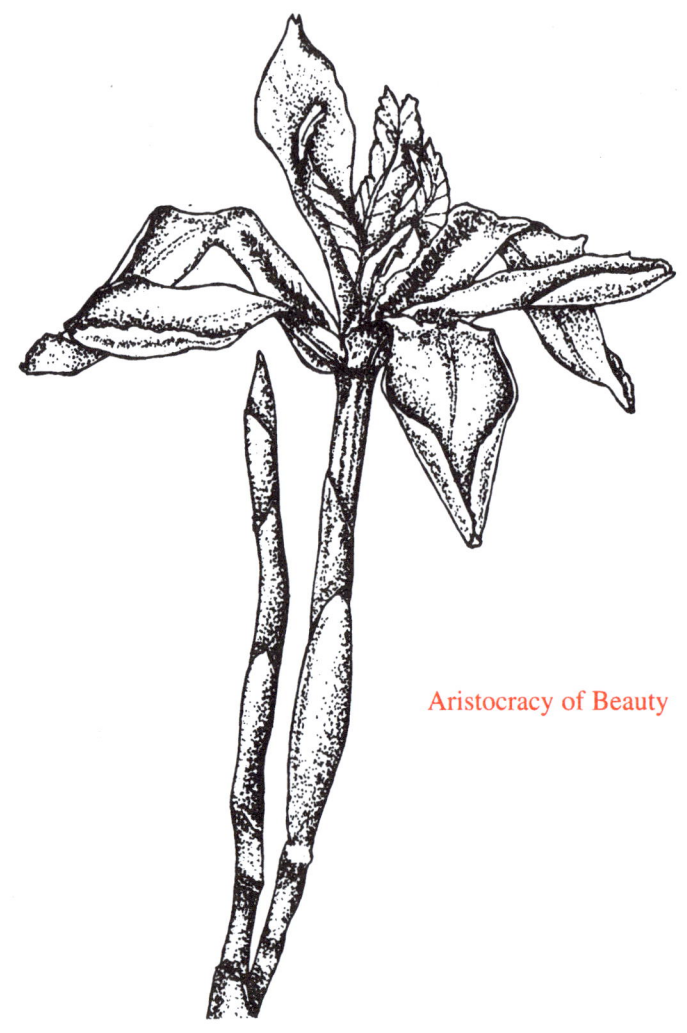

Aristocracy of Beauty

In the physical world, of all things it is beauty which best expresses the Divine. The physical world is the world of form, and the perfection of form is beauty. . . . Its true role is to put the whole of manifested nature into contact with the Eternal through the perfection of form, harmony, and through a sense of the ideal which raises you towards something higher.

Morea
    African iris, Fortnight lily
    short erect scape bearing waxy white
    iris-like flowers with petals marked
    golden-orange; rhizomatous plant

Aristocracy of Beauty
So perfect a form as to compel admiration!

Morinda pubescens
> Awl tree
> small fragrant white star-shaped flowers with thick petals and short corolla tube, appearing singly from a hard rounded base; tree

Peace in the Sex Centre
Indispensable for beginning the Yoga.

Moringa
> Drumstick tree
> airy clusters of small fragrant white flowers with recurved petals and yellow throat; household tree

Hygienic Organisation
Cleanliness, order, utility.

Muntingia calabura
> Calabur, Singapore cherry
> small white rotate flowers and round red fruits; tree

Primitive Succulence
Pleasing to a simple taste.

Murraya paniculata
> Cosmetic-bark tree, Orange jessamine, Satinwood
> clusters of small very fragrant white star-shaped flowers with recurved petals; shrub

Peace in the Vital
The result of the abolition of desires.

Mussaenda
> small yellow star-shaped flower surrounded by one or five conspicious sepals, white, yellow, pink or red; shrub

Mental Goodwill
Likes to show off a little, but is very useful.

Myosotis sylvatica
> Forget-me-not
> clusters of tiny exquisite sky-blue flowers; low seasonal plant

Lasting Remembrance
The remembrance of that which has helped the being to progress.

To Live only for the Divine

Myrtus communis
Myrtle
small white flower with innumerable delicate stamens; shrub

To Live Only for the Divine
This means to have overcome all the difficulties of the individual life.

Some give their soul to the Divine, some their life, some offer their work, some their money. A few consecrate all of themselves and all they have — soul, life, work, wealth; these are the true children of God.

The preoccupation with universal beauty even in its aesthetic forms has an intense power for refining and subtilising the nature, and at its highest it is a great force for purification.

* * *

A complete and universal appreciation of beauty and the making entirely beautiful our whole life and being must surely be a necessary character of the perfect individual and the perfect society.

Narcissus
: Daffodil, Trumpet narcissus
scape bearing an umbel of fragrant yellow-shaded flowers, each with a trumpet emerging from spreading petals; bulbous plant

Power of Beauty
Beauty has its full power only when it is surrendered to the Divine.

Narcissus poeticus
: Poet's narcissus, Polyanthus narcissus
cream-white petals with white trumpet edged orange

Beauty Aspiring for the Supramental Realisation
Beauty is not sufficient in itself, it wants to become divine.

The One whom we adore as the Mother is the divine Conscious Force that dominates all existence.

* * *

She is the golden bridge, the wonderful fire.
The luminous heart of the Unknown is she,
A power of silence in the depths of God;
She is the Force, the inevitable Word,
The magnet of our difficult ascent,
The Sun from which we kindle all our suns,
The Light that leans down from the unrealised Vasts,
The joy that beckons from the impossible,
The Might of all that never yet came down.

* * *

The Avatar is always a dual phenomenon of divinity and humanity; the Divine takes upon himself the human nature with all its outward limitations and makes them the circumstances, means, instruments of the divine consciousness and the divine power, a vessel of the divine birth and the divine works.

Nelumbo nucifera 'Alba'
    Sacred lotus
    pointed bud on long stem opening into large fragrant many-petalled white flower with narrow stamens and unique golden centre; aquatic rhizomatous plant

Aditi—the Divine Consciousness
Pure, immaculate, gloriously powerful.

Nelumbo
    pink, single or double flowers

Avatar—the Supreme Manifested in a Body upon Earth
The pink lotus is the flower of Sri Aurobindo.

Avatar—the Suprmeme Manifested in a Body upon Earth

Nerine sarniensis
   Guernsey Lily
   umbels of trumpet-shaped white, pink or red flowers with narrow twisting recurved petals and long stamens; bulbous plant

Exclusivism
The capacity to do several things at the same time.

Nerium oleander
   Oleander, Rosebay
   terminal clusters of mildly fragrant single pink salverform flowers with delicate corona and light yellow throat; tall shrub

Sweetness of Thought Turned Exclusively towards the Divine
Pretty, joyful, sweet and calm sheltered from all conflict!

Sweetness of Thought Turned Exclusively Towards the Divine

Nerium oleander
   double, pink

Surrender of All Falsehood
Let us offer our falsehoods to the Divine so that He may change them into joyous Truth.

Nerium oleander
   single, very deep pink or deep red

Changing of Wrong Movements into Right
An extreme goodwill always ready to be transformed.

Nerium oleander
: single, pale pink

Contemplation of the Divine
Exclusively occupied with its joyful contemplation.

Nerium oleander
: single, white

Quiet Mind
The best way of learning.

Nerium oleander
: double, white

Perfect Quietness in the Mind
An essential condition for true progress.

Nerium oleander
: single white flower with elongated petals

Quietness Established in the Mind
The essential condition for transformation.

Nicotiana alata
: Flowering tobacco, Jasmine tobacco several colours of salverform flowers; seasonal herbaceous plant

Common Sense
It is very practical and avoids making mistakes, but lacks flight.

Nicotiana plumbaginifolia
: smaller white flowers; countryside seasonal plant

Certitude
Assured and calm, it never argues.

Nierembergia
: Cupflower
small blue-violet cup-shaped flower with a very slender corolla tube; low perennial

Vital Joy in Matter
The reward for abolishing egoism.

Nyctanthes arbor-tristis (*Pl. 4*)
: fragrant white star-shaped salverform flower with orange corolla tube; large shrub

Aspiration
Innumerable, obstinate, repeating itself untiringly.

Wealth

All wealth belongs to the Divine and those who hold it are trustees, not possessors. It is with them today, tomorrow it may be elsewhere. All depends on the way they discharge their trust while it is with them, in what spirit, with what consciousness in their use of it, to what purpose.

Nymphaea
    Water lily
    many colours of large or small star-shaped flowers with numerous petals and yellow centre; aquatic rhizomatous plant

Wealth
True wealth is that which one offers to the Divine.

Nymphaea
    fragrant lavender to mauve flowers

Emotional Wealth
The only true emotional wealth is love from the Divine.

Nymphaea
    yellow flowers

Generous Wealth
Likes to be given and spread far and wide.

Nymphaea
    white flowers shaded pink

Wealth under the Psychic Influence
Wealth ready to return to its true possessor—the Divine.

Nymphaea
    large vivid pink flowers

Wealth in the Vital
Comes willingly to generous natures.

Nymphaea
    variously coloured flowers with prominent yellow centres

Supramentalised Wealth
Wealth put at the service of the Divine.

Nymphaea
    large white flower with golden centre

Integral Wealth of Mahalakshmi
Wealth of feeling and action in all fields of activity—intellectual, psychological and material.

Nymphaea (*Pl. 13*)
    fragrant blue flowers with golden centre

Wealth in the Mind of Light
Open to all higher ideas.

Nymphaea
    magenta or dark red flowers

Wealth in the Most Material Vital
Can be stable only after conversion.

Ochna kirkii (*Pl. 2*)
    Bird's-eye bush, Mickey Mouse plant small glossy black fruits set on a little red dome and surrounded by persistant sepals; shrub

Greed for Money
The surest way to decrease one's consciousness and narrow one's nature.

By knowledge we seek unity with the Divine in his conscious being: by works we seek also unity with the Divine in his conscious being, not statically, but dynamically, through conscious union with the divine Will; but by love we seek unity with him in all the delight of his being.

* * *

To be constantly and integrally at one with Thee is to have the assurance that we shall overcome every obstacle and triumph over all difficulties, both within and without.

Joy of Union with the Divine

Ocimum basilicum
   Sweet basil
   spikes of very small white flowers set in green calyces; aromatic herb

Joy of Union with the Divine
Lavishly scented, it fills the heart with joy.

Ocimum basilicum
   Basil
   heads or spikes of very small white to light mauve labiate flowers with green or purple calyces; aromatic plant

Discipline
Sets the example and hopes to be followed.

Ocimum canum
>spikes of small white flowers set in furry calyces, leaves have lemon fragrance; medicinal plant

Conquering Fervour
An ardour which fears no obstacles.

Ocimum sanctum
>Rama tulsi, Krishna tulsi
>tiny pale mauve or cream-white flowers set in green or dark maroon calyces; sacred plant with medicinal properties

Devotion
Modest and fragrant, it gives itself without seeking for anything in return.

Mental Chastity

Odontonema strictum
>racemes of small red salverform flowers; small shrub

Matter Aspiring for the Supramental Guidance
Dissatisfied and troubled, Matter asks for a powerful guide to put it in order.

Oncoba spinosa
>fragrant white saucer-shaped flower with prominent centre of innumerable yellow stamens; small tree

Mental Chastity
Precious and magnificent in its purity.

Compassion and gratitude are essentially psychic virtues. They appear in the consciousness only when the psychic being takes part in active life.

The vital and the physical experience them as weaknesses, for they curb the free expression of their impulses, which are based on the power of strength.

As always, the mind, when insufficiently educated, is the accomplice of the vital being and the slave of the physical nature, whose laws, so overpowering in their half-conscious mechanism, it does not fully understand. When the mind awakens to the awareness of the first psychic movements, it distorts them in its ignorance and changes compassion into pity or at best into charity, and gratitude into the wish to repay, followed, little by little, by the capacity to recognise and admire.

It is only when the psychic consciousness is all-powerful in the being that compassion for all that needs help, in whatever domain, and gratitude for all that manifests the divine presence and grace, in whatever form, are expressed in all their original and luminous purity, without mixing compassion with any trace of condescension or gratitude with any sense of inferiority.

Operculina turpethum
pure white funnel-shaped flower with prominent light green calyx; heavy creeper

Integral Gratitude
The whole being offers itself to the Lord in absolute trust.

Operculina turpethum
Wood rose
light green rattlebox fruit and buff-coloured persistent calyx

Call of the Divine Grace
Not loud but persistent and very perceptible to those who know how to listen.

Call of the Divine Grace

Orchidaceae
Orchid
several colours and shapes of exquisite flowers with five petals, a central lip and column; epiphytic or terrestrial plant

Attachment to the Divine
Wraps itself around the Divine and finds all its support in Him, so as to be sure of never leaving Him.

What is called "new birth" is the birth into the spiritual life, the spiritual consciousness; it is to carry in oneself something of the spirit which, individually, through the soul, can begin to rule the life and be the master of existence. But in the supramental world, the spirit will be the master of this entire world and all its manifestations, all its expressions, consciously, spontaneously, naturally.

* * *

We can, simply by a sincere aspiration, open a sealed door in us and find... that Something which will change the whole significance of life, reply to all our questions, solve all our problems and lead us to the perfection we aspire for without knowing it, to that Reality which *alone* can satisfy us and give us lasting joy, equilibrium, strength, life.

Origanum majorana
Knotted marjoram, Sweet marjoram
sprigs bearing small aromatic leaves, tiny white to light mauve flowers clustered on mature stems; perennial aromatic herb

The New Birth
Birth of the true consciousness—that of the Divine Presence in us.

Ornithogalum umbellatum (*Pl. 2*)
: Star-of-Bethlehem, Summer snowflake
short scape bearing a raceme of small white star-shaped flowers; bulbous plant

Beauty in Collective Simplicity
Each element plays its role in the whole.

The first determining element of the Siddhi is, therefore, the intensity of the turning, the force which directs the soul inward. The power of aspiration of the heart, the force of the will, the concentration of the mind, the perseverance and determination of the applied energy are the measure of that intensity.

Orthosiphon
: erect spikes bearing very small rose-purple flowers with elongated stamens; low countryside perennial

Aspiration for Spiritual Intensity
Bold, elegant, persistent.

Orthosiphon (*Pl. 12*)
: small white flowers and elongated pale lavender stamens; low shrub

Spiritual Intensity
It is an intensity without violence—the ardour it gives you manifests without big gestures and loud words.

Oxalis
: Wood sorrel
groups of small lavender-pink to rose-purple rotate flowers on a short scape; countryside rhizomatous groundcover

Candid Simplicity in the Vital
One of the most difficult qualities for the vital to acquire.

Pachira rosea (also Careya)
: large cream-white flower with innumerable red-tipped stamens; tree

Liberation
The disappearance of the ego.

Aspiration for the Supramental Guidance in the Subconscient

Pachystachys coccinea
    Cardinal's-guard
    terminal heads of bright red labiate flowers with elongated corolla tubes set in prominent green bracts; shrub

Aspiration for Supramental Guidance in the Subconscient
Intense need of order, light and knowledge in the subconscient penumbra.

The subconscient is to be penetrated by the light and made a sort of bed-rock of truth, a store of right impressions, right physical responses to the Truth. Strictly speaking, it will not be subconscient at all, but a sort of bank of true values held ready for use.

Paeonia
: Peony
: several colours of showy fragrant rotate flowers with numerous petals and a yellow centre; shrub

Beauty in Art
A beauty that displays itself and allows one to contemplate on it.

Pancratium
: fragrant white funnel-shaped flower with pointed petals borne singly on a short scape; bulbous plant

Occultism
Does not truly blossom except when it is surrendered to the Divine.

Pandanus tectorius
: Screw pine
: highly fragrant tiny powdery cream-yellow flowers in dense branching spikes; large countryside semi-aquatic plant with long leaves

Spiritual Perfume
It has an extraordinary power of attraction.

Pandorea jasminoides
: Bower plant
: clusters of mildly fragrant pale pink to white salverform flowers with slightly curved corolla tube and deep pink throat; creeper

Opening of the Emotive Centre to the Light
An important event in human development.

Papaver
: Poppy
: several colours of cup-shaped flowers with numerous stamens and delicately crinkled petals, borne on a thin stalk; seasonal plant

Spontaneous Joy of Nature
It is man who has brought pain to Nature.

Parkia pedunculata
: Mungo tree, Nittu tree
: large round head of minute cream-white flowers, borne on apendulous stalk; tree

Boastfulness
Boasting, boasting—one of the greatest obstacles to progress! It is a foolishness to be carefully avoided if one aspires for true progress.

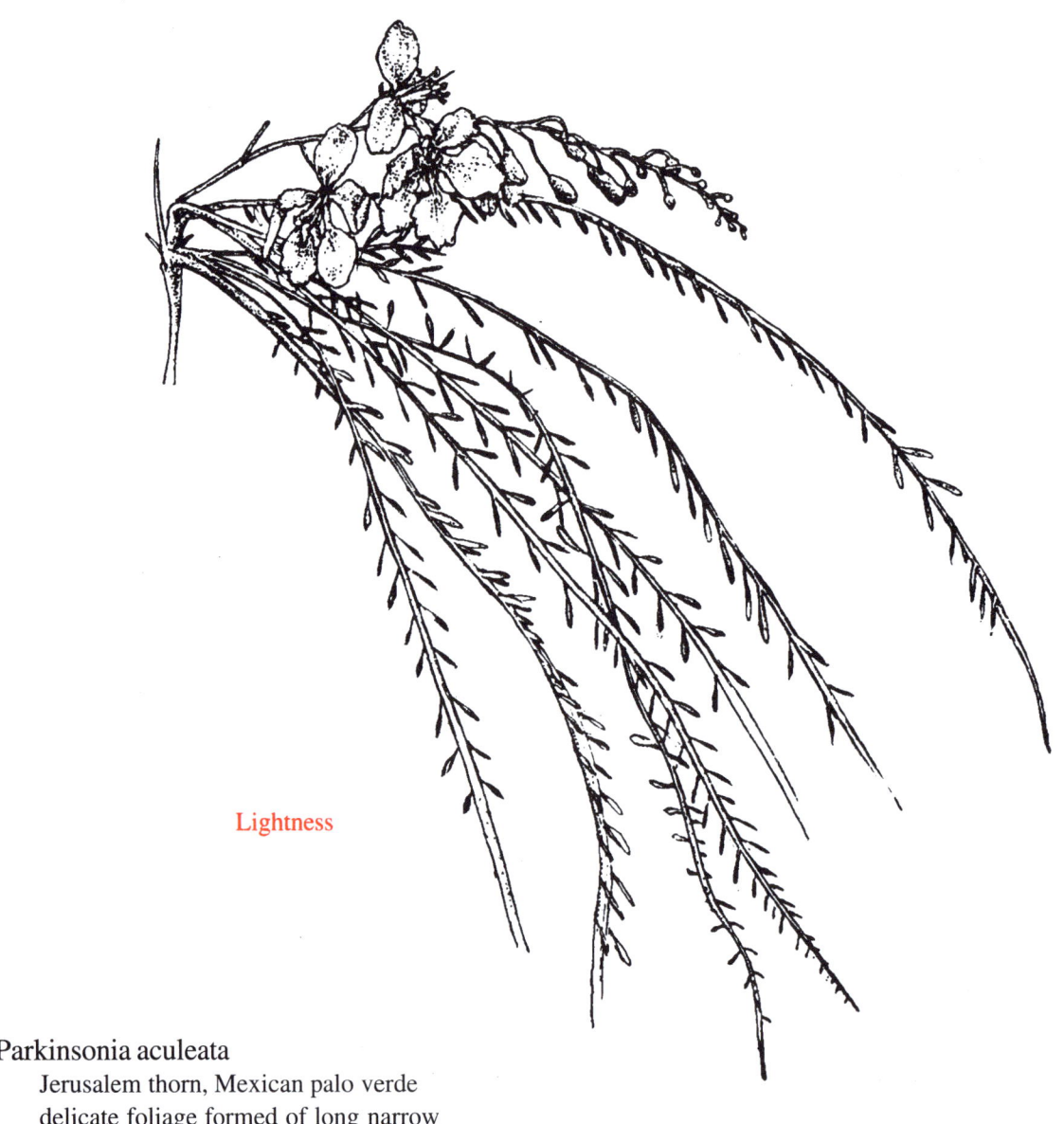

Lightness

Parkinsonia aculeata
>Jerusalem thorn, Mexican palo verde delicate foliage formed of long narrow stalks bearing tiny leaflets, loose axillary racemes of small fragrant light yellow flowers; small thorny tree

Lightness
Charming, but thorny at times!

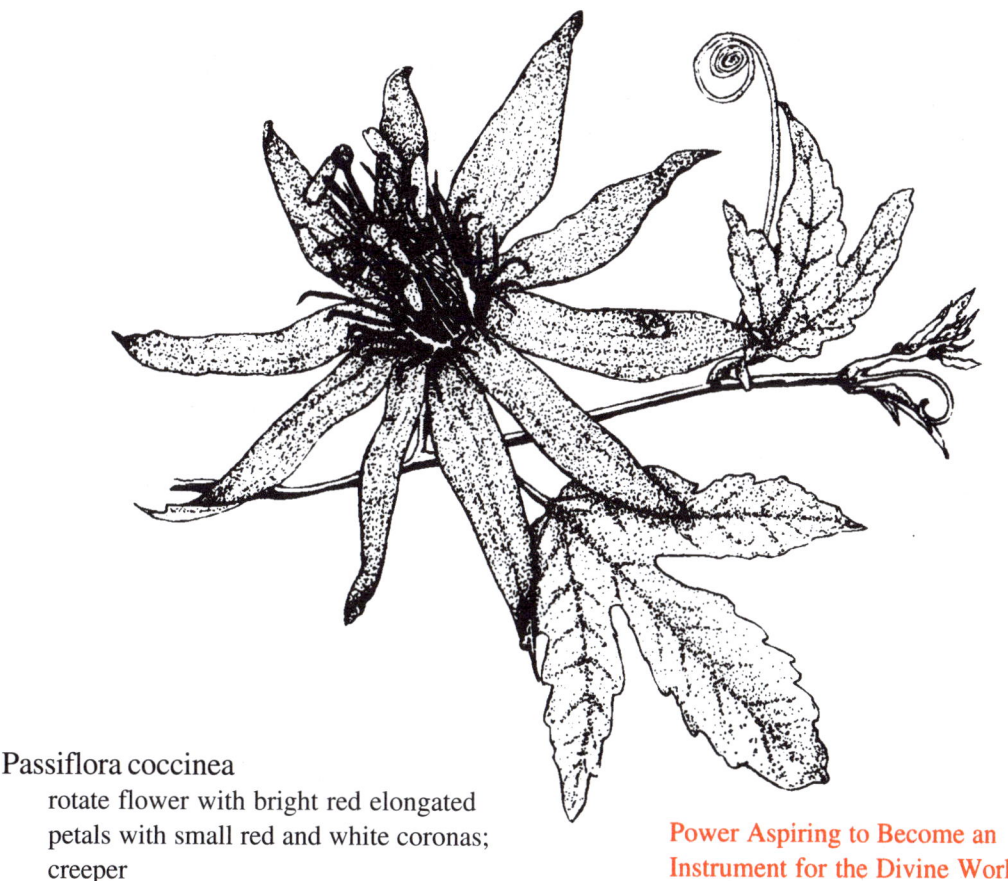

Passiflora coccinea
  rotate flower with bright red elongated petals with small red and white coronas; creeper

Power Aspiring to Become an Instrument for the Divine Work
Opening to a higher consciousness, power awakens to the need of being at the service of the Divine.

Passiflora incarnata (*Pl. 11*)
  intensely fragrant flower with prominent violet corona banded white; heavy creeper

Silence
The ideal condition for progress.

Passiflora foetida
  flowers with white petals and corona; countryside creeper

Integral Silence
The source of true force.

There comes a time when one begins to be almost ready, when one can feel in everything, every object, in every movement, in every vibration, in all the things around—not only people and conscious beings, but things, objects; not only trees and plants and living things, but simply any object one uses, the things around one—this delight, this delight of being, of being just as one is, simply being. And one sees that all this vibrates like that. One touches a thing and feels this delight....

One moves in the midst of things and it is as though they were all singing to you their delight. There comes a time when it becomes very familiar in the life around you. Of course, I must admit that it is a little more difficult to feel it in human beings, because there are all their mental and vital formations which come into the field of perception and disturb it. There is too much of this kind of egoistic asperity which gets mixed with things, so it is more difficult to contact the Delight there.

Pavetta indica
> large rounded heads of small fragrant salverform flowers with long styles; countryside shrub

Radiating Peace in the Cells
A happy contagion.

Pelargonium hortorum
> Geranium
> rounded clusters of single or double flowers in various colours; low perennial or light climber

Spiritual Happiness
Calm and smiling, nothing can disturb it.

Peltophorum pterocarpum
> Copper-pod, Rusty shield-bearer
> terminal panicles of fragrant golden-yellow rotate flowers with delicately crinkled petals and bright yellow stamens; tree

Service
To be at the service of the Divine is the surest means of attaining realisation.

Pentapetes phoeniceae
> small bright red saucer-shaped flower with erect ribbonlike stamens; countryside seasonal plant

Vigilance
Indispensable for all true progress.

Pentas
: Egyptian star-cluster
terminal clusters of small white salverform flowers; low shrub

Movements in the Light
This is possible only with a great sincerity.

Pentas
: mauve to pale purple flowers

Light in the Vital Movements
This certainly means the beginning of wisdom.

Pentas
: vivid pink flowers

Psychic Light in the Physical Movements
The first step towards the transformation of the physical.

Pentas
: bright red flowers

Psychic Light in the Material Movements
The essential condition for transformation.

Pereskia (*Pl. 3*)
: Leaf cactus, Rose cactus
small clusters of pink rotate flowers with numerous yellow stamens and a fleshy base; rambling thorny climber

Never Tell a Lie
The absolute condition for safety on the path.

Pergularia odoratissima
: West Coast creeper
discreet pendulous clusters of small intensely fragrant greenish-yellow salverform flowers with thick petals; creeper

Vital Plenitude
Cannot be obtained except by conversion.

Petrea (*Pl. 8*)
: Queen's-wreath
pendulous racemes bearing small purple salverform flowers set in pale lilac star-shaped calyces; creeper or shrub

Spiritual Power of Healing
Opening and receptivity to the Divine Influence.

Petunia
: Garden petunia
many colours of delicate mildly fragrant salverform flowers; low seasonal plant

Enthusiasm
True enthusiasm is full of a peaceful endurance.

Petunia
: double flowers

Joyous Enthusiasm
The best way of facing life.

Petunia
: white flowers

Integral Enthusiasm
The whole being does everything with ardour.

Petunia
: red flowers

Physical Enthusiasm
The body takes a lively interest in life and action.

Petunia
: bi-coloured single flowers in several combinations

Enthusiasm in Action
All actions are done with warmth and energy.

Petunia
: bi-coloured double flowers

Joyous Enthusiasm in Action
Action will become joyously enthusiastic when governed by the Supermind.

Petunia
: double white flowers

Joyous Integral Enthusiasm
To ardour is united the joy of doing things well.

Petunia
: double red flowers

Joyous Physical Enthusiasm
The whole being lives only to serve the Divine.

Petunia
deep pink to mauve flowers

Vital Enthusiasm
Care must be taken that it is in the right direction.

Petunia
lavender flowers with deeper veins of the same colour

Enthusiasm in the Higher Vital
The vital being takes a living interest in what it does.

Petunia
deep rich velvety purple flowers

Enthusiasm in the Most Material Vital
Needed to face the difficulties of life successfully.

Petunia
light pink flowers

Psychic Enthusiasm
A state which only the Divine can bring about.

Petunia
double deep pink to mauve flowers

Joyous Vital Enthusiasm
Very valuable if it persists in spite of difficulties.

Petunia
double lavender flowers with deeper coloured veins

Joyous Enthusiasm in the Higher Vital
The result of perfect surrender to the Divine.

Petunia
double deep rich velvety purple flowers

Joyous Enthusiasm in the Most Material Vital
When governed by the Supermind the most material vital will find its joy in an enthusiastic action.

Petunia
double light pink flowers

Joyous Psychic Enthusiasm
An assurance of success in spite of obstacles.

Skill in Work

Whatever work you do, do it as perfectly as you can.
That is the best service to the Divine in man.

Phlox drummindii
    Annual phlox
    terminal clusters of small salverform
    lowers, several colours; low seasonal plant

Skill in Works
Must be used knowingly.

Phlox
    very light pink flowers with indented
    petals

Artistic Work
Work at the service of beauty.

Phlox
    starred flowers in several colours with
    fringed petals

Radiating Skill in Work
When the instruments of work—the hands, the eyes, etc. become conscious and the attention is controlled, the capacity for work seems to be limitless.

Phlox
    white

Skill in Integral Work
All that is done is done well, whatever the work undertaken.

No matter what you want to do, the first thing is to put consciousness in the cells of your hand. If you want to play, if you want to work, if you want to do anything at all with your hand, unless you push consciousness into the cells of your hand you will never do anything good. . . . And this is felt. You feel it. You can acquire it. All sorts of exercises may be done to make the hand conscious and there comes a time when it becomes so conscious that you can leave it to do things; it does them by itself without your little mind having to intervene.

Phlox
yellow

Skill in Mental Work
To know how to observe in silence is the source of its skilfulness.

Phlox
carmine red

Skill in Physical Work
Skilful hands, a clear vision, a concentrated attention, an untiring patience and what one does is done well.

Phlox
bright red

Skill in Material Work
Skilful hands, precise care, a sustained attention and one compels Matter to obey the Spirit.

Phlox
purple to mauve

Skill in Vital Work
This is the seat of all capacities and all skills which need only discipline to be realised.

Phlox
light mauve

Skill in Emotive Work
When work becomes attractive and is done with joy, how much better it is.

Phlox
light pink

Skill in Psychic Work
Listen silently to the command that comes from the Supreme Lord and you will have the capacity to carry it out.

Physalis alkekengi
>Chinese-lantern plant, Winter cherry
fruit enclosed in an orange-red persistent calyx; shrub

Sun-drop
Luminous and pretty it brings joy.

Pimpinella major
>Lady's lace
lacey umbels of tiny white flowers; seasonal plant

Purity in the Blood
Can only be obtained by the absence of desires.

Krishna's Ananda

Krishna is the Eternal's Personality of Ananda; because of him all creation is possible, because of his play, because of his delight, because of his sweetness.

Platycodon grandiflorus
>Balloon flower, Chinese bellflower
blue semi-double bell-shaped flowers with short white stamens; herbaceous perennial

Unostentatious Certitude
It does not flaunt nor try to convince anyone.

Plumbago auriculata
>Cape plumbago
terminal clusters of delicate light blue salverform flowers; rambler or shrub

Krishna's Ananda
Manifold, abundant and so full of charm!

Plumbago auriculata 'Alba'
  white flowers

Presence
Consciousness seeking for the Presence.

Plumbago indica
  deep pink flowers in terminal spikes; spreading shrub

Organisation of the Being around the Psychic
The first stage of transformation.

Plumbago zeylanica
  small white flowers; spreading countryside shrub

First Appearance of Purity in the Inconscient
The sign that the Inconscient is on the way to becoming conscious.

To become a conscious instrument, capable of identification and conscious, willed movements, you must have this inner organisation; otherwise you will always be running into a chaos somewhere, a confusion somewhere or an obscurity, an unconsciousness somewhere. And naturally your action, even though guided exclusively by the Divine, will not have the perfection of expression it has when one has acquired a conscious organisation around this divine Centre....

Beginning this work of organising your being and all its movements and all its elements around the central Consciousness and Presence, this is the surest and most complete cure, and the most comforting, for all possible boredom. It gives life a tremendous interest and an extraordinary diversity. You no longer have the time to get bored.

Only, one must persevere.

And what adds to the interest of the thing is that this kind of work, this harmonisation and organisation of the being around the divine Centre can only be done in a physical body and on earth. That is truly the essential and original reason for physical life. For, as soon as you are no longer in a physical body, you can no longer do it *at all*.

Plumeria rubra
>Champa, Frangipani, Pagoda tree, Temple tree
>clusters of fragrant rotate funnel form flowers with soft velvety petals in a large variety of colour combinations; shrub or tree

Psychological Perfection
There is not one psychological perfection but five. They are sincerity, faith, devotion, aspiration and surrender.*

Such qualities as faith, sincerity, aspiration, devotion, etc. make up the perfection indicated in our language of the flowers. In ordinary language it would mean something else such as purity, love, benevolence, fidelity and a host of other virtues.

Plumeria rubra
>red with orange centre, petals streaked orange

Psychological Perfection in the Course of Fulfilment
The state of those who undertake the Yoga seriously.

Plumeria rubra
>flowers with fruit-like fragrance, predominantly white with light pink border and red or reddish-pink streak on one lower edge of petals

Psychological Perfection in Matter
The first step towards transformation.

Plumeria obtusa
>white with yellow centre and slender recurved petals; shrub

Integral Psychological Perfection
One of the indispensable conditions for transformation.

Plumeria obtusa
>white with yellow centre and broad petals; shrub

Perfect Psychological Perfection
Psychological perfection in all parts of the being.

---

* Extract from a talk by the Mother, see Introduction.

Podranea ricasoliana
> Pink trumpet vine
> clusters of fragrant pink trumpet-shaped flowers with cream white throat lined red, white calyces; creeper

> ***To Know How to Listen***
> *To be attentive and silent.*

Flowers speak to us when we know how to listen to them—it is a subtle and fragrant language.

Fire

Poinciana pulcherrima
> Barbados pride
> erect panicles of showy orange-red flowers with long stamens; shrub

> ***Fire***
> *Does not fear any obstacle.*

Poinciana pulcherrima
> bright yellow flowers

> ***Fire in the Mind***
> *An ardour that sets ideas ablaze!*

The New Creation

What is there new that we have yet to accomplish? Love, for as yet we have only accomplished hatred and self-pleasing; Knowledge, for as yet we have only accomplished error and perception and conceiving; Bliss, for as yet we have only accomplished pleasure and pain and indifference; Power, for as yet we have only accomplished weakness and effort and a defeated victory; Life, for as yet we have only accomplished birth and growth and dying; Unity, for as yet we have only accomplished war and association.

In a word, godhead; to remake ourselves in the divine image.

Polianthes tuberosa
    Tuberose
    long scapes bearing single white highly fragrant tubular flowers with waxy petals; bulbous plant

The New Creation
Strong, lasting and fragrant, it rises straight towards the sky.

Polianthes tuberosa (*Pl. 15*)
    double flowers

The Perfect New Creation
Clustered, manifold and complete, it asserts its right to be.

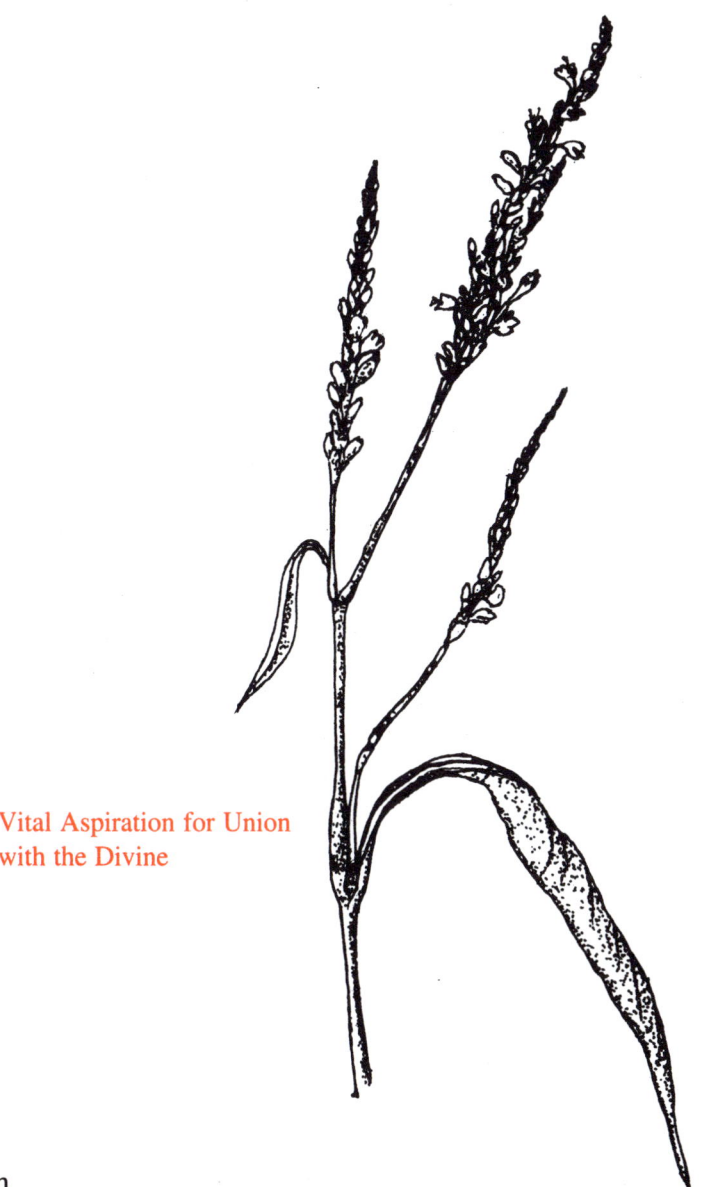

Vital Aspiration for Union with the Divine

Polygonum
    Fleece flower, Knotweed
    clusters of tiny pink flowers on slender erect or branching spikes; countryside perennial semi-aquatic plant

Aspiration of the Vital for Union with the Divine
It rises straight up in an intense and concentrated movement.

It is to offer all the vital nature and its movements to the Divine so that it may be purified and only the true movements in consonance with the Divine Will may be there and all egoistic desires and impulses disappear.

Porana paniculata
> Bridal-bouquet, Snow creeper
> delicate branching racemes of very small white salverform flowers; creeper

Ether
Charming and ethereal, it is bound to please.

Porana volubilis
> dense cascading racemes of small white bell-shaped flowers

Water
Fluid, abundant and pure.

There is a point where all the virtues are united: it is a point that goes beyond the ego. If we take this faithfulness, if we take devotion, take love, the meaning of service, all these things, when they are above the egoistic level, they meet, in the sense that they give themselves and do not expect anything in exchange. And if you climb one step higher, instead of its being done with the idea of duty and abnegation, it is done with an intense joy which carries within itself its own reward, which needs nothing in exchange, for it carries its joy in itself. But then, for that you must have climbed quite high and must no longer have that turning back upon yourself which, of all things, pulls you down lowest....

One must have gone far beyond all that, left it very far behind oneself, in order to truly have the joy of faithfulness, the joy of self-giving, which does not care at all, no, indeed, not at all, in any way, whether it is properly received or gets the adequate response. Not to expect anything in exchange for what one does, not to expect anything, not through asceticism or a sense of sacrifice but because one has the joy of the consciousness one is in and that is enough; this is much better than all one can receive, from whomsoever it be.

Portlandia grandiflora (*Pl. 14*)
> large white fragrant trumpet-shaped flower with waxy petals edged pink; shrub

Joy of Integral Faithfulness
That link of love which makes all faithfulness so easy.

Portlandia grandiflora
> fully white flower

Peace of Integral Faithfulness
Be faithful to the Divine and you will enjoy a constant peace.

Portulaca
  Rose moss, Sun plant
  many colours of small single or double
  rose-like flowers with delicate petals;
  seasonal succulent

Sri Aurobindo's Compassion
*Innumerable, always present and
efficacious in every instance.*

Why is the flower symbolising your compassion so delicate and why does it wither away so soon?

No, the compassion does not wither with its symbol—flowers are the moment's representations of things that are in themselves eternal.

Primula
  Primrose
  clusters of showy salverform flowers in a
  wide range of colours; low perennial

Growth
It will multiply and assert its right to be.

Prosopis glandulosa (*Pl. 6*)
  Mesquite
  catkins of tiny mildly fragrant
  lemon-yellow flowers; thorny countryside
  shrub or high hedge

Logic in Thoughts
Likes coherent discourses.

Prunus dulcis
  Almond tree
  clusters of single white or rosy pink rotate
  flowers covering the tree in Spring; tree

Smile of Nature
Nature rejoices at her beauty!

Prunus subhirtella
  Japanese flowering cherry, Oriental cherry
  clusters of small single or double light pink
  flowers covering the tree in Spring; tree

Smile of Beauty
Nature is happy to be beautiful.

Pseuderanthemum
    erect clusters of small salverform flowers with rounded petals; shrub with plain or variously coloured and variegated foliage

Organisation
Indispensable for all good work.

Pseuderanthemum
    white with red centre; long narrow green leaves

Aspiration for Organisation
Clear and methodical, order at the cost of multiplicity.

Pseuderanthemum
    white

Integral Organisation
The first requisite for transformation.

Pseuderanthemum
    white covered with magenta dots and centre; white and green vareiegated leaves

Material Organisation
Manifold and well-organised to face difficulties.

Pseuderanthemum
    magenta with small white dots; pink to dark red variegated foliage

Organisation in the Vital
Indispensable for all realisation.

Pseuderanthemum
    white with small red dots towards the centre; yellow veined foliage

Organisation of Details
Indispensable for all lasting accomplishment.

Pseuderanthemum (*Pl. 8*)
    white dotted maroon with long corolla tube and one petal marked maroon at centre, appearing singly or in pairs

Result of Harmonious Organisation
More effective than showy!

Pseudocalymna alliaceum
    Garlic-vine
    showy clusters of lavender-violet
    trumpet-shaped flowers changing to light
    mauve, nearly white; creeper

Collective Emotions Open to the Divine
Crowds answering the impulsion coming from the Divine; an event marking the great stages of terrestrial life.

If mankind only caught a glimpse of what infinite enjoyments, what perfect forces, what luminous reaches of spontaneous knowledge, what wide calms of our being lie waiting for us in the tracts which our animal evolution has not yet conquered, they would leave all and never rest till they had gained these treasures. But the way is narrow, the doors are hard to force, and fear, distrust and scepticism are there, sentinels of Nature to forbid the turning away of our feet from less ordinary pastures.

Psidium guajava
    Guava tree
    fragrant white rotate flower with
    numerous stamens; fruit tree

Steadfastness
What it has chosen it keeps and does not like to change.

Pterospermum acerifolium (*Pl. 5*)
    large fragrant cream-white trumpet-shaped
    flower with separate petals and thick
    downy calyx; tree

Realisation of the Supramental Riches
It can manifest only after human consciousness is transformed.

An Old Chaldean Legend

Long ago, very long ago, in the desert land that is now Arabia, a divine being incarnated on earth to awaken it to the Supreme Love. As one would expect, he was persecuted by men, misunderstood, suspected, hunted after. Mortally wounded by his assailants, he wished to die alone, quietly, so that his work might be accomplished; and, pursued by them, he fled. Suddenly in the broad barren plain, a tiny bush of pomegranate appeared. The Saviour stole under its low branches in order to give up his body in peace; and at once the bush expanded miraculously, increased itself, widened, became deep and luxuriant in such a way that when the pursuers passed by they did not even suspect that the One whom they were chasing was hidden there, and they continued on their way.

While, drop by drop, the sacred blood fell, fertilising the soil, the bush covered itself with marvellous flowers, scarlet, enormous—clusters of petals, innumerable drops of blood....

These are the flowers that, for us, express and hold the Divine Love.

Punica
  Pomegranate tree
  single flower with round vermilion petals, innumerable stamens and a fleshy apricot to light reddish-orange calyx; shrub

Divine Sacrifice
For the Divine is it not a supreme sacrifice to renounce the beatitude of His unity in order to create the painful multiplicity of the world?

Punica (*Pl. 8*)
  hard round light pink or blood-red fruit with innumerable seeds

Divine Love Spreading over the World
Innumerable, succulent, it gives strength and life untiringly.

Punica
  fully double vermilion flower

Divine Love
A flower reputed to bloom even in the desert.

Punica
  fully double white flower

Unmanifest Divine Love
The splendour of that marvellous love which the Divine keeps for the pure in heart.

Pyrostegia venusta
> Flame vine
> massive cascading clusters of orange tubular flowers with recurved velvety petals; heavy creeper

Supramental Rain
Happy are those who receive it!

Let me be consumed with this love divine, love powerful, infinite, unfathomable, in every activity, in all the worlds of being!

Quamoclit coccinea
> Star Ipomoea
> orange-red star-shaped salverform flowers; creeper

Opening of the Physical to the Divine Love
The surest way to find happiness.

Quamoclit pennata
> Cypress vine, Cardinal climber
> scarlet flowers

Love in the Physical for the Divine
Modest in appearance but tenacious and charming, it does not make a fuss and is very faithful.

Quassia amara
> Bitterwood, Surinam quassia
> long racemes of small glowing crimson-pink candlelike flowers; shrub

Splendour and Opulence in the Material Life
It can become widespread only by transformation.

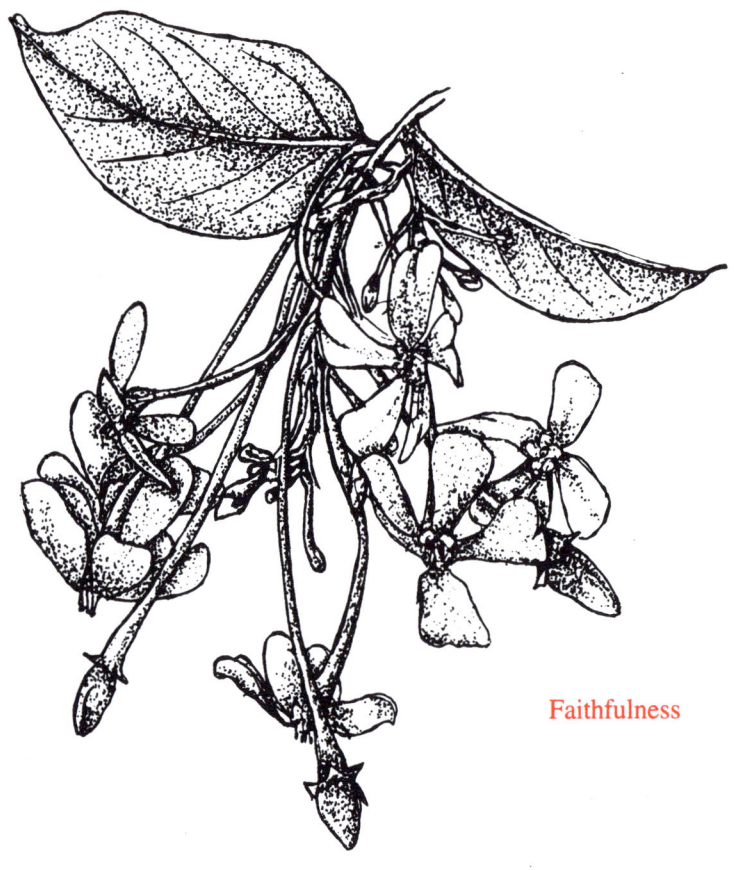

Faithfulness

This is faithfulness, to admit and to manifest no other movements but only the movements prompted and guided by the Divine.

Quisqualis indica
> Rangoon creeper
> dense pendulous clusters of fragrant white
> rotate flowers changing through pink to
> red, long tubular calyces; heavy climber

Faithfulness
*We can count on you; you never fail
us when we need you!*

Randia
> rounded clusters of fragrant cream-white salverform flowers with long erect styles; shrub

Order
To put a thing in its place gives it its true value.
A thing apparently meaningless acquires its full value when it is put in its true place.

Mahasaraswati is the Mother's Power of Work and her spirit of perfection and order.... Moulding and remoulding she labours each part till it has attained its true form, is put in its exact place in the whole and fulfils its precise purpose. In her constant and diligent arrangement and rearrangement of things her eye is on all needs at once and the way to meet them and her intuition knows what is to be chosen and what rejected and successfully determines the right instrument, the right time, the right conditions and the right process.

Ravenia spectabilis (*Pl. 9*)
> deep rose-pink solitary salverform flower with one larger petal and very short corolla tube; shrub

Happy Heart
Smiling, peaceful, wide open, without a shadow!

Reseda odorata
> Mignonette
> very small intensely fragrant light yellow or green-yellow flowers in loose erect racemes; seasonal plant

Benevolence
Makes life fragrant without attracting attention.

Abundance of Beauty

Rhododendron
Azalea
dense clusters of delicate open bell-shaped or funnelform flowers in a variety of colours; shrub or small tree

Abundance of Beauty
A beauty that blossoms abundantly and without reserve.

Rhoeo spathacea (*Pl. 1*)
: Moses-in-a-boat, Purple-leaved spiderwort small white flowers set in reddish-violet boat-shaped bracts; low succulent with erect violet-green leaves

The more we advance on the way, the more the need of the Divine Presence becomes imperative and indispensable.

Divine Presence
It hides from the ignorant eye its ever-present magnificence!

Carelessness and negligence and indolence she [Mahasaraswati] abhors; all scamped and hasty and shuffling work, all clumsiness and *à peu pres* and misfire, all false adaptation and misuse of instruments and faculties and leaving of things undone or half done is offensive and foreign to her temper. When her work is finished, nothing has been forgotten, no part has been misplaced or omitted or left in a faulty condition; all is solid, accurate, complete, admirable.

Rondeletia
: light terminal corymbs of small orange-red or deep pink salverform flowers; shrub

Mahasaraswati's Perfection in Works
It is not satisfied with makeshift.

Love for the Divine

The psychic love is pure and full of self-giving without egoistic demands, but it is human and can err and suffer.

Rosa
: Rose
: single or double fragrant flowers in a great variety of colours; soft velvety petals arranged in spirals of one or more whorls; shrub or climber

Love for the Divine
The vegetal kingdom gathers together its most beautiful possibilities to offer them to the Divine

Rosa
: The Mother described this rose as a beautiful, large and multi-coloured one

Love from the Divine
There is one rose that is Love from the Divine

Rosa canina
: Brier rose, Eglantine
: clusters of single fragrant light pink roses

Psychic Soaring of Nature
Nature has a soul which blossoms very prettily!

Rosa chienensis
: small white roses tinged pink

Affection for the Divine
A sweet and confident tenderness giving itself unfailingly to the Divine.

Rosa chinensis 'Viridiflora'
: small roses with green sepals instead of petals

Timidity in Attachment to the Divine
Full of life, but not knowing how to change this life into an offering to the Divine.

Rosa
: small reddish-pink roses

Psychic Love for the Divine
Strong and faithful, it has a beauty that does not belie.

Rosa chinensis
: China rose
: small roses in clusters of two or three, very light pink fading to white

Tenderness for the Divine
Sweet, charming, of delicate form—a blossoming smile!

Rosa
    pink roses, except 'Surrender' and 'Perfect Surrender'

Loving Surrender
A state that can be obtained by surrendering to the Divine.

Surrender is giving oneself to the Divine—to give everything one is or has to the Divine and regard nothing as one's own, to obey only the Divine will and no other, to live for the Divine and not for the ego.

Detailed surrender means the surrender of all the details of life, even the smallest and the most insignificant in appearance. And this means to remember the Divine in all circumstances; whatever we think, feel or do, we must do it for Him as a way of coming close to Him, to be more and more what He wants us to be, capable of manifesting His will in perfect sincerity and purity, to be the instruments of His Love.

Rosa 'Edward' (*Pl. 14*)
    Country rose, Damask rose
    highly fragrant semi-double pink roses

Surrender
To will what the Divine wills is supreme wisdom.

Rosa chinensis 'Minima'
    Fairy rose, Old China rose
    tiny pink roses

Detailed Surrender
A surrender which does not leave anything aside.

Rosa 'Prosperity'
    white roses in small pendulous clusters; climber with very few thorns

Pure Spiritual Surrender
Candid, simple, spontaneous and complete in its multiplicity.

Rosa 'Paul Neyron'
    highly fragrant large pink roses

Perfect Surrender
The indispensable condition for arriving at identification.

Rosa x rehderana
: Polyantha rose
various colours of single or double roses
in erect clusters

Communion with the Divine
For one who truly has it, all circumstances become an occasion for it.

Rosa
: bicoloured roses

Balance of the Nature in Love for the Divine
Passive and active, calm and ardent, sweet and strong, silent and expressed.

Rosa 'Confidence'
: salmon-coloured roses

Beauty Offers itself in Service to the Divine
Incomparable splendour, it becomes a modest servitor.

Rosa
: orange roses

Flaming Love for the Divine
Ready for all heroism and all sacrifices.

Rosa
: red roses

Human Passions Changed into Love for the Divine
May they become a real fact, and their abundance will save the world.

Rosa
: lavender or mauve roses

Humility in the Love for the Divine
Delicate, effective and surrendered, but very persistent in its feelings.

Rosa
: solitary pure white roses

Integral Love for the Divine
Pure, complete and irrevocable, it is a love that gives itself for ever.

Since we have decided to reserve love in all its splendour for our personal relationship with the Divine, we shall replace it in our relations with others by a total, unvarying, constant and egoless kindness and goodwill that will not expect any reward or gratitude or even any recognition. However others may treat you, you will never allow yourself to be carried away by any resentment; and in your unmixed love for the Divine, you will leave him sole judge as to how he is to protect you and defend you against the misunderstanding and bad will of others.

Rosa
yellow roses

Mental Love for the Divine
The nature offers its love in a fragrant blossoming.

Rosa 'Peace'
cream or yellow roses tinged pink

Mental Love under the Psychic Influence
Under the psychic influence the mind knows how to express its love for the Divine in magnificent terms.

Rosa
yellow roses tinged red or orange

Mental Surrender
This happens when the mind has understood that it is only an instrument.

Rosa 'Father's Day'
small light orange roses in dainty clusters

Supramental Attachment for the Divine
Manifold and smiling, repeating itself endlessly.

All our earth starts from mud and ends in sky,
And Love that was once an animal's desire,
Then a sweet madness in the rapturous heart,
An ardent comradeship in the happy mind,
Becomes a wide spiritual yearning's space.
A lonely soul passions for the Alone,
The heart that loved man thrills to the love of God,
A body is his chamber and his shrine.

Rudbeckia hirta
: Black-eyed Susan, Gloriosa daisy medium-sized yellow to brown compositae flower with dark cone-shaped centre; seasonal plant

   First Turning of the Vital towards the Divine Light
   The vital prepares itself to be transformed.

Ruellia ciliosa
: small pale blue-mauve salverform flowers appearing singly or in pairs; low countryside perennial

Krishna's Light in the Physical Mind
The physical mind loses all rigidity and becomes supple and charming.

Ruellia tuberosa
: mauve flowers with violet centre; erect perennial

   Krishna's Light in the Vital
   The light that directs the vital towards the Truth.

The descent of Krishna would mean the descent of the overmind Godhead preparing, though not itself actually, the descent of supermind and Ananda. Krishna is the Anandamaya; he supports the evolution through the overmind leading it towards the Ananda.

* * *

[Krishna's light] is a special light—in the mind it brings clarity, freedom from obscurity, mental error and perversion; in the vital it clears out all perilous stuff and where it is, there is a pure and divine happiness and gladness.

Ruellia elegans
: carmine flowers

   Heroic Action
   Fights for the true and the beautiful without fear of obstacles and oppositions!

Here is the flower we have called "Aspiration in the Physical for the Divine's Love." By the "Physical" I mean the physical consciousness, the most ordinary outward-going consciousness, the normal consciousness of most human beings, which sets such great store by comfort, good food, good clothes, happy relationships, etc., instead of aspiring for the higher things. Aspiration in the physical for the Divine's Love implies that the physical asks for nothing else save that it should feel how the Divine loves it. It realises that all its usual satisfactions are utterly insufficient. But there cannot be a compromise: if the physical wants the Divine's Love it must want that alone and not say, "I shall have the Divine's Love and at the same time keep my other attachments, needs and enjoyments...."

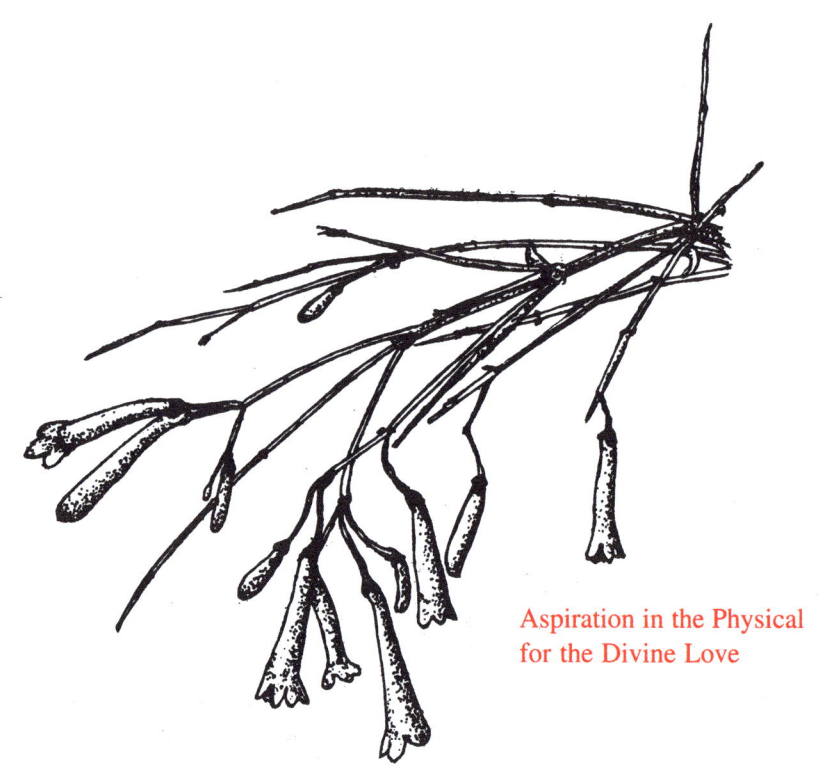

Aspiration in the Physical for the Divine Love

Russelia equisetiformis
　Coral plant, Fountain plant
　small red candle-shaped flowers in light cascading racemes; spreading herbaceous perennial

Aspiration in the Physical for the Divine Love
Manifold and intense, it is difficult to satisfy.

Russelia sarmentosa
　very small fire-red flowers in tiers of ascending whorls

Spiritual Aspiration in the Physical
Comes in fits and starts to oppose and overcome the resistances which do not succeed in making it give in.

Saintpaulia ionantha
African violet
several colours of small single or double rotate flowers appearing between soft decorative foliage; compact perennial succulent

Correct Movements
All movements coming from the correct inspiration.

Saintpaulia
purple flowers

Correct Movements in the Vital
At once the cause and the result of conversion.

Salix discolor
Pussy-willow
soft silky pearl-grey catkins turning bright yellow; tree

The Future
A promise yet unrealised!

To know, possess and be the divine being in an animal and egoistic consciousness, to convert our twilit or obscure physical mentality into the plenary supramental illumination, to build peace and a self-existent bliss where there is only a stress of transitory satisfactions besieged by physical pain and emotional suffering, to establish an infinite freedom in a world which presents itself as a group of mechanical necessities, to discover and realise the immortal life in a body subjected to death and constant mutation,—this is offered to us as the manifestation of God in Matter and the goal of Nature in her terrestrial evolution.

The first movement of aspiration is this: you have a kind of vague sensation that behind the universe there is something which is worth knowing, which is probably (for you do not yet know it) the only thing worth living for, which can connect you with the Truth; something on which the universe depends but which does not depend upon the universe, something which still escapes your comprehension but which seems to you to be behind all things.

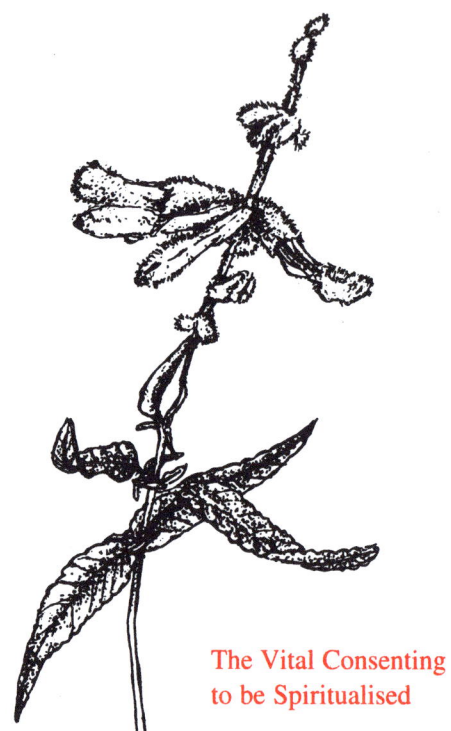

The Vital Consenting to be Spiritualised

Salvia
    several colours of small tubular labiate flowers on erect spikes or curving racemes; seasonal herbaceous plant

Aspiration for Spirituality
Conscious of the advantages of spiritualisation

Salvia leucantha
    Mexican bush salvia
    small white to pale mauve velvety flowers with purple calyces

The Vital Consenting to Be Spiritualised
A great victory over the lower nature.

Salvia farinacea
    Blue sage
    very small violet-blue flowers with light blue-grey calyces

Krishna's Light in the Overmind
The Overmind ready to be divinised.

Salvia splendens
    Scarlet sage
    scarlet red flowers and calyces

Matter Consenting to Be Spiritualised
The beginning of wisdom.

Sambucus
: Elder, Elderberry
tiny fragrant cream-white flowers in large rounded clusters, small tree

Charm
Envelops and conquers by its inexhaustible sweetness.

Sanchezia speciosa
: long spikes of yellow tubular flowers set in reddish bracts, leaves veined white; shrub

Foresight
A perception which is under the Divine Influence.

Spirituality is in its essence an awakening to the inner reality of our being, to a spirit, self, soul which is other than our mind, life and body, an inner aspiration to know, to feel, to be that, to enter into contact with the greater Reality beyond and pervading the universe which inhabits also our own being, to be in communion with It and union with It, and a turning, a conversion, a transformation of our whole being as a result of the aspiration, the contact, the union, a growth or waking into a new becoming or new being, a new self, a new nature.

Sansevieria (*Pl. 14*)
: Bowstring hemp
long spikes bearing intensely fragrant cream-white flowers with narrow corolla tube and recurved silky petals; rhizomatous decorative plant with thick sturdy variegated leaves

Joy of Spirituality
The reward of sincere efforts.

Sansevieria
: larger flowers

Power of Spirituality
True spirituality transforms life.

Saponaria officinalis
: Bouncing Bet, Silene saponaria
light airy clusters of very small white or pink starlike flowers; seasonal or tuberous perennial

Right Use of the Granted Grace
No deformation, no diminution, no exaggeration—a clear sincerity.

Absence of Grief

"How shall he be deluded, whence shall he have sorrow who sees everywhere the Oneness?"

Saraca indica
> Ashoka, Sorrowless tree of India
> fragrant clusters of apricot to orange-red
> salverform flowers with long stamens; tree

Absence of Grief
*The contemplation that takes you
above suffering.*

Scabiosa atropurpurea
> Pincushions, Sweet scabious
> small rounded heads of mildly fragrant
> light mauve flowers with striking white
> anthers; countryside or cultivated seasonal
> plant

Blessings
*Pure and innumerable, manifesting
itself boundlessly.*

Scabiosa
> deep purple flowers

Blessings on the Material World
*Puissant and innumerable, they
answer all needs.*

Selenicereus
Moon cereus, Night-blooming cereus
large striking white funnel-shaped cactus flower with many petals and innumerable stamens; climbing cactus

The Supramental Riches
The riches that are at the command of the Supramental Being and as yet unknown to man.

If mankind only caught a glimpse of what infinite enjoyments, what perfect forces, what luminous reaches of spontaneous knowledge, what wide calms of our being lie waiting for us in the tracts which our animal evolution has not yet conquered, they would leave all and never rest till they had gained these treasures.

Senecio (*Pl. 5*)
Groundsel
mildly fragrant cream-white tassel-like head on an erect stalk; spreading succulent

Observation
Likes to prolong its attention in order to see better.

Sesamum indicum
Gingelly, Sesame
erect racemes of small white pendulous tubular flowers with spreading petals and pale pink throat; economic seasonal plant

Conciliation
Likes smooth contacts.

Sesbania grandiflora
Agati, Vegetable humming-bird
large white, pink or red papilionacous flowers opening singly or in pairs; small tree

Beginning of Realisation
Full of promise and hope, it emanates confidence and joy!

Setcreasea purpurea
Purple heart
small mauve-pink flowers set in two half-folded dark purple bracts, dark purple leaves; spreading succulent

The Vital Governed by the Presence
The vital force is made peaceful and is disciplined by the Divine Presence.

Sinningia
> Gloxinia
> several colours of elegant velvety
> bell-shaped flowers set above velvety
> foliage; compact tuberous perennial

Broadening of the Being
All the parts of the being broaden in order to progress.

Sinningia
> white flowers

Balanced Use of the Integral Power
It is true that power can only become integral when it is used in equilibrium.

Sinningia
> purple flowers

Broadening of the Most Material Vital
The limitations of the ego begin to be shaken.

Sinningia
> white flowers covered with innumerable purple dots

Organised Emotive Broadening
The broadening should not result from an instinctive impulse but from a conscious organisation.

Solandra maxima
> Chalice vine, Cup-of-gold vine
> large mildly fragrant cream to light
> yellow chalice-shaped flower; heavy
> climber

Absolute Truthfulness
Must govern one's life if one wants to be close to the Divine.

Solanum seaforthianum
: delicate pendulous clusters of light blue star-shaped flowers with erect stamens; creeper

Seeking for All Support in the Divine
The Divine alone is the support that never fails.

Seeking for all Support in the Divine

Never seek a support elsewhere than in the Divine. Never seek satisfaction elsewhere than in the Divine. Never seek the satisfaction of your needs in anyone else except the Divine—never, for anything at all. All your needs can be satisfied only by the Divine. All your weaknesses can be borne and healed only by the Divine. He alone is capable of giving you what you need in everything, always, and if you try to find any satisfaction or support or help or joy or... Heaven knows what, in anyone else, you will always fall on your nose one day, and that always hurts, sometimes even hurts very much.

This courage, this heroism which the Divine wants of us, why not use it to fight against one's own difficulties, one's own imperfections, one's own obscurities? Why not heroically face the furnace of inner purification?…

Solanum torvum
>light clusters of white star-shaped flowers; countryside vegetable shrub

Fearlessness
Without fear and without hesitation it will obey the command of the Divine.

Solanum melongena
>Aubergine, Brinjal, Eggplant
>small lavender-blue cup-shaped flower; seasonal vegetable plant

Fearlessness in the Vital
Goes straight to its goal and does not fear inclemency.

Solanum surattense
>purple star-shaped flower; low thorny countryside seasonal plant

Vital Courage
Must be controlled in order to do good.

Solanum rantonnetii
>violet rotate flower; shrub

Remembrance
The constant remembrance of the Divine is indispensable for transformation.

Solidago
> Goldenrod
> tiny yellow flowers in tall feathery spikes; rhizomatous perennial

Mental Sincerity
The essential condition for integral honesty.

Mental Sincerity

Sincerity is progressive, and as the being progresses and develops, as the universe unfolds in the becoming, sincerity too must go on perfecting itself endlessly....

To be perfectly sincere it is indispensable not to have any preference, any desire, any attraction, any dislike, any sympathy or antipathy, any attachment, any repulsion. One must have a total, integral vision of things, in which everything is in its place and one has the same attitude towards all things: the attitude of true vision.

Do not imagine that truth and falsehood, light and darkness, surrender and selfishness can be allowed to dwell together in the house consecrated to the Divine. The transformation must be integral, and integral therefore the rejection of all that withstands it.

Spathiphyllum
: Spathe flower
cream-white to pale green spathe with white spadix borne on a long scape; rhizomatous perennial with decorative foliage

Aspiration for Purity
Purity is perfect sincerity and one cannot have it unless the being is entirely consecrated to the Divine.

Spathodea campanulata
: African tulip tree, Scarlet-bell tree
clusters of large apricot to reddish-orange bell-shaped flowers with fiery border; tree

Passion
It is a force, but is dangerous and cannot be used unless it is perfectly surrendered to the Divine.

Spathoglottis plicata
: Ground orchid
small white orchids on a long erect scape; terrestrial rhizomatous plant

Integral Attachment for the Divine
On the right way towards realisation.

Spathoglottis
: light mauve to deep violet flowers

Vital Attachment for the Divine
Manifold and abundant in its multiplicity.

Humility

Sporobolus capillaris
   Dropseed
   delicate airy panicles of branching spikelets
   bearing minute flowers, light green-brown
   to maroon; countryside grass

Humility
Adorable in its simplicity.

To be humble means for the mind, the vital and the body never to forget that *without the Divine* they know nothing, are nothing and can do nothing; without the Divine they are nothing but ignorance, chaos and impotence.

Stachytarpheta
: very small flowers sparsely arranged on long ascending spikes, light blue, pink or purple; low perennial shrub

Spiritual Ascension of the Vital
It is more fanciful and less regular [than Spiritual Ascension].

Stapelia
: Carrion flower, Starfish flower
large dark purple or maroon star-shaped flower with innumerable yellow rings, malodorous; low succulent with fleshy stem and minute leaves

Conquest of the Armies
Brutal and material, it does not bring joy.

Stemmadenia galeottiana
: fragrant white salverform flower with rounded petals; small tree

Purity in Action
When action is initiated by the Divine Will it is pure.

Sternbergia
: large yellow or orange-yellow flowers

Supramental Invocation
The spontaneous attitude of the Supermind before the Divine.

Strelitzia reginae (*Pl. 16*)
: Bird-of-paradise
scapes bearing spectacular orange, yellow and blue flowers resembling the head of a crested bird; rhizomatous perennial

Supramental Bird
It remains just where it has descended!

Strobilanthes kunthianus
: Kurunji
small blue-violet funnel-shaped flowers set in short bracteate spikes blossoming profusely once in twelve years; low shrub

The Power of a Perfect Endurance
Shows itself rarely but is very precious.

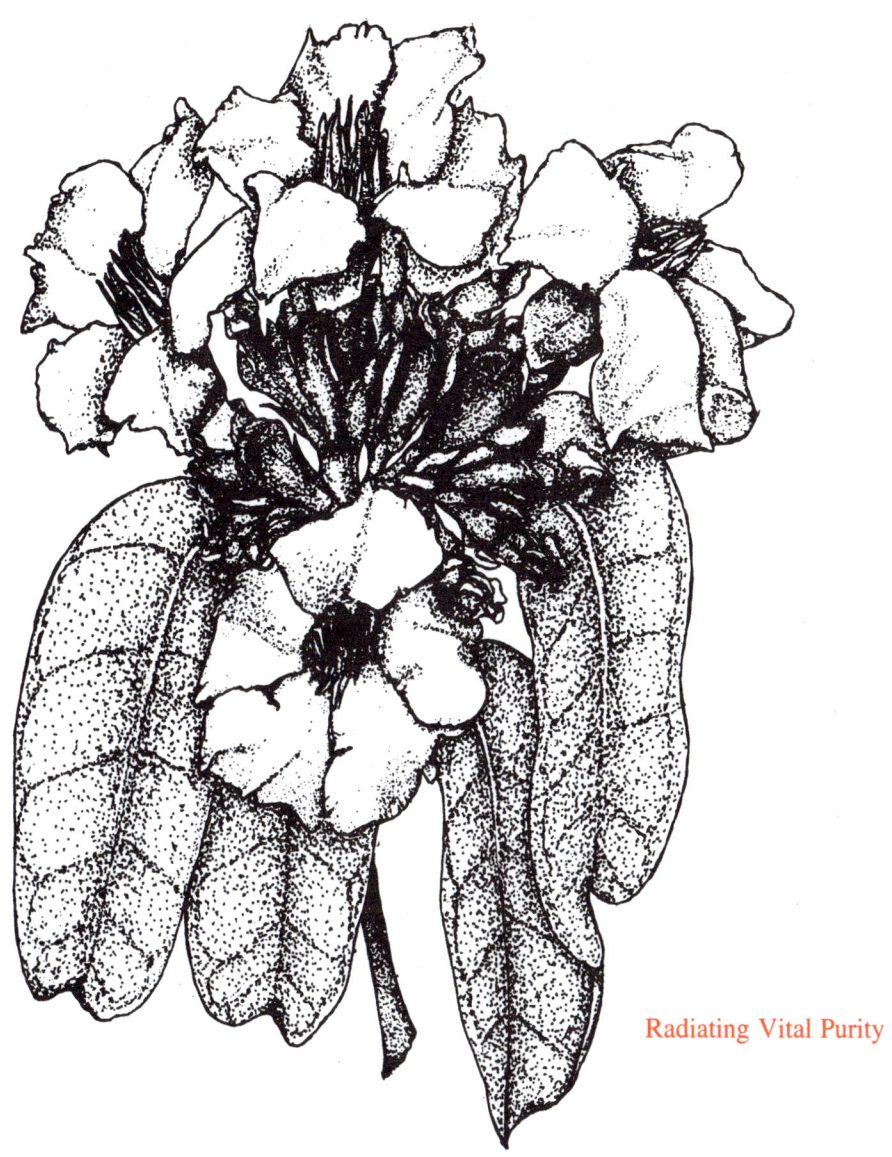

Radiating Vital Purity

Strophanthus
    small white salverform flower with purple ribbonlike petals; robust climber

Spreading of the Manifestation
The Divine Manifestation radiates.

Strophanthus gratus
    Cream fruit
    clusters of fragrant white to light pink trumpet-shaped flowers with prominent light maroon corona; heavy climber or spreading shrub

Radiating Vital Purity
It is possible only by perfect consecration of the vital.

Cease inwardly from thought and word, be motionless within you, look upward into the light and outward into the vast cosmic consciousness that is around you. Be more and more one with the brightness and the vastness. Then will Truth dawn on you from above and flow in you from all around you.

But only if the mind is no less intense in its purity than its silence. For in an impure mind the silence will soon fill with misleading lights and false voices, the echo or sublimation of its own vain conceits and opinions or the response to its secret pride, vanity, ambition, lust, greed or desire.

Syringa
    Lilac
    showy clusters of small very fragrant lilac or white waxy flowers; shrub

Distinction
Of a refined beauty, it is sufficient to itself.

Syzygium jambos (*Pl. 9*)
    Rose apple, Star apple
    small clusters of delicate white rotate flowers with innumerable stamens; fruit tree

Mastery
Know what the Divine wills and you will have mastery.

Tabernaemontana (*Pl. 7*)
    Crape gardenia, Eye flower, Pin-wheel flower
    clusters of single white salverform flowers with yellow centre and narrow corolla tube; shrub or small tree

Mental Purity
A mirror that does not distort.

Tabernaemontana 'Flore-pleno'
    semi-double white salverform flower with curling petals

Integral Mental Purity
Silent, attentive, receptive, concentrated on the Divine—such is the path of purity.

Tabernaemontana 'Flore-pleno'
    fully double fragrant white flower with soft crapelike petals

Perfect Mental Purity
A spotless mirror constantly turned towards the Divine.

That which can easily change its form is 'plastic'. Figuratively, it is suppleness, a capacity of adaptation to circumstances and necessities. When I ask you to be plastic in relation to the Divine, I mean not to resist the Divine with the rigidity of preconceived ideas and fixed principles.

* * *

The physical being and physical consciousness must be very plastic to be able to lend themselves to all the necessary changes, so as to be of one kind one day and another the next, and so on.

Tagetes
Marigold
light yellow to gold or red-maroon
double compositae flowers; seasonal plant

Plasticity
Always ready for the necessary progress.

Tagetes erecta
large lemon yellow flowers

Mental Plasticity
Indispensable for true knowledge.

Tagetes erecta 'Spun Yellow'
Chrysanthemum marigold
small to large yellow flowers with finely frilled florets

Energy of a Plastic Mind
Does not draw back from any effort to progress.

Tagetes erecta
large orange or golden flowers

Supramentalised Plasticity
One of the steps on the way to transformation.

Tagetes patula
French marigold
medium-sized yellow or orange flowers streaked maroon

Physical Plasticity
One of the important conditions for transformation.

Tagetes patula
French marigold
small or miniature light yellow, gold or red-maroon flowers

Detailed Plasticity
The plasticity needed to always progress.

Talinum
>　Fame-flower, Jewels-of-Opar, Puchero
>　tiny pink rotate flowers in light airy clusters, followed by tiny yellow round fruits; low succulent

>　***Vital Fantasy***
>　*Ephemeral and of no importance.*

Tarenna asiatica
>　clusters of small highly fragrant cream-white starlike flowers; countryside shrub

>　***Humility before the Divine in the Physical Nature***
>　*The first attitude needed for transformation.*

It [the physical mind] is the instrument of understanding and ordered action on physical things. Only instead of being obscure and ignorant and fumbling as now or else guided only by an external knowledge it has to become conscious of the Divine and to act in accordance with an inner light, will and knowledge putting itself into contact and an understanding unity with the physical world.

Tecoma stans
>　Yellow-bells, Yellow elder
>　showy clusters of mildly fragrant bright yellow trumpet-shaped flowers with or without orange or maroon throat; large shrub or tree

>　***Physical Mind***
>　*Becomes a good instrument of action when it is content to be that alone.*

Tecoma alata
>　Trumpet bush
>　smaller yellow flowers with orange or light maroon corolla tube and throat; shrub

>　***Higher Mind***
>　*Its superiority consists in its capacity to open to the Divine Light.*

Power of Truth in the Subconscient

Tecomaria capensis
    Cape honeysuckle
    erect clusters of bright orange tubular
    flowers with recurved petals; shrub

Power of Truth in the Subconscient
It can act only when sincerity is
perfect.

If you call for the Truth and yet something in you chooses what is false, ignorant and undivine or even simply is unwilling to reject it altogether, then always you will be open to attack and the Grace will recede from you. Detect first what is false or obscure in you and persistently reject it, then alone can you rightly call for the divine Power to transform you.

Desire nothing but the purity, force, light, wideness, calm, Ananda of the divine consciousness and its insistence to transform and perfect your mind, life and body. Ask for nothing but the divine, spiritual and supramental Truth, its realisation on earth and in you and in all who are called and chosen and the conditions needed for its creation and its victory over all opposing forces.

Tectona grandis
    Teak tree
    mildly fragrant tiny cream-white rotate
    flowers in large airy cloudlike panicles;
    large tree

Renunciation of Desire
The essential condition for realisation.

Terminalia catappa
    Indian almond, Tropical almond
    short spikes of tiny white starlike flowers;
    large tree

Spiritual Aspiration
Rises like an arrow caring neither for obstacles nor laggards!

Thespesia populnea
    Portia tree
    bright yellow deep cup-shaped flower with
    crapelike petals, changing to carmine; tree

Health
Not to be preoccupied with it but to leave it to the Divine!

Thevetia peruviana
Yellow oleander
fragrant yellow funnel-shaped flower;
large shrub

Mind
Its true value lies in its surrender to the Divine.

The nature of Mind as we know it is an Ignorance seeking for knowledge; it is a knower of fractions and worker of divisions striving to arrive at a sum, to piece together a whole,—it is not possessed of the essence of things or their totality.

* * *

The transformation of the Ignorance into the integral Knowledge, the growth in us of a spiritual intelligence ready to receive a higher light and canalise it for all the parts of our nature is an intermediate necessity of great importance.

Thevetia peruviana
white flowers

Purified Mind
Mind ready to surrender to the Divine.

Thevetia
light orange flowers

Supramentalised Mind
Mind has become an instrument for transformation.

Thunbergia alata
>Black-eyed Susan
>yellow-orange to orange salverform flowers with nearly black centre; creeper

>**Obscurity Offering Itself to Be Transformed**
>*Obscurity tired of being obscure.*

Obscurity Offering Itself to Be Transformed

Thunbergia alata 'Julietta'
>pure golden-yellow flowers

>**Transformation Makes the Obscurity Disappear**
>*Obscurity will disappear more and more as the transformation progresses.*

Transformation Makes the Obscurity Disappear

Thunbergia erecta
   Bush clock vine, King's mantle
   deep violet salverform flowers with
   rounded petals and yellow throat; shrub

Opening of the Material Vital to the Light
One of the essential conditions for peace.

Thunbergia erecta
   pure white

Integral Opening to the Light
The assurance of the peace and the joy to come.

Thunbergia grandiflora
   Blue trumpet vine
   medium to large lavender-blue flowers

Krishna's Light in the Mind
A charming way of becoming intelligent!

Thunbergia erecta (*Pl. 7*)
   variegated white and lavender

Opening of the Higher Vital to the Light
Existing only for the Divine, the vital knows no other master.

Thunbergia grandiflora
   Clock vine
   pendulous clusters of white salverform
   flowers with recurved corolla tubes;
   creeper

Opening to the Light
Co-operates with all that leads towards the Light.

Thunbergia fragrans
   small delicate white salverform flowers;
   rambling creeper

Purity in the Emotive Centre
Indispensable for progress.

Thunbergia kirkii (*Pl. 15*)
   very small lavender-blue salverform
   flowers; low shrub

Opening to Sri Aurobindo's Force
The help of Sri Aurobindo is constant; it is for us to know how to receive it.

Mental Simplicity

Thymopylla tenuiloba
   Dahlberg daisy, Golden-fleece
   very small yellow compositae flowers set
   among finely frilled aromatic leaves;
   seasonal groundcover

Mental Simplicity
Does not like complications.

I have always found that this one [Mental Simplicity] has a cleansing fragrance; when you breathe it, ah, everything becomes clean—it's wonderful! Once I cured myself of the onset of a cold with it—this can be done when you catch it at the very beginning. It fills you completely, the nose, the throat.

Tithonia diversifolia (*Pl. 2*)
   Perennial sunflower
   large yellow sunflower with long separate
   petals; shrub

**First Movement of the Riches
towards the Divine**
The sure sign of conversion.

Tithonia rotundifolia
   Mexican sunflower
   striking orange-red sunflower with velvety
   petals; seasonal plant

**Physical Consciousness Turned
Entirely towards the Divine**
*It thirsts for the Divine and wants Him
alone.*

Torenia fournieri
    Bluewings
    erect racemes of white, mauve or lavender two-lipped flowers with yellow spot on throat giving the impression of a peacock feather; low seasonal

Krishna's Play
A power of progress veiling itself behind appearances.

Torenia fournieri
    purple flowers with pale lavender-blue corolla tube

Krishna's Play in Matter
Beauty, love and joy are comrades! It is a play that widens and makes for progress.

Torenia fournieri 'alba'
    ivory-white flowers

Krishna's Integral Play
All the parts of the being respond to His influence.

Trachymene coeruleus
    Blue lace flower
    rounded heads of very small light lavender-blue rotate flowers; seasonal plant

Perfect Working of the Mind
Can happen when the mind is resolved to exclusively fulfil its role.

Tribulus terrestris
    Puncture vine, Burr-nut
    very small yellow rotate flower; countryside groundcover

First Mental Awakening in Matter
It has preceded and prepared the future of man upon earth.

Trifolium
    Clover
    small white, pink or violet rounded heads of tiny papilionaceous flowers; countryside groundcover

Kindness of Nature
She is kind when she is loving

Mental Honesty

It is a mind that does not attempt to deceive itself. And in fact it is not an "attempt", for it succeeds very well in doing it!

It would seem that in the ordinary psychological constitution of man, the almost constant function of the mind is to give an acceptable explanation of what goes on in the "desire-being", the vital, the most material parts of the mind and the subtlest parts of the body.

Tristellateia australis
    showy racemes of small bright yellow
    rotate flowers; creeper

Mental Honesty
One does not try to deceive others nor to deceive oneself.

Tropaeolum majus
> Nasturtium
> cream-yellow, red or maroon rotate flowers with corona, spreading petals and prominent spur; low seasonal plant with aromatic leaves

Promise of Realisation
The best encouragement.

Tropaeolum
> yellow flowers

Promise of Realisation in the Mind
The mind must be silent to allow the Supramental Consciousness to take its place.

Tropaeolum
> dark red to maroon flowers

Promise of Realisation in Matter
The best encouragement for doing what is necessary.

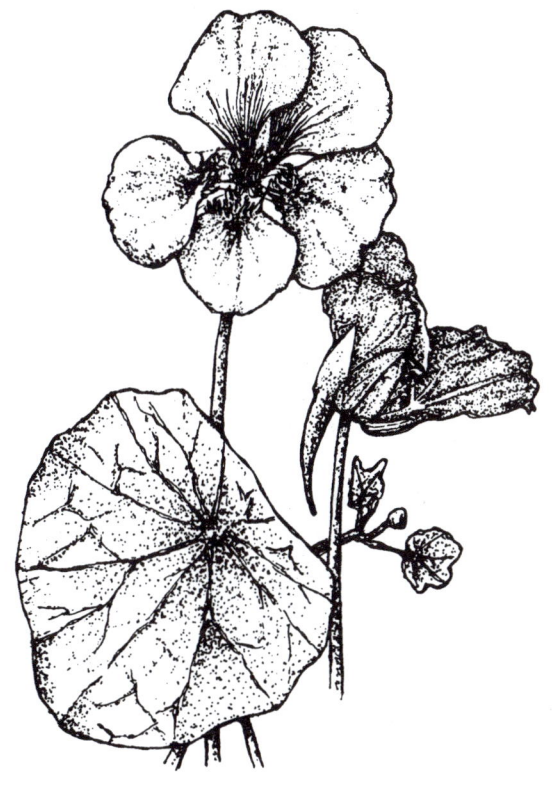

Promise of Realisation

Tropaeolum
> red to light maroon flowers with yellow border

Promise of Realisation in the Physical
Courage to face the long labour.

Tropaeolum
> yellow flowers with red centre

Promise of Realisation in the Physical Mind
A good encouragement for the necessary effort.

Tulipa
: Tulip
  many colours and forms of cup-shaped flowers each on a short scape; bulbous plant

  Blossoming
  The result of trust and success.

Turnera ulmifolia elegans (*Pl. 2*)
: cream-white flowers with maroon centre; perennial groundcover

  Awakening of the Physical Mind
  It wants to know and opens wide in order to understand.

Turnera ulmifolia
: Yellow alder, Sage rose, West Indian holly yellow rotate flowers with delicate petals; low countryside shrub

  Wakefulness in the Mind
  Let it turn to the Light and to the Light alone.

Typhonium divaricatum
: large maladorous red-maroon spathe and bright red spadix coming out from the ground; countryside rhizomatous plant

  Gossip
  Dark and pointed, this flower hurts more than it charms.

The physical mind is that which is fixed on physical objects and happenings, sees and understands these only, and deals with them according to their own nature, but can with difficulty respond to the higher forces.... To enlighten the physical mind by the consciousness of the higher spiritual and supramental planes is one object of this yoga, just as to enlighten it by the power of the higher vital and higher mental elements of the being is the greatest part of human self-development, civilisation and culture.

Psychic Tranquility

Vallaris solanacea
    clusters of small white fragrant bell-shaped flowers; heavy creeper

Psychic Tranquillity
By its very nature the psychic is calm and tranquil.

We shall endure tranquilly the action and impact on us of men and things and forces, the pressure of the Gods and the assaults of Titans; we shall face and engulf in the unstirred seas of our spirit all that can possibly come to us down the ways of the soul's infinite experience.

Emmotional Attachment for the Divine

Vanda caerulea
> Blue orchid
> racemes of large light blue fragrant orchids with violet lip; epiphytic orchid

Attachment in the Emotive Vital for the Divine
An artistic and graceful attachment that can be a little fanciful.

Vanda teres
> medium-sized pale lavender-pink fragrant orchid with golden-yellow lip

Emotional Attachment for the Divine
Cups of flowering feelings offered to the Divine!

Vanda tessellata
> long racemes of fragrant olive-lavender orchids with curly petals speckled ochre-brown and prominent lavender lip

Detailed Attachment for the Divine
Manifold, scrupulous, neglecting nothing, meticulous—always ready to make another effort.

The only way of being truly free is to make your surrender to the Divine entire, without reservation, because then all that binds you, ties you down, chains you, falls away naturally from you and has no longer any importance. . . .

And it is this freedom that I want of you—free from all attachment, all ignorance, all reaction; free from everything except a total surrender to the Divine.

Verbena hybrida
> Perennial verbena
> erect clusters of small salverform flowers
> in several colours; low spreading seasonal
> or perennial plant

Thoroughness
Indispensable for all true progress.

Verbena
> carmine with cream centre

Artistic Thoroughness
Neglects nothing in its search for perfection.

Thoroughness

Verbena
> dark red

Physical Thoroughness
Takes great care of details in the execution of work.

Verbena
> violet

Vital Thoroughness
The vital must become calm and docile.

Verbena
white

Integral Thoroughness
Nothing is neglected in order to reach the Divine Goal.

Verbena
pink

Psychic Thoroughness
With untiring patience it works for the perfection of the being.

Verbena tenuisecta
Moss verbena
elongated clusters of smaller light pink salverform flowers; low spreading seasonal plant

Aspiration for Conquest of the Enemies in the Vital
A will concentrated and not noisy, acting quietly but effectively.

Verbena
purple

Will to Conquer the Vital Enemies
Indispensable for the mastery over desires.

Verbena
white

Conquest over the Vital Enemies
Of modest appearance, it has an enduring power.

Every morning may our thought rise fervently towards Thee, asking Thee how we can manifest and serve Thee best.

Vernonia eleagnaefolia
: Curtain creeper
airy clusters of tiny pale lavender to white compositae flowers changing to soft fluffy heads; heavy creeper

Aspiration for the Divine Consciousness
O precious flower, blossom forth never to close again!

Viburnum plicatum
: Japanese snowball
large round clusters of small white rotate flowers; shrub

Collective Purity
A very precious achievement, but difficult to obtain.

Viola odorata
: Violet
very fragrant small purple flower with recurved petals and short spur hidden behind small rounded leaves; low rhizomatous plant

Modesty
Is satisfied with its own charm and does not draw attention.

Thoughts Turned Towards the Divine

Viola
    Pansy
    several colours of small, soft velvety flowers with five rounded petals, some mildly fragrant; low rhizomatous plant

Thoughts Turned towards the Divine
A certitude of beauty.

Viola
    cream-yellow flowers

Integrally Pure Thoughts
An effect of the Divine Grace.

Viscum album
: Mistletoe
tiny white flowers, small pearl-white berries and oval leaves; perennial parasitic shrub

Sign of the Spirit
"I am here", says the Spirit.

Vitis vinifera
: Cultivated grape
clusters of grapes, green, red or black

Divine Ananda
Abundant, succulent, nourishing, full of vigour.

Vittadinia australis
: Creeping daisy
very small white compositae flowers; creeping groundcover

Integral Simplicity
The simplicity that is the consequence of perfect sincerity.

As soon as all effort disappears from a manifestation, it becomes very simple, with the simplicity of a flower opening, manifesting its beauty and spreading its fragrance without clamour or vehement gesture. And in this simplicity lies the greatest power, the power which is least mixed and least gives rise to harmful reactions.

Wedelia
: small double yellow compositae flowers; low perennial shrub or groundcover

Detailed Perseverance
To continue the work begun for as long as is necessary.

Wisteria sinensis
: Chinese wisteria
small lavender papilionaceous flowers in long pendulous clusters; heavy deciduous creeper

Poet's Ecstasy
Rare and charming is your presence!

Truth is a difficult and strenuous conquest. One must be a real warrior to make this conquest, a warrior who fears nothing, neither enemies nor death, for with or against everybody, with or without a body, the struggle continues and will end by Victory.

Wormia bourbridgii
    medium-sized lemon-yellow open cup-shaped flower with white crown; shrub

Effort towards the Truth
Should exist in all men of goodwill.

Wrightia tinctoria
    light clusters of small fragrant white star-shaped flowers with white coronas; tree

Religious Thought
Can only be used when liberated from the influence of religions.

Yucca
    large erect branching spikes with fragrant white bell-shaped flowers; perennial shrub blooming once in its lifetime

Initiation
It is unique in the whole of its existence.

Zebrina pendula
    Inch plant, Wandering Jew
    very small violet flower emerging singly from a folded bract, small purple leaves striped green; succulent groundcover or hanging-basket plant

Quiet Strength in the Vital
Does not like to attract attention.

Prayer

Flowers are the prayers of the vegetal kingdom

A prayer, a master act, a king idea
Can link man's strength to a transcendent Force.
Then miracle is made the common rule.

Zephyranthes
    Fairy lily, Rain lily
    several colours of small funnel-shaped
    flowers each borne on a short scape,
    sometimes mildly fragrant; bulbous plant

Prayer
Self-giving is true prayer.

Zephyranthes
    white flowers

Integral Prayer
The whole being is concentrated in a single prayer to the Divine.

Zephyranthes
    yellow flowers

Mental Prayer
Spontaneous in a mind aspiring for transformation.

Zephyranthes
    deep pink flowers

Vital Prayer
The vital implores for its purification.

Zephyranthes
    large pink flowers

Psychic Prayer
Spontaneous and fervent.

Endurance

Zinnia
> many colours of small, medium or large double compositae flowers; erect seasonal plant

> **Endurance**
> *Going to the very end of the effort without fatigue or relaxing.*

Supramental Sun

Mastery   *Happy Heart*

Faith

Perfect Radiating Psychology

Supramental Action *Success in Supramental Work*

The New World

Cheerfulness in Work done for the Divine   *Sex Centre Aspiring to be Purified*

Unselfishness   *Silence*

Sweetness of the Power Surrendered to the Divine

Spiritual Intensity

Krishna's Play in the Vital

Gratitude

Spiritual Speech

Miracle

Divine Smile

Aspiration in the Physical for the Supramental Light

Wealth in the Mind of Light

Joy of Spirituality

Realisation

Surrender

Friendship with the Divine

Joy of Integral Faithfulness

Beauty of Tomorrow Manifesting the Divine

The Perfect New Creation

Opening to Sri Aurobindo's Force   *Perfect Radiating Purity*

Supramental Bird

Supramental Influence

The most important is a steady, quiet endurance that does not allow any upsetting or depression to interfere with your progress. The sincerity of the aspiration is the assurance of the victory.

* * *

To maintain one's endurance in spite of all oppositions, the support must be unshakable, and *one support* alone is unshakable, that of the reality, the Supreme Truth.

Zinnia
cream with or without red centre

Ananda of Endurance
To have the knowledge and the power to bear and endure is certainly the source of a firm joy.

Zinnia
royal purple

Courageous Endurance
Strong and energetic, it never complains.

Zinnia
white

Integral Endurance
Unfailingly it will go on till the very end of its task.

Zinnia
bright coral pink

Joyous Endurance
It keeps smiling whatever happens.

Zinnia
variegated or multi-coloured

Manifold Endurance
Whatever the endurance needed, it is always there to fulfil its role.

Zinnia
lemon yellow

Mental Endurance
It is never discouraged by the difficulty of problems to be resolved.

Zinnia
violet-red

Vital Endurance
Wht do obstacles matter, we shall always go forward!

Zinnia
mauve-pink

Endurance of the Higher Vital
Whatever the circumstances, it does not fail.

Zinnia
dark red

Physical Endurance
Knows neither fatigue nor exhaustion.

Zinnia
pink

Psychic Endurance
It will smile at life whatever its difficulties may be.

Zinnia
light green

Spontaneous Endurance
Smiling, effortless and natural.

Zinnia
orange

Victorious Endurance
It will last to the end of the combat.

Zinnia
golden-yellow

Supramentalised Endurance
With such an attitude difficulties lose their power to harrass you.

Zinnia angustifolia
very small single white, yellow or orange semi-double compositae flowers; seasonal groundcover

Detailed Endurance
Nothing is so small as to be neglected; the same attention is given to all circumstances.

Previously Used Names

The Mother would often give a message orally to a disciple or write a meaning below a picture sent to her and return the envelope with her blessings. Other names have evolved as time went by with changes she made. Here are some of them.

Botanical Name (Message)	Previous Name
Amaranthus caudatus (Fearlessness in Action)	Fearlessness in the Vital
Bauhinia purpurea (Stability in the Vital)	Stability in the Higher Vital Vital Contentment
Calonyction alba (Entire Self-giving)	Consecration
Celosia plumosa (Aspiraion for Immortality)	Spiritual Aspiration in the Vital
Clitoria ternatea (Radha's Consciosness)	Loving Consecration Radha's Absolute Consecration Integral Radha's Consciousness Devotional Movement in Radha's Consciousness
Convallaria (Power of Purity)	Joy of spiritual purity
Dahlia (Pride)	Mental Pride Vital Pride
Digitalis (Regularity)	Regularity* (*This flower appears under Martynia annua)
Gaillardia pulchella (Successful Future)	Future success under the Supramental Influence
Gaillardia pulchella 'picta' (Cheerfulness)	Cheerfulness in artistic Work
Hibiscus sp.	Power over the Things of the Earth* (*A very old name)
Lathyrus odorata (Gentleness)	Kindness
Lavendula*	Vital cleanliness (*A very old name)
Linium grandifolium	Good Temper
Gloriosa superba (No Quarrels)	Occult Power over the Adverse Forces* (*A very old name)
Solandra maxima (Absolute Truthfulness)	Truthfulness* (*The Mother would have preferred this)
Tecoma alata (Higher Mind)	Supramental Victory * (*The Mother changed to Higher Mind)

Flowers Originally Named for Auroville*

Air of Auroville	Miracle
Beauty of Auroville	Beauty of the New Creation
Blossoming of Auroville	Blossoming of the New Creation
Charm of Auroville	Charm of the New Creation
Concentration of Auroville	Concentration of the New Creation
Continuous Perseverance and Action	Power of Perseverance
Effort of Auroville	Power of Effort
Firmness of Auroville	Firmness of the New Creation
Ideal of Auroville	Ideal of the New Creation
Manifold Power of Auroville	Manifold Power of the New Creation
Progress of Auroville	Progress of the New Creation
Realisation of Auroville	Realisation of the New Creation
Spiritual Beauty of Auroville	Power of Spiritual Beauty
Success of Auroville	Power of Success
Sweetness of Auroville	Sweetness of the Power Surrendered to the Divine
Usefulness of Auroville	Usefulness of the New Creation

* An international township situated near Puducherry which aspires to realise human unity in diversity.

Pl.17

Pl.18

The Symbolism of Colour

What is it in a flower which makes it take and reflect a certain colour?

The scientists say that it is the composition of its atoms but I say that it is the nature of its aspiration.

The Mother

*

[The meaning of a colour may vary] with the field, the combination, the character and shades of the colour, the play of forces.

Sri Aurobindo

*

When we study the messages given by the Mother we find that certain colours correspond to certain planes of consciousness, to certain levels of the being. This becomes clear when we read the explanation Sri Aurobindo gives to colours seen in visions. Besides he has indicated in his various writings the levels of our being corresponding to those used also by the Mother when naming the flowers. They are given here in ascending order: the Inconscient, the Subconscient, the Physical proper, the Vital, including the material- physical- Vital, the emotional and the higher Vital. Next is the Mind with its own proper levels, ascending from the physical Mind to the awakened or illumined Mind and continuing upwards towards the intuitive Mind and the Overmind. There are still higher degrees above the normal reaches of our consciousness; these are the Mind of Light and the Supermind or the Truth-Consciousness. Behind all these planes of our being stands the Psychic, the true soul.

But colour alone does not determine the message of a flower. The shape and size of the flower, its intensity of fragrance can often be as important. Even the manner of blossoming is important. In certain plants it may be the inflorescence that is more striking and significant than the individual flower. Often enough, though not always, it is the use of the plant or its character that may be expressed in the flower's message. The meaning may coincide with its use in religious ceremonies.

The following Plates have been designed to show the colours of some of the planes of our being and help the reader, as far as possible, to begin to feel and become aware of these subtle vibrations.

Plate I shows the colours of the Supermind, the Mind and the Psychic region. For comparison, the colours of Krishna and that of the emotive centre have been included.

Plate II continues with the other parts of the Vital and the Physical, which represents our body.

In Plate I first comes 'Krishna's Ananda' (Cape plumbago — *Plumbago capensis*, I.1). Light blue is Krishna's colour and also that of Sri Aurobindo.

Orange and golden-yellow are the colours of the Supermind and of the Supramental qualities. For example, 'Supramentalised Psychological Perfection' (Champaka, *Michelia champaca*, I, 2).

'Mind' (Yellow Oleander, *Thevetia peruviana*, I, 3). It is usually a lemon yellow, since yellow, shading orange, can also indicate light. The significance of higher mind or intuitive mind may be given to cream-yellow flowers such as 'Voice of the Higher Mind' (*Anemopaegma paraense*, I, 4). Shades of blue may also indicate the mind, especially with Krishna's influence: 'Krishna's Light in the Mind' (Clock-vine, *Thunbergia grandiflora* I, 5). However, there are exceptions — 'Charity' (*Commelina*) for example, is a large delicate blue flower.

Light pink is the colour of the psychic region. The Plate shows 'Psychic Prayer' (*Zephyranthes*, I, 6). It is sometimes difficult to distinguish the colour of the psychic from that of the emotive centre. The emotive centre is often expressed by light mauve or lilac-pink. For example, 'Offering of the Emotions' (Hollyhock, *Alcea*, I, 7).

In Plate II the darker colours denoting the Vital and the Physical are shown.

The vital being is usually divided into three layers. First, the higher vital — lavender, deep mauve or deep carmine, as 'Power in the Higher Vital' (Shrub Althaea, *Hibiscus syriacus*, II, 1). Second, the vital proper which is dark red as in the 'Vital Centre' (*Canna*, II, 3), or blue as in 'Spiritual Awakening of the Vital' (*Coleus*, II, 2). The coloured leaves of the same plant express 'Strength in the Vital'. Third, the lower material vital which is denoted by dark blue, violet blue or dark purple as in 'Opening of the Material Vital to the Light' (*Thunbergia erecta*, II, 4).

Red is the colour of the Physical, usually a clear bright red — for example, 'Aspiration in the Physical for the Divine Love' (Fountain plant, *Russelia equisetiformis*, II, 5).

Lastly, the colour of Matter or the Inconscient may be a very dark maroon red, as in 'First Response of the Inconscient to the Supramental Action' (Sausage tree, *Kigelia pinnata*). It is not illustrated here.

The Flower Game

From the end of 1929 to the middle of 1930, the Mother played a flower game with a small group of disciples. Arranging a few flowers in her hand, she made up a sentence in English based on the significances she had given and asked the disciples to guess it. These flower-game sentences are given here with the significances in italics. However the last two are flower-messages given much later. The first was probably inspired by the Mother and put up with pictures on a board in the Ashram dispensary; the other, given in French, was written by the Mother below two pressed flowers sent to her. Minor changes have been made to render the text more readable.

*

The *divine solicitude* is with you—meaning, you are getting all the help you need.. But keep up your *aspiration*, remain *faithful* and the *wrong movement will be changed into the right*, so that the *victorious love* may manifest.

*

The *divine solicitude* is supporting you in the *disinterested work* through which you will attain *transformation*.

*

By *loving consecration* and *faithful service* allow the *divine protection* to be with you in your *aspiring concentration* for *integral transformation* [four flowers together].

*

Love the victor will manifest when there will be established through the five-fold *psychological perfection* [these were Sincerity, Faith, Devotion, Aspiration and Surrender] and when, through *loving consecration* [Radha's consciousness], there will be a complete *love of the physical for the Divine,* and complete *faithfulness* to the Divine.

*

Open with *devotion* your *vital being* to *Radha's influence* and you will get *vital peace*, the peace which leads to *transformation*.

*

Peace in the vital is at once the basis of the *aspiration* and the condition for the *beginning of realisation.*

*

To keep *Agni* burning always in the *psychic centre* is an indispensable condition for the *transformation.*

*

Aspire for *integral and absolute loving consecration* in which will be established *faithfulness* and *purity*, the forerunners of *transformation.*

*

With s*imple sincerity, offer* your *vital being* to the Divine and the *realisation will begin.*

*

To an *aspiration for the Divine Love* supported by *faithfulness* and *sincerity in the vital*, the *Divine Love* will surely answer.

*

The *devotion* that accompanies *Radha's absolute consecration*,—this alone has the power of bringing down *Krishna's light in the mind.*

*

Only by the constant flaming up of *Agni* can integral *loving consecration* be realised; and only by this *absolute loving consecration* can it be established permanently.

*

Peace in the vital, the peace on which is based the *beginning of realisation*, leading to *transformation*—the goal.

*

Aspire for *gratitude*—without gratitude the *mind* cannot get *purified.*

*

Realise an *integral silence* in the being and a complete force of *faith* in this silence; then only can *power* descend and bring *mastery over the things of the earth.*

*

Aspiration and *faithful devotion* firmly established in a *peaceful vital being* and crowned by a *simple sincerity* are some of the most essential conditions for a *beginning of realisation*.

*

Only to those who have a true *humility* will *power* be given.

*

The power of *Agni* will keep the *aspiration flaming in the physical being*. Then can be founded and established in a *vital opened to Radha's influence*, the true *supramentalised friendship with the Divine*.

*

Approach the Divine with *loving gratitude* and you will meet the *Divine's Love*.

*

Let your *aspiration* for *progress* be *cheerful* and you will get the *ananda* of *progress*.

*

Let the *divine cheerfulness suffuse your work*. So your *mind will be purified* and this will bring the *beginning of realisation*.

*

Agni steadily burning within will firmly found in you *faithfulness* and a *devoted loving consecration to the Divine*. This is the surest way to *transformation*.

*

Let *faithfulness* to the Divine be your *tapasya*. Then there will *begin to come a realisation* of the true *supramentalised friendship with the Divine*.

*

The *generosity* of your *absolute self-giving* will bring to you the *revelation* of the *generosity* of the *Divine's love*.

*

Reach through *aspiration* the *intuitive mind*; then you will know what is meant by *transformation*.

*

Peace in the physical cells leads first to *health* and then to *transformation*.

*

Advance on the way with *peace in the physical being* as your ground and *simple sincerity* as your means and, sooner or later, you are bound to reach *identification with the divine consciousness* [Consciousness One with the Divine Consciousness].

*

Surrender to the Divine and *integral transformation* are the two great steps leading to *the perfect New Creation*.

*

Open the vital to Radha's influence; it will establish in you an *absolute loving consecration* to the Divine. Then there will come an *integral opening of your being* which will hasten the manifestation of the *victorious love*.

*

With *simple sincerity, faithfulness* and *purity, open your vital being to the Divine's Love*.

*

Devoted loving consecration [Radha's consciousness], *faithfulness, purity* and *peace in the vital*, these four are the conditions most important for conquest of the *power over the most material vital*.

*

A *mind quiet* and filled with the *sweetness of thoughts exclusively turned towards the divine* is the gate through which there will be the constant *connection between the supramental light and the material being*.

*

Be *simply sincere* in your *obedience* to the Divine. This will take you far on the way to *transformation*.

*

The *power in the mind*, complete *mastery over the sex-centre, supramentalised psychological perfection, perfect transformation, victorious love*—these belong to and will come with the *supramental future*.

*

Wakefulness, resolution and an *integral even basis in the physical* are initial conditions for the *realisation*.

Aspiration in the physical for the Divine's Love, a complete *opening of the physical being to the Divine's Love* and the *turning of the whole physical consciousness towards the Divine* are the conditions for the last and entire *transformation*.

*

A transformed *life-energy* is the *dynamic power* for *transformation*.

*

Only if you have *faith* and *vital confidence in the Divine*, can the *Divine help* come to you.

*

In the *sincerity* of your effort towards *silence* lies the assurance of a *purified mind*.

*

Let *patience* and *endurance* be your companions on the way to physical *transformation*.

*

Turn your *consciousness to the Supramental light* and, through a *pure mind*, let the *Supramental influence* permeate your sex-centre. Then you will obtain *mastery over the sex-centre*.

*

With *aesthetic taste* and *vital purity* build up *vital harmony*. This will make possible the manifestation of the *supramental beauty in the physical*.

*

Let the *flame* of *devotion* help you to have the *patience* needed for *transformation*.

*

Open your *vital generously* to the Divine with *simple sincerity* and *thoroughness* and keep up the *spirit to conquer the vital enemies*. So can be established a *perfect and integral purity*.

*

The complete *opening of the vital to the Divine* leading to its entire *conversion* and to the *transformation* of the *power in the higher vital* and the *conquest of* [low vital movements like] *greed for food* and sexual desire are the necessary conditions for bringing into the physical the principle of *eternal youth*.

*

You must *get rid of the rising of the desires in the vital* and establish *purity in the cells* before you can be fit to enjoy divine *prosperity*.

*

A *consciousness luminous without obscurity*, turned towards the *Supramental light* and full of a *Supramental plasticity* are the conditions for the *manifestation of the Supramental light* upon earth.

*

Let the *integral offering* of your being be the form of your *purified worship*.

*

By *integral endurance*, perfect *mental plasticity* and the organisation of an *integral progress*, *conquer the vital enemies*.

*

By *vital stability*, by *purified life-energy* and the *Supramental influence in the cells* it will be possible for the *body consciousness to undergo the Supramental transformation* which will fix the *ananda in the sex-centre*.

*

Be completely *obedient* to the *Divine's Love*. This will *transform* your being till it becomes *supramentally plastic*.

*

First *aspire for vital purity* and fix firmly a thorough *stability in the vital*. Then only can you in truth make the *offering of your vital being* to the Divine.

*

Silence all outside noise, *aspire* for the *Divine's help*; *open integrally* to it when it comes and *surrender* to its action, and it will effectively bring about your *transformation*.

*

Resolutely keep up the *spirit to conquer the vital enemies* who stand in the way of the *opening of your vital to the Divine's Love*. The *Divine's Love* is the sure maker of *vital harmony* which will lead to a very *successful future*.

*

Let *gold* be turned to the *service* of the Divine; so it will be a *purified gold* and take its true place in *Krishna's play in the material*.

*

Surrender all falsehood; your *physical mind will be converted* and a mental *victory* won.

*

Plasticity brings that *sweetness of thought* which helps you to *surrender*. Through that the *consciousness turns to the Divine*. Then *purity* comes. In *purity* you *realise* the Divine. He grants you *power* and perfect *health*.

*

Let us be *humble* so that we may be able to open ourselves to the *Divine Love* in its marvellous action.

Classified List of Significance

ABOLITION
Abolition of the Ego — 97

ABSENCE
Absence of Desire — 24
Absence of Grief — 220

ABUNDANCE — 80
Abundance of Beauty — 208
Abundant Expression — 55
Emotional Abundance — 150
Material Abundance — 109

ACCOMPLISHMENT — 165

ACTION
Divine will Acting in the Inconscient — 65
Divine Will Acting in the Subconscient — 65
Enthusiasm in Action — 190
Fearlessness in Action — 13
First Response of the Subconscient to the Supramental Action — 146
Heroic Action — 215
Joyous Enthusiasm in Action — 190
Mind of Light Acting in Matter — 51
Organisation of Action in Life — 72
Power of Action — 122
Purity in Action — 228
Supramental Action — 28
Supramentalised Psychic Activity — 42
True Action in the Material Vital — 72

ADITI
Aditi—the Divine Consciousness — 172

ADORATION — 74

ADVERSE SUGGESTION
Power to Reject Adverse Suggestions — 71

AFFECTION
Affection for the Divine — 211

AGNI — 115

AIR — 57

ALCHEMY — 134

ANANDA — 115
Ananda in the Centres — 45
Ananda in the Physical — 115
Ananda in the Physical Body — 45
Ananda of Endurance — 255
Divine Ananda — 250
Krishna's Ananda — 194
Poet's Ecstasy — 250

APPEARANCE
First Appearance of Purity in the Inconscient — 195
First Emergence of the Psychic in Matter — 146

APPLICATION — 100

ARISTOCRACY — 85
Aristocracy of Beauty — 140, 168

ARMIES
Conquest of the Armies — 228

ART — 101
Artistic Sensibility — 138
Artistic Taste — 138
Artistic Thoroughness — 246
Artistic Work — 192
Beauty in Art — 185
Supramental Artistic Genius — 112

ASCENSION — 153
Spiritual Ascension — 61
Spiritual Ascension of the Vital — 228

ASPIRATION — 175
Aspiration for Conquest of the Enemies in the Vital — 247
Aspiration for Immortality — 54
Aspiration for Integral Immortality — 6
Aspiration for Organisation — 202
Aspiration for Purity — 226
Aspiration for Silence in the Mind — 95
Aspiration for Silence in the Physical Mind — 95
Aspiration for Spiritual Intensity — 183
Aspiration for Spirituality — 218
Aspiration for Supramental Guidance in the Subconscient — 184
Aspiration for the Divine Consciousness — 248
Aspiration for the Right Attitude — 66
Aspiration for Trust in the Divine — 23
Aspiration for Vital Purity — 92
Aspiration in the Physical — 142
Aspiration in the Physical for the Divine Love — 216
Aspiration in the Physical for the Supramental Light — 142
Aspiration of the Mind for the Supramental Guidance — 147
Aspiration of the Vital for Union with the Divine — 199
Beauty Aspiring for the Supramental Realisation — 171
Flame of Aspiration — 5
Matter Aspiring for the Supramental Guidance — 179
Mental Aspiration — 142
Nature Aspires to Be Supramentalised — 137
Physical Aspiration for Immortality — 54
Power Aspiring to Become an Instrument for the Divine Work — 187
Power of Collective Aspiration — 134
Psychic Aspiration — 142
Sex Centre Aspiring to Be Purified — 16
Soaring of Aspiration — 63
Spiritual Aspiration — 234
Spiritual Aspiration in the Physical — 216
Spontaneous Aspiration of Nature towards the Divine — 59
Triple Aspiration — 48
Vital Aspiration for Immortality — 54

ATTACHMENT
Attachment in the Emotive Vital to the Divine — 245
Attachment of the Cells to the Divine — 94
Attachment of the Material Vital

to the Divine 95
Attachment to the
   Divine 30, 53, 182
Beauty of the Attachment to the
   Divine 53
Detailed Attachment to the
   Divine 245
Emotional Attachment to the
   Divine 245
Integral Attachment to the
   Divine 226
Lasting Attachment 110
Mental Attachment to the Divine 88
Supramental Attachment for the
   Divine 214
Timidity in Attachment to the
   Divine 211
Vital Attachment to the Divine 226

ATTEMPT
Attempt at Vital Goodwill 143
Attempt towards Continuity 4
Attempt towards Immortality 54
Attempt towards Protection 35

ATTRACTION
Attraction for the Light 82

AVATAR
Avatar—the Supreme Mani-
   fested in a Body upon Earth 172

AWAKENING
Awakening and First Response of
   Nature to the Supramental
   Manifestation 146
Awakening of the Physical
   Mind 242
Emotions Awake to the First
   Contact with the Divine 5
First Mental Awakening in
   Matter 239
Psychic Awakening in Matter 89
Spiritual Awakening of the Vital 72
Wakefulness in the Mind 242

BALANCE 29
Balance of the Nature in the
   Love for the Divine 213
Balanced Use of the Integral
   Power 222
Integral Balance 29
Mental Balance 29
Perfect Balance 30
Perfect Integral Balance 30
Perfect Mental Balance 30
Perfect Psychic Balance 30
Psychic Balance 29

BEAUTY
Abundance of Beauty 208
All-powerful Charm of an
   Alluring Beauty 115
Aristocracy of Beauty 140, 168
Beauty Arising from
   Consecration 21
Beauty Aspiring for the Supra-
   mental Realisation 171
Beauty in Art 185
Beauty in Collective Simplicity 183
Beauty of Supramental Love 115
Beauty of Supramental Youth 115
Beauty of the Attachment to the
   Divine 53
Beauty of the New Creation 115
Beauty of Tomorrow 115
Beauty of Tomorrow Mani-
   festing the Divine 116
Beauty Offers itself in Service
   to the Divine 213
Emotional Beauty in the Cells 152
Joy of Beauty 138
Modesty of Beauty 109
Nature Makes an Offering of
   her Beauty 137
Power of Beauty 171
Power of Spiritual Beauty 125
Pride of Beauty 134
Pure Sense of Beauty 138
Smile of Beauty 201
Spiritual Beauty 153
Spontaneous Beauty 139
Static Beauty 44
Supramental Beauty in the
   Physical 127
Victorious Beauty 128

BEGINNING
Beginning of Realisation 221
Beginning of Realisation in
   Matter 96

BEING, THE
Broadening of the Being 222
Combined Offering of Two
   Parts of the Being 9
Integral Opening of the Being
   towards the Divine 26
Organisation of the Being
   around the Psychic 195

BELIEF 65

BENEVOLENCE 207

BIRD
Bird of Paradise 113
Supramental Bird 228

BIRTH
Birth of True Mental Sincerity 160
New Birth 182

BLESSINGS 221
Blessings on the Material World 221

BLOOD
Light in the Blood 14, 100
Purity in the Blood 194

BLOSSOMING 242
Blossoming of Nature 44
Blossoming of the Emotional
   Being 107
Blossoming of the New
   Creation 116

BOASTFULNESS 185

BODY (see PHYSICAL)

BOLDNESS 55
Mental Boldness 55
Physical Boldness 55
Spontaneous Boldness 55
Vital Boldness 55

BRAVERY(see also COURAGE,
   FEARLESSNESS) 13

BROADENING
Broadening of the Being 222
Broadening of the Most
   Material Vital 222
Organised Emotive Broadening 222

CALL
Call of the Divine Grace 162, 180
Joy's Call 44

CARE	58	

CELLS
Attachment of the Cells to the
  Divine — 94
Emotional Beauty in the Cells — 152
Light in the Cells — 152
Peace in the Cells — 143
Purity in the Cells — 152
Radiating Peace in the Cells — 188
Supramental Influence in
  the Cells — 152

CENTRES, THE
Ananda in the Centres — 45
Complexity of the Centres — 45
Emotive Centre — 47
Future Supramental Centre — 47
Illumined Mind Centre — 47
Intuitive Mind Centre — 47
Mastery of Sex — 16
Opening of the Emotive Centre
  to the Light — 185
Peace in the Sex Centre — 169
Physical Centre — 47
Psychic Centre — 47
Purified Sex Centre — 16
Purity in the Emotive Centre — 237
Sex Centre Aspiring to Be
  Purified — 16
Supramental Influence in the
  Sex Centre — 75
Tranquillity of the Sex Centre
  When under the Influence of
  the Supramental Light — 75
Transformed Sex Centre — 39
Vital Centre — 47

CERTITUDE — 175
Certitude of Victory — 51
Unostentatious Certitude — 194

CHANGE (*see also* TURNING)
Changing of Wrong Movements
  into Right — 174
Human Passions Changed into
  Love for the Divine — 213

CHARITY — 73

CHARM — 219
All-powerful Charm of an
  Alluring Beauty — 115

Charm of the New Creation — 116

CHASTITY — 61
Mental Chastity — 179

CHEERFULNESS — 102
(*see also* JOY)
Cheerfulness in Work for the
  Divine — 74
Mental Cheerfulness — 102

CLARITY
Clear Mind — 20
Seeking for Clarity — 103

COLLABORATION — 88

COLLECTIVE
Beauty in Collective Simplicity — 183
Collective Emotions Open to
  the Divine — 203
Collective Harmony — 134
Collective Purity — 248
Power of Collective Aspiration — 134

COMMON SENSE — 175

COMMUNION
Communion with the Divine — 213

COMPASSION
Sri Aurobindo's Compassion — 201

CONCENTRATION — 99
Concentration of the New
  Creation — 116

CONCILIATION — 221

CONNECTION
Connection between the Light
  and the Physical — 45
Connection between the Supermind and the Physical — 45

CONQUEST
Aspiration for Conquest of the
  Enemies in the Vital — 247
Conquering Fervour — 179
Conquest of the Armies — 228
Conquest over the Greed
  for Food — 90

Conquest over the Vital
  Enemies — 247
Will to Conquer the Vital
  Enemies — 247

CONSCIOUSNESS
Aditi—the Divine
  Consciousness — 172
Aspiration for the Divine
  Consciousness — 248
Body Consciousness Under-
  going the Supramental
  Transformation — 112
Consciousness One with the
  Divine Consciousness — 116
Consciousness Turned towards
  the Light — 112
Consciousness Turned towards
  the Supramental Light — 112
First Conscious Reception of
  the Light in Nature — 73
Intensity of the Consciousness
  in the Full Supramental Light — 112
Physical Consciousness Turned
  Entirely towards the Divine — 238
Power of Consciousness — 122
Power of the Psychic
  Consciousness — 125
Power of the Supramental
  Consciousness — 126
Radha's Consciousness — 68
Radha's Consciousness in the
  Vital — 68
Solid Steadfastness in the
  Material Consciousness — 32
Supramental Consciousness — 127

CONSECRATION
Beauty Arising from
  Consecration — 21
Entire Self-Giving — 44
Purity Arising from Perfect
  Consecration — 154
Vital Consecration — 113

CONSENT
Consent of the Vital — 36
Enthusiastic Vital Consent — 36
Matter Consenting to Be
  Spiritualised — 218
Vital Consenting to Be
  Spritualised — 218

CONTEMPLATION	Absence of Desire 24	Aspiration for Trust in the
Contemplation of the Divine 175	Integral Renunciation of	Divine 23
	Vital Desires 15	Aspiration of the Vital for
CONTINENCE 61	Renunciation of Desire 234	Union with the Divine 199
	Renunciation of Emotional	Attachment in the Emotive
CONTINUITY	Desires 15	Vital to the Divine 245
Attempt towards Continuity 4	Renunciation of Vital Desires 15	Attachment of the Cells to the
Material Continuity 5		Divine 94
Physical Continuity 4	**DETACHMENT**	Attachment of the Material Vital
Vital Continuity 5	Detachment from All That Is	to the Divine 95
	not the Divine 139	Attachment to the
CONTROL 32		Divine 30, 53, 182
Controlled Power 116	**DETAILS**	Balance of the Nature in the
	Detailed Attachment to the	Love for the Divine 213
CONVERSION 130	Divine 245	Beauty of the Attachment to
Conversion of the Aim of Life	Detailed Endurance 256	the Divine 53
from the Ego to the Divine 69	Detailed Gratitude 162	Beauty of Tomorrow
Conversion of the Emotional	Detailed Knowledge 3	Manifesting the Divine 116
Being 131	Detailed Obedience 88	Beauty Offers itself in Service
Conversion of the Higher Mind 157	Detailed Perseverance 250	to the Divine 213
Conversion of the Mind 131	Detailed Plasticity 231	Call of the Divine Grace 162, 180
Conversion of the Physical 131	Detailed Surrender 212	Cheerfulness in Work for
Conversion of the Physical	Organisation of Details 202	the Divine 74
Mind 131		Collective Emotions Open
Conversion of the Vital 131	**DETERMINATION** 149	to the Divine 203
Integral Conversion 131		Communion with the Divine 213
Integral Conversion with the	**DEVOTION** 179	Consciousness One with the
Help of the Psychic 131	Devotional Attitude 6	Divine Consciousness 116
Power in the Converted Mind 123		Constant Remembrance of
Total Conversion 131	**DIGNITY** 84	the Divine 156
	Dignity in the Physical 84	Contemplation of the Divine 175
COURAGE (*see also* BRAVERY,	Dignity of the Emotions 84	Conversion of the Aim of Life
FEARLESSNESS) 44	Mental Dignity 84	from the Ego to the Divine 69
Courageous Endurance 255	Psychic Dignity 84	Detachment from All That is
Courageous Goodwill 135	Supramentalised Mental Dignity 84	Not the Divine 139
Integral Courage 44		Detailed Attachment to the
Vital Courage 224	**DISCIPLINE** 178	Divine 245
		Disinterested Work Done
CREATION	**DISINTERESTED**	for the Divine 76
Creation Word 60	Disinterested Work Done for	Disinterested Work Done for
New Creation 198	the Divine 76	the Divine in the Vital 76
Perfect New Creation 198	Disinterested Work Done for	Divine Ananda 250
	the Divine in the Vital 76	Divine Grace 117
CURIOSITY 133		Divine Help 158
Mental Curiosity 133	**DISTINCTION** 230	Divine Knowledge 159
Physical Curiosity 133	Distinction of the Vital 161	Divine Presence 209
		Divine Purity 141
DELICACY 74	**DIVINE** (*see also* DIVINE LOVE)	Divine Sacrifice 204
	Aditi—the Divine	Divine Smile 162
DESCENT	Consciousness 172	Divine Solicitude 158
Descent of the Light 150	Affection for the Divine 211	Divine Solicitude Rightly
	Aspiration for the Divine	Understood 158
DESIRES	Consciousness 248	Emotional Attachment to the

Divine	245	
Emotions Awake to the First Contact with the Divine	5	
Energy Turned towards the Divine	153	
Exclusive Turning of All Movements towards the Divine	99	
First Movement of the Riches towards the Divine	238	
First Response of the Inconscient to the Divine Force	148	
First Turning of the Vital towards the Divine Light	215	
Flaming Love for the Divine	213	
Friendship with the Divine	45	
Human Passions Changed into Love for the Divine	213	
Humility before the Divine in the Physical Nature	232	
Humility in the Love for the Divine	213	
Integral Attachment to the Divine	226	
Integral Intimacy with the Divine	151	
Integral Love for the Divine	213	
Integral Opening of the Being towards the Divine	26	
Integral Trust in the Divine	23	
Intimacy with the Divine	151	
Intimacy with the Divine in the Physical	151	
Intimacy with the Divine in the Psychic	151	
Intimacy with the Divine in the Vital	151	
Joy of Union with the Divine	178	
Love for the Divine	211	
Love from the Divine	211	
Love in the Physical for the Divine	205	
Mental Attachment to the Divine	88	
Mental Love for the Divine	214	
Mental Trust in the Divine	23	
Opening of the Vital to the Divine Love	99	
Physical Consciousness Turned Entirely towards the Divine	238	
Power Aspiring to Become an Instrument for the Divine Work	187	
Progressive Friendship with the Divine	45	
Psychic Love for the Divine	211	
Right Use of the Granted Grace	219	
Road to the Divine	91	
Seeking for All Support in the Divine	223	
Spontaneous Aspiration of Nature towards the Divine	59	
Steps to the Supreme	157	
Supramental Attachment for the Divine	214	
Supramental Friendship with the Divine	45	
Sweetness of the Power Surrendered to the Divine	127	
Sweetness of Thought Turned Exclusively towards the Divine	174	
Tenderness for the Divine	211	
Thoughts Turned towards the Divine	249	
Timidity in Attachment to the Divine	211	
To Live Only for the Divine	170	
Trust in the Divine	23	
Trust in the Vital Mind for the Divine	24	
Trust of the Emotive Vital in the Divine	24	
Vital Attachment to the Divine	226	
Vital Governed by the Presence	221	
Vital Trust in the Divine	24	
Will in Course of Uniting with the Divine Will	129	
Will One with the Divine Will	129	

DIVINE LOVE 204
Aspiration in the Physical for the Divine Love 216
Divine Love Governing the World 37
Divine Love Spreading over the World 204
Opening of the Physical to the Divine Love 205
Unmanifest Divine Love 204

DIVINE WILL
Divine Will Acting in the Inconscient 65
Divine Will Acting in the Subconscient 65
Will in Course of Uniting with the Divine Will 129
Will One with the Divine Will 129

DREAMS 12

DYNAMIC
Purified Dynamic Life Energy 60

EARTH (*see also* WORLD)
Avatar—the Supreme Manifested in a Body upon Earth 172
Supramental Immortality Upon Earth 112

EFFORT
Effort towards the Truth 251
Power of Effort 123
Striving towards Integral Wisdom 39
Striving towards Wisdom 39

EGO
Abolition of the Ego 97
Conversion of the Aim of Life from the Ego to the Divine 69

ELEGANCE
Elegance in the Emotions 27
Fragile Elegance 14

ELEMENTS
Agni 115
Air 57
Earth (*see* EARTH)
Ether 200
Fire 197
Flame 120
Water 200

EMOTIONS (*see also* SENTIMENTAL)
Attachment in the Emotive Vital to the Divine 245
Blossoming of the Emotional Being 107
Collective Emotions Open to the Divine 203
Conversion of the Emotional Being 131
Dignity of the Emotions 84
Elegance in the Emotions 27
Emotional Abundance 150
Emotional Attachment to the Divine 245

Emotional Beauty in the Cells	152	Enemies	247	Divine	174
Emotional Opening	27	**ENERGY**		**EXISTENCE**	
Emotional Protection	33	Energy of a Plastic Mind	231	Psychic Power in Existence	126
Emotional Receptivity	104	Energy Turned towards		The Aim of Existence Is	
Emotional Sincerity	22	the Divine	153	Realised	53
Emotional Wealth	176	Life Energy	59		
Emotions Awake to the First		Life Energy in the Vital	59	**EXPRESSION**	
Contact with the Divine	5	Organised Material Energy	35	Abundant Expression	55
Emotive Centre	47	Purified Dynamic Life Energy	60	Eloquence	12
Offering of the Emotions	9	Specialised Detailed Energy	60	Expressive Silence	154
Opening of the Emotive Centre		Supramentalised Life Energy	60	Gossip	242
to the Light	185			Joyful Expression	55
Opening of the Emotive Vital	27	**ENLIGHTENED**		Mental Voice	107
Organised Emotive Broadening	222	Enlightened Prudence	93	Never Tell a Lie	189
Psychic Influence in the		Working of the Enlightened		Power of Expression	18
Emotions	147	Mind	76	Power of Integral Expression	18
Purity in the Emotive Centre	237			Power of Manifold Expression	18
Refinement of Emotions	37	**ENTERPRISES**		Power of Mental Expression	18
Renunciation of Emotional		Material Enterprises	53	Power of Physical Expression	18
Desires	15			Power of Psychic Expression	18
Richness of Feelings	93	**ENTHUSIASM**	190	Power of Vital Expression	18
Skill in Emotive Work	193	Enthusiasm in Action	190	Progressive Expression	18
Transparency of the Emotive		Enthusiasm in the Higher Vital	191	Seeking for Clarity	103
Vital	42	Enthusiasm in the Most		Sharp Tongue	19
Trust of the Emotive Vital in		Material Vital	191	Spiritual Speech	21
the Divine	24	Enthusiastic Vital Consent	36	To Know How to Listen	197
		Integral Enthusiasm	190	To Know What Has to be Said	12
ENDEAVOUR		Joyous Enthusiasm	190	Voice of the Higher Mind	14
Cheerful Endeavour	19	Joyous Enthusiasm in Action	190		
		Joyous Enthusiasm in the		**FACULTY**	
ENDURANCE	254	Higher Vital	191	Formative Faculty in the Mind	80
Ananda of Endurance	255	Joyous Enthusiasm in the Most		Formative Faculty in the Vital	80
Courageous Endurance	255	Material Vital	191		
Detailed Endurance	256	Joyous Integral Enthusiasm	190	**FAIRIES**	
Endurance of the Higher Vital	256	Joyous Physical Enthusiasm	190	Joy in Fairyland	148
Integral Endurance	255	Joyous Psychic Enthusiasm	191	Light in Fairyland	148
Joyous Endurance	255	Joyous Vital Enthusiasm	191	Fairy Freshness	110
Manifold Endurance	255	Physical Enthusiasm	190		
Mental Endurance	255	Psychic Enthusiasm	191	**FAITH**	119
Physical Endurance	256	Vital Enthusiasm	191		
Power of a Perfect Endurance	228			**FAITHFULNESS**	206
Psychic Endurance	256	**EQUANIMITY**	135	Incorruptible Faithfulness	49
Spontaneous Endurance	256			Joy of Integral Faithfulness	200
Supramentalised Endurance	256	**ETERNAL**		Peace of Integral Faithfulness	200
Victorious Endurance	256	Eternal Smile	119		
Vital Endurance	256	Eternal Youth	119	**FANTASY**	
				Mental Fantasy	86
ENEMIES		**ETHER**	200	Vital Fantasy	232
Aspiration for Conquest of the					
Enemies in the Vital	247	**EXCLUSIVISM**	174	**FEARLESSNESS** (*see also*	
Conquest over the Vital		Sweetness of Thought Turned		BRAVERY, COURAGE)	224
Enemies	247	Exclusively towards the		Fearlessness in Action	13
Will to Conquer the Vital					

Fearlessness in the Vital	224	

FERVOUR
Conquering Fervour 179

FIRE 197
Fire in the Mind 197

FIRST
Awakening and First Response of Nature to the Supramental Manifestation 146
Emotions Awake to the First Contact with the Divine 5
First Appearance of Purity in the Inconscient 195
First Conscious Reception of the Light in Nature 73
First Emergence of the Psychic in Matter 146
First Mental Awakening in Matter 239
First Movement of the Riches towards the Divine 238
First Response of the Inconscient to the Divine Force 148
First Response of the Subconscient to the Supramental Action 146
First Sign of Krishna's Light in Matter 100
First Turning of the Vital towards the Divine Light 215

FLAME 120
Flame of Aspiration 5
Flaming Love for the Divine 213

FOOD
Conquest over the Greed for Food 90

FORCE
Opening to Sri Aurobindo's Force 237

FORCES
Vegetal Goodwill towards the Supramental Forces 81

FORESIGHT 219
(*see also* PREVISION)

FORTUNE (*see also* WEALTH) 56

FRANKNESS 103

FRIENDSHIP
Friendship with the Divine 45
Progressive Friendship with the Divine 45
Supramental Friendship with the Divine 45

FULFILMENT
Psychological Perfection in the Course of Fulfilment 196

FUTURE, THE 217
Beauty of Tomorrow 115
Beauty of Tomorrow Manifesting the Divine 116
Future Supramental Centre 47
Power in Service of the Future 125
Power of the Future 123
Successful Future 102

GENEROSITY 136
Generosity in the Physical 136
Generosity in the Vital 136
Generous Wealth 177
Manifold Generosity 136
Psychic Generosity 136
Psycho-physical Generosity 136

GOAL, THE
Aim of Existence is Realised 53
Conversion of the Aim of Life from the Ego to the Divine 69

GODHEAD 121

GODS
Protection of the Gods 35

GOLD 28
Purified Gold 28

GOODWILL 155
Attempt at Vital Goodwill 143
Benevolence 207
Courageous Goodwill 135
Mental Goodwill 169
Vegetal Goodwill towards the Supramental Forces 81

GRACE, THE
Call of the Divine Grace 162, 180
Divine Grace 117
Right Use of the Granted Grace 219

GRATITUDE 139
Detailed Gratitude 162
Integral Gratitude 180
Mental Gratitude 162

GREED
Conquest over the Greed for Food 90
Greed for Money 177

GRIEF
Absence of Grief 220

GROUPING 65

GROWTH 201

GUARDIAN, THE 5

GUIDANCE
Aspiration for Supramental Guidance in the Subconscient 184
Aspiration of the Mind for the Supramental Guidance 147
Matter Aspiring for the Supramental Guidance 179
Matter under the Supramental Guidance 110

HABITS
Refinement of Habits 106

HAPPINESS
Spiritual Happiness 188

HARMONY 17
Collective Harmony 134
Harmony in the Material Vital 17
Harmony in the Vital 17
Integral Harmony 17
No Quarrels 106
Power of Harmony 123
Result of Harmonious Organisation 202

HEALING
Material Power to Heal 39
Spiritual Power of Healing 189

274

HEALTH 234
Hygienic Organisation 169

HEART
Happy Heart 207

HELP 83
Divine Help 158

HEROISM
Heroic Action 215
Heroic Thought 139

HONESTY
Honesty in the Physical Mind 103
Mental Honesty 240
Vital Honesty 147

HOPE 143
Nature's Hope for Realisation 159

HUMILITY 227
Humility before the Divine
  in the Physical Nature 232
Humility in the Love for
  the Divine 213

IDEA 50
Idealism 56
Ideal of the New Creation 121

ILLUMINED
Illumined Mind Centre 47
Illumined Transparency 41

IMAGINATION 50

IMITATION
Mental Spirit of Imitation 157

IMMORTALITY
Aspiration for Immortality 54
Aspiration for Integral
  Immortality 6
Attempt towards Immortality 54
Conscious Vital Immortality 108
Integral Immortality 13, 108
Physical Aspiration for
  Immortality 54
Supramental Immortality 108
Supramental Immortality
  Upon Earth 112
Vital Aspiration for Immortality 54
Vital Immortality 108

INCONSCIENT
Divine Will Acting in the
  Inconscient 65
First Appearance of Purity
  in the Inconscient 195
First Response of the Inconscient to the Divine Force 148

INFLUENCE
Krishna's Influence in the
  Subconscient 78
Mental Love under the Psychic
  Influence 214
Psychic Influence in the
  Emotions 147
Supramental Influence 91
Supramental Influence in
  the Cells 152
Supramental Influence in the
  Sex Centre 75
Supramental Influence in the
  Subconscient 77
Tranquility in the Sex centre
  when under the Influence
  of the Supramental Light 75
Wealth under the Psychic
  Influence 177

INITIATION 251

INSPIRATION 19
Lasting Inspiration 19

INTEGRAL
Aspiration for Integral
  Immortality 6
Balanced Use of the Integral
  Power 222
Entire Self-Giving 44
Integral Attachment to
  the Divine 226
Integral Balance 29
Integral Conversion 131
Integral Conversion with the
  Help of the Psychic 131
Integral Courage 44
Integral Endurance 255
Integral Enthusiasm 190
Integral Even Basis in
  the Physical 64
Integral Gratitude 180

Integral Harmony 17
Integral Immortality 13, 108
Integral Intimacy with
  the Divine 151
Integral Love for the Divine 213
Integral Mental Purity 230
Integral Offering 9
Integral Offering of the Vital 10
Integral Opening of the Being
  towards the Divine 26
Integral Opening to the Light 237
Integral Organisation 202
Integral Prayer 253
Integral Progress 52
Integral Progress in Matter 53
Integral Progress in the Vital 53
Integral Protection 33
Integral Psychological
  Perfection 196
Integral Purity 145
Integral Receptivity 105
Integral Renunciation of
  Vital Desires 15
Integral Revelation 75
Integral Silence 187
Integral Simplicity 250
Integral Solace 167
Integral Tapasya 86
Integral Thoroughness 247
Integral Transparency 41
Integral Trust in the Divine 23
Integral Unconditional Offering 139
Integral Wealth of Mahalakshmi 177
Integral Wisdom 7
Integrally Pure Thoughts 249
Joy of Integral Faithfulness 200
Joy of Integral Peace 76
Joyous Integral Enthusiasm 190
Krishna's Integral Play 239
Peace of Integral Faithfulness 200
Perfect Integral Balance 30
Power of Integral Expression 18
Power of Integral Purity 124
Skill in Integral Work 192
Striving towards Integral
  Wisdom 39
Total Conversion 131

INTENSITY
Aspiration for Spiritual Intensity 183
Intensity of the Consciousness
  in the Full Supramental Light 112
Spiritual Intensity 183

INTIMACY
Integral Intimacy with
   the Divine 151
Intimacy with the Divine 151
Intimacy with the Divine in
   the Physical 151
Intimacy with the Divine in
   the Psychic 151
Intimacy with the Divine in
   the Vital 151
Intimacy with Universal Nature 151

INTUITIVE
Intuitive Knowledge 39
Intuitive Mind Centre 47

INVENTIONS 83, 103

INVOCATION
Supramental Invocation 228

JOY (see also CHEERFULNESS)
Cheerful Endeavour 19
Cheerfulness 102
Glad Remembrance 62
Happy Heart 207
Joy in Fairyland 148
Joy of Beauty 138
Joy of Integral Faithfulness 200
Joy of Integral Peace 76
Joy of Spirituality 219
Joy of Union with the Divine 178
Joy of Vegetal Nature in
   Answer to the New Light 40
Joy of Victory 14
Joy's Call 44
Joyful Expression 55
Joyous Endurance 255
Joyous Enthusiasm 190
Joyous Enthusiasm in Action 190
Joyous Enthusiasm in the
   Higher Vital 191
Joyous Enthusiasm in the
   Most Material Vital 191
Joyous Integral Enthusiasm 190
Joyous Physical Enthusiasm 190
Joyous Psychic Enthusiasm 191
Joyous Vital Enthusiasm 191
Mental Cheerfulness 102
Spritual Happiness 188
Spontaneous Joy of Nature 185
Vital Joy in Matter 175

KINDNESS
Kind Mind 157
Kindness of Nature 239

KNOWLEDGE 154
(see also UNDERSTANDING)
Detailed Knowledge 3
Divine Knowledge 159
Intuitive Knowledge 39
Supramental Knowledge 3
To Know How to Listen 197

KRISHNA
Krishna's Play 239
First Sign of Krishna's Light
   in Matter 100
Krishna's Ananda 194
Krishna's Influence in the
   Subconscient 78
Krishna's Integral Play 239
Krishna's Light in the Mind 237
Krishna's Light in the
   Overmind 218
Krishna's Light in the
   Physical Mind 215
Krishna's Light in the Senses 68
Krishna's Light in the
   Subconscient 95
Krishna's Light in the Vital 215
Krishna's Play in Matter 239
Krishna's Play in the Vital 93

LASTING
Lasting Inspiration 19
Lasting Remembrance 169

LEARNING
Thirst to Learn 166

LIBERATION 183
LIberation in the Vital 32

LIFE
Aim of Existence is Realised 53
Conversion of the Aim of Life
   from the Ego to the Divine 69
Life Energy 59
Life Energy in the Vital 59
Organisation of Action in Life 72
Purified Dynamic Life Energy 60
Splendour and Opulence in the
   Material Life 205
Supramentalised Life Energy 60

To Live Only for the Divine 170
Vital Will Manifesting in Life 94
Will Manifesting in Life 94

LIGHT 57
Aspiration in the Physical for
   the Supramental Light 142
Attraction for the Light 82
Connection between the Light
   and the Physical 45
Consciousness Turned towards
   the Light 112
Consciousness Turned towards
   the Supramental Light 112
Descent of the Light 150
First Conscious Reception of
   the Light in Nature 73
First Sign of Krishna's Light
   in Matter 100
First Turning of the Vital
   towards the Divine Light 215
Integral Opening to the Light 237
Intensity of the Consciousness
   in the Full Supramental Light 112
Joy of Vegetal Nature in Answer
   to the New Light 40
Krishna's Light in the Mind 237
Krishna's Light in the
   Overmind 218
Krishna's Light in the
   Physical Mind 215
Krishna's Light in the Senses 68
Krishna's Light in the
   Subconscient 95
Krishna's Light in the Vital 215
Light in Fairyland 148
Light in the Blood 14, 100
Light in the Cells 152
Light in the Vital 57
Light in the Vital Movements 189
Light of the Purified Power 121
Light without Obscurity 988
Mind of Light Acting in Matter 51
Movements in the Light 189
Opening of the Emotive Centre
   to the Light 185
Opening of the Higher Vital to
   the Light 237
Opening of the Material Vital to
   the Light 237
Opening to the Light 237
Psychic Light in the Material
   Movements 189

Psychic Light in the Physical Movements	189	
Psychic Light in the Subconscient	78	
Response of the Mind to the Supramental Light	21	
Response of the Physical Mind to the Supramental Light	21	
Seeking the Light in the Lower Vital	136	
Supramental Light in the Subconscient	77	
Tranquility of the Sex Centre when under the Influence of the Supramental Light	75	
Wealth in the Mind of Light	177	

LIGHTNESS 186

LOGIC
Logic in Thoughts 201

LOVE (*including* DIVINE LOVE)
Aspiration in the Physical for the Divine Love	216
Balance of the Nature in the Love for the Divine	213
Beauty of Supramental Love	115
Divine Love	204
Divine Love Governing the World	37
Divine Love Spreading over the World	204
Flaming Love for the Divine	213
Human Passions Changed into Love for the Divine	213
Humility in the Love for the Divine	213
Integral Love for the Divine	213
Love for the Divine	211
Love from the Divine	211
Love in the Physical for the Divine	205
Loving Surrender	212
Mental Love for the Divine	214
Mental Love under the Psychic Influence	214
Opening of the Physical to the Divine Love	205
Opening of the Vital to the Divine Love	99
Psychic Love for the Divine	211
Unmanifest Divine Love	204
Victorious Love	128
Works of Love	136

MAHALAKSHMI
Integral Wealth of Mahalakshmi 177

MAHASARASWATI
Mahasaraswati's Perfection in Works 209

MANIFESTATION
Avatar—the Supreme Manifested in a Body upon Earth	172
Awakening and First Response of Nature to the Supramental Manifestation	146
Divine Love Spreading over the World	204
Spreading of the Manifestation	229
Supramental Manifestation	110
Vital Will Manifesting in Life	94
Will Manifesting in Life	94

MANIFOLD
Manifold Endurance	255
Manifold Generosity	136
Manifold Power of the New Creation	121
Manifold Protection	33
Manifold Receptivity	105
Power of Manifold Expression	18

MARVEL
Scented Marvel 82

MASTERY 230
Mastery of Sex 16

MATTER
Attachment of the Material Vital to the Divine	95
Beginning of Realisation in Matter	96
Blessings on the Material World	221
Broadening of the Most Material Vital	222
Constant Progress in Matter	52
Enthusiasm in the Most Material Vital	191
First Emergence of the Psychic in Matter	146
First Mental Awakening in Matter	239
First Sign of Krishna's Light in Matter	100
Harmony in the Material Vital	17
Integral Progress in Matter	53
Joyous Enthusiasm in the Most Material Vital	191
Krishna's Play in Matter	239
Material Abundance	109
Material Continuity	5
Material Enterprises	53
Material Organisation	202
Material Power to Heal	39
Matter Aspiring for the Supramental Guidance	179
Matter Consenting to be Spiritualised	218
Matter Prepares Itself to Receive the Supramental	96
Matter under the Supramental Guidance	110
Mind of Light Acting in Matter	51
Offering of the Material Vital	10
Offering of the Most Material Vital	10
Opening of the Material Vital to the Light	237
Organised Material Energy	35
Promise of Realisation in Matter	241
Psychic Awakening in Matter	89
Psychic Governing Matter	96
Psychic Light in the Material Movements	189
Psychological Perfection in Matter	196
Skill in Material Work	193
Solid Steadfastness in the Material Consciousness	32
Splendour and Opulence in the Material Life	205
Success in the Most Material Vital	109
True Action in the Material Vital	72
Vital Joy in Matter	175
Wealth in the Most Material Vital	177

MENTAL
Birth of True Mental Sincerity	160
First Mental Awakening in Matter	239
Integral Mental Purity	230
Mental Aspiration	142

Mental Attachment to the Divine	88	
Mental Balance	29	
Mental Boldness	55	
Mental Chastity	179	
Mental Cheerfulness	102	
Mental Curiosity	133	
Mental Edurance	255	
Mental Fantasy	86	
Mental Goodwill	169	
Mental Gratitude	162	
Mental Honesty	240	
Mental Love for the Divine	214	
Mental Love under the Psychic Influence	214	
Mental Opening	27	
Mental Plasticity	231	
Mental Prayer	253	
Mental Promise	1	
Mental Purity	230	
Mental Receptivity	105	
Mental Simplicity	238	
Mental Sincerity	225	
Mental Spirit of Imitation	157	
Mental Suggestions of Organisation	7	
Mental Surrender	214	
Mental Tapasya	86	
Mental Trust in the Divine	23	
Mental Voice	107	
Mentalised Power	1, 121	
Perfect Mental Balance	30	
Perfect Mental Purity	230	
Power of Mental Expression	18	
Skill in Mental Work	193	
Supramentalised Mental Dignity	84	

MIND — 235

Aspiration for Silence in the Mind — 95
Aspiration for Silence in the Physical Mind — 95
Aspiration of the Mind for the Supramental Guidance — 147
Attentive Mind — 51
Awakening of the Physical Mind — 242
Clear Mind — 20
Conversion of the Higher Mind — 157
Conversion of the Mind — 131
Conversion of the Physical Mind — 131
Energy of a Plastic Mind — 231
Fire in the Mind — 197
Formative Faculty in the Mind — 80
Heroic Thought — 139
Higher Mind — 232
Honesty in the Physical Mind — 103
Illumined Mind Centre — 47
Integrally Pure Thoughts — 249
Intuitive Mind Centre — 47
Kind Mind — 157
Krishna's Light in the Mind — 237
Krishna's Light in the Physical Mind — 215
Logic in Thoughts — 201
Mind of Light Acting in Matter — 51
Perfect Quietness in the Mind — 175
Perfect Working of the Mind — 239
Physical Mind — 232
Power in the Converted Mind — 123
Promise of Realisation in the Mind — 241
Promise of Realisation in the Physical Mind — 241
Purified Mind — 235
Quiet Mind — 175
Quietness Established in the Mind — 175
Reason — 20
Religious Thought — 251
Response of the Mind to the Supramental Light — 21
Solace in the Mind — 167
Supramentalised Mind — 235
Voice of the Higher Mind — 14
Wakefulness in the Mind — 242
Wealth in the Mind of Light — 177
Wisdom in the Physical Mind — 39
Working of the Enlightened Mind — 76

MIND OF LIGHT

Mind of Light Acting in Matter — 51
Wealth in the Mind of Light — 177

MIRACLE — 162

MODESTY — 248
Modesty of Beauty — 109

MOVEMENTS

Changing of Wrong Movements into Right — 174
Correct Movements — 217
Correct Movements in the Vital — 217
Exclusive Turning of All Movements towards the Divine — 99
First Movement of the Riches towards the Divine — 238
Light in the Vital Movements — 189
Movements in the Light — 189
Psychic Light in the Material Movements — 189
Psychic Light in the Physical Movements — 189

MULTITUDE — 70

NATURE
Awakening and First Response of Nature to the Supramental Manifestation — 146
Balance of the Nature in the Love for the Divine — 213
Blossoming of Nature — 44
First Conscious Reception of the Light in Nature — 73
Humility before the Divine in the Physical Nature — 232
Intimacy with Universal Nature — 151
Joy of Vegetal Nature in Answer to the New Light — 40
Kindness of Nature — 239
Nature Aspires to Be Supramentalised — 137
Nature Makes an Offering of Her Beauty — 137
Nature's Hope for Realisation — 159
Psychic Soaring of Nature — 211
Smile of Nature — 201
Spontaneous Aspiration of Nature towards the Divine — 59
Spontaneous Joy of Nature — 185

NERVES
Peace in the Nerves — 109

NEW CREATION, THE — 198
Beauty of the New Creation — 115
Blossoming of the New Creation — 116
Charm of the New Creation — 116
Concentration of the New Creation — 116
Firmness of the New Creation — 119
Ideal of the New Creation — 121
Manifold Power of the New Creation — 121

Perfect New Creation	198	
Progress of the New Creation	126	
Realisation of the New Creation	126	
Usefulness of the New Creation	127	

NOBILITY 85

OBEDIENCE 88
Detailed Obedience 88
Perfect Obedience 88

OBSCURITY
Light without Obscurity 98
Obscurity Offering Itself to Be
   Transformed 236
Offering of All Obscurities 10
Transformation Makes the
   Obscurity Disappear 236

OBSERVATION 221

OCCULTISM 185

OFFERING 9
Beauty Offers itself in Service
   to the Divine 213
Combined Offering of Two Parts
   of the Being 9
Integral Offering 9
Integral Offering of the Vital 10
Integral Unconditional Offering 139
Nature Makes an Offering of
   Her Beauty 137
Obscurity Offering Itself to Be
   Transformed 236
Offering of All Obscurities 10
Offering of the Emotions 9
Offering of the Material Vital 10
Offering of the Most
   Material Vital 10
Offering of the Physical 9
Offering of the Vital 10
Psychic Offering 9

OPENING 26
Collective Emotions Open to
   the Divine 203
Emotional Opening 27
Integral Opening of the Being
   towards the Divine 26
Integral Opening to the Light 237
Mental Opening 27

Opening of the Emotive Centre
   to the Light 185
Opening of the Emotive Vital 27
Opening of the Higher Vital to
   the Light 237
Opening of the Material Vital
   to the Light 237
Opening of the Physical to
   the Divine Love 205
Opening of the Vital to the
   Divine Love 99
Opening to Sri Aurobindo's
   Force 237
Opening to the Light 237
Vital Opening 32

OPTIMISM 58

ORDER 207

ORGANISATION 202
Aspiration for Organisation 202
Hygienic Organisation 169
Integral Organisation 202
Material Organisation 202
Mental Suggestions of
   Organisation 7
Organisation in the Vital 202
Organisation of Action in Life 72
Organisation of Details 202
Organisation of the Being
   around the Psychic 195
Organised Emotive Broadening 222
Organised Material Energy 35
Organised Team-Work 24
Result of Harmonious
   Organisation 202

OVERMIND
Krishna's Light in the
   Overmind 218

PASSION 226
Human Passions Changed
   into Love for the Divine 213

PATH, THE
Perfect Path 72
Road to the Divine 91
Steps to the Supreme 157

PATIENCE 165

Vital Patience 7

PEACE 82
Joy of Integral Peace 76
Peace in the Cells 143
Peace in the Nerves 109
Peace in the Physical 44
Peace in the Sex Centre 169
Peace in the Vital 169
Peace of Integral Faithfulness 200
Psychic Peace 132
Radiating Peace in the Cells 188

PERCEPTION
Accurate Perception 44

PERFECT
Perfect Balance 30
Perfect Integral Balance 30
Perfect Mental Balance 30
Perfect Mental Purity 230
Perfect New Creation 198
Perfect Obedience 88
Perfect Path 72
Perfect Psychic Balance 30
Perfect Psychological Perfection 196
Perfect Quietness in the Mind 175
Perfect Radiating Purity 103
Perfect Surrender 212
Perfect Tapasya 37
Perfect Vigilance 157
Perfect Working of the Mind 239
Power of a Perfect Endurance 228
Purity Arising from Perfect
   Consecration 154

PERFECTION
Integral Psychological
   Perfection 196
Mahasaraswati's Perfection
   in Works 209
Perfect Psychological Perfection 196
Perfect Radiating Psychology 58
Psychological Perfection 196
Psychological Perfection
   in Matter 196
Psychological Perfection in
   the Course of Fulfilment 196
Supramentalised Psychological
   Perfection 162
Thirst for Perfection 31
Vital's Possibility of
   Perfection, the 6

PERFUME
Scented Marvel 82
Spiritual Perfume 185

PERSEVERANCE 39
Detailed Perseverance 250
Power of Perseverance 124

PHYSICAL
Ananda in the Physical 115
Ananda in the Physical Body 45
Aspiration in the Physical 142
Aspiration in the Physical for
  the Divine Love 216
Aspiration in the Physical for the
  Supramental Light 142
Avatar—the Supreme Mani-
  fested in a Body upon Earth 172
Body Consciousness Under-
  going the Supramental
  Transformation 112
Connection between the Light
  and the Physical 45
Connection between the Super-
  mind and the Physical 45
Conversion of the Physical 131
Conversion of the
  Physical Mind 131
Dignity in the Physical 84
Generosity in the Physical 136
Humility before the Divine in
  the Physical Nature 232
Integral Even Basis in
  the Physical 64
Intimacy with the Divine
  in the Physical 151
Joyous Physical Enthusiasm 190
Love in the Physical for
  the Divine 205
Offering of the Physical 9
Opening of the Physical to
  the Divine Love 205
Peace in the Physical 44
Physical Aspiration for
  Immortality 54
Physical Boldness 55
Physical Centre 47
Physical Consciousness Turned
  entirely towards the Divine 238
Physical Continuity 4
Physical Curiosity 133
Physical Endurance 256
Physical Enthusiasm 190

Physical Mind 232
Physical Plasticity 231
Physical Protection 35
Physical Receptivity 105
Physical Thoroughness 246
Power of Physical Expression 18
Promise of Realisation in
  the Physical 241
Psychic Light in the
  Physical Movements 189
Psycho-physical Generosity 136
Response of the Physical Mind
  to the Supramental Light 21
Skill in Physical Work 193
Spiritual Aspiration in
  the Physical 216
Supramental Beauty in
  the Physical 127
Transparency in the Phyiscal 42
Wisdom in the Physical Mind 39

PLASTICITY 231
Detailed Plasticity 231
Energy of a Plastic Mind 231
Mental Plasticity 231
Physical Plasticity 231
Supramentalised Plasticity 231

PLENITUDE
Vital Plenitude 189

POET
Poet's Ecstasy 250

POWER
Aesthetic Power 114
Balanced Use of the
  Integral Power 222
Controlled Power 116
Dynamic Power 118
Effective Power of
  the Supermind 118
Enlightened Individual Power 118
Individual Power 118
Light of the Purified Power 121
Manifold Power of the
  New Creation 121
Material Power to Heal 39
Mentalised Power 1, 121
Power Aspiring to Become an
  Instrument for the
  Divine Work 187
Power in Service of the Future 125

Power in the Converted Mind 123
Power in the Higher Vital 124
Power of Action 122
Power of a Perfect Endurance 228
Power of Beauty 171
Power of Collective Aspiration 134
Power of Consciousness 122
Power of Effort 123
Power of Expression 18
Power of Harmony 123
Power of Integral Expression 18
Power of Integral Purity 124
Power of Manifold Expression 18
Power of Mental Expression 18
Power of Perseverance 124
Power of Physical Expression 18
Power of Progress 124
Power of Psychic Expression 18
Power of Purity 74
Power of Spiritual Beauty 125
Power of Spirituality 219
Power of Success 126
Power of the Future 123
Power of the Psychic
  Consciousness 125
Power of the Supramental
  Consciousness 126
Power of Truth in the
  Subconscient 233
Power of Vital Expression 18
Power to Progress 124
Power to Reject Adverse
  Suggestions 71
Psychic Power in Existence 126
Puissance of Realisation 126
Spiritual Power of Healing 189
Sweetness of the Power
  Surrendered to the Divine 127

PRAYER 253
Integral Prayer 253
Mental Prayer 253
Psychic Prayer 253
Vital Prayer 253

PRESENCE 195
Divine Presence 209
Vital Governed by the Presence 221

PREVISION 65
Foresight 219

PRIDE 84

Pride of Beauty	134	the Help of the Psychic	131	Perfection	196
		Intimacy with the Divine in		Perfect Psychological Perfection	196
PROGRESS	52	the Psychic	151	Perfect Radiating Psychology	58
Constant Progress in Matter	52	Joyous Psychic Enthusiasm	191	Psychological Perfection	196
Integral Progress	52	Mental Love under the		Psychological Perfection	
Integral Progress in Matter	53	Psychic Influence	214	in Matter	196
Integral Progress in the Vital	53	Organisation of the Being		Psychological Perfection in	
Power of Progress	124	around the Psychic	195	the Course of Fulfilment	196
Power to Progress	124	Perfect Psychic Balance	30	Supramentalised Psychological	
Progress of the New Creation	126	Power of Psychic Expression	18	Perfection	162
Progressive Expression	18	Power of Psychic			
Progressive Friendship with		Consciousness	125	PURITY	145
the Divine	45	Psychic Aspiration	142	Aspiration for Purity	226
Uninterrupted but Spasmodic		Psychic Awakening in Matter	89	Aspiration for Vital Purity	92
Progress	52	Psychic Balance	29	Collective Purity	248
Vital Progress	52	Psychic Centre	47	Divine Purity	141
		Psychic Dignity	84	First Appearance of Purity	
PROMISE	1	Psychic Endurance	256	in the Inconscient	195
Mental Promise	1	Psychic Enthusiasm	191	Integral Mental Purity	230
Promise of Realisation	241	Psychic Generosity	136	Integral Purity	145
Promise of Realisation		Psychic Governing Matter	96	Integrally Pure Thoughts	249
in Matter	241	Psychic Influence in		Light of the Purified Power	121
Promise of Realisation in		the Emotions	147	Mental Purity	230
the Mind	241	Psychic Light in the Material		Perfect Mental Purity	230
Promise of Realisation in		Movements	189	Perfect Radiating Purity	103
the Physical	241	Psychic Light in the Physical		Power of Integral Purity	124
Promise of Realisation in		Movements	189	Power of Purity	74
the Physical Mind	241	Psychic Light in		Psychic Purity	145
Promise of Renewal	103	the Subconscient	78	Pure Sense of Beauty	138
Vital Promise	1	Psychic Love for the Divine	211	Pure Spiritual Surrender	212
		Psychic Offering	9	Purified Dynamic Life Energy	60
PROSPERITY	75	Psychic Peace	132	Purified Gold	28
Unselfish Prosperity	75	Psychic Power in Existence	126	Purified Mind	235
		Psychic Prayer	253	Purified Senses	68
PROTECTION	33	Psychic Protection	35	Purified Sex Centre	16
Attempt towards Protection	35	Psychic Purity	145	Purity Arising from Perfect	
Discreet Protection	33	Psychic Receptivity	105	Consecration	154
Emotional Protection	33	Psychic Soaring of Nature	211	Purity in Action	228
Integral Protection	33	Psychic Thoroughness	247	Purity in the Blood	194
Manifold Protection	33	Psychic Tranquility	243	Purity in the Cells	152
Physical Protection	35	Psychic Transparency	41	Purity in the Emotive Centre	237
Protection of the Gods	35	Psychic Work	51	Radiating Purity	103
Psychic Protection	35	Psycho-physical Generosity	136	Radiating Vital Purity	229
Triple Protection	35	Receptivity of the		Sex Centre Aspiring to Be	
Vital Protection	35	Supramentalised Psychic	105	Purified	16
		Skill in Psychic Work	193	Spring Purity	76
PRUDENCE	93	Supramentalised Psychic		Vital Purity	92
Enlightened Prudence	93	Activity	42		
		Wealth under the Psychic		QUIETNESS (*see also*	
PSYCHIC		Influence	177	TRANQUILLITY)	
First Emergence of the Psychic				Perfect Quietness in the Mind	175
in Matter	146	PSYCHOLOGY		Quiet Mind	175
Integral Conversion with		Integral Psychological		Quietness Established in	

the Mind	175
Quiet Strength in the Vital	251

RADHA

Radha's Consciousness	68
Radha's Consciousness in the Vital	68

RADIATING

Perfect Radiating Psychology	58
Perfect Radiating Purity	103
Radiating Peace in the Cells	188
Radiating Purity	103
Radiating Skill in Work	192
Radiating Vital Purity	229
Spreading of the Manifestation	229

RAIN

Supramental Rain	205

REALISATION

REALISATION	86
Aim of Existence Is Realised	53
Beauty Aspiring for the Supramental Realisation	171
Beginning of Realisation	221
Beginning of Realisation in Matter	96
Beginning of the Supramental Realisation	38
Nature's Hope for Realisation	159
Promise of Realisation	241
Promise of Realisation in Matter	241
Promise of Realisation in the Mind	241
Promise of Realisation in the Physical	241
Promise of Realisation in the Physical Mind	241
Puissance of Realisation	126
Realisation of the New Creation	126
Realisation of the Supramental Riches	203

REASON 20

RECEPTIVITY

RECEPTIVITY	104
Emotional Receptivity	104
First Conscious Reception of the Light in Nature	73
Integral Receptivity	105
Manifold Receptivity	105
Mental Receptivity	105
Physical Receptivity	105
Psychic Receptivity	105
Receptivity of the Supramentalised Psychic	105
Supramentalised Receptivity	105
Vital Receptivity	105

REFINEMENT 37

Refined Taste	147
Refinement of Emotions	37
Refinement of Habits	105
Refinement of Sensations	51

REGULARITY 159

RELIGION

Religious Thought	251

REMEMBRANCE 224

Constant Remembrance of the Divine	156
Glad Remembrance	62
Lasting Remembrance	169
Remembrance of Sri Aurobindo	155
Sentimental Remembrance	89
Subconscient Remembrance	83

RENEWAL

Promise of Renewal	103

RENUNCIATION

Integral Renunciation of Vital Desires	15
Power to Reject Adverse Suggestions	71
Renunciation of Desire	234
Renunciation of Emotional Desires	15
Renunciation of Vital Desires	15

REPENTANCE 58

RESOLUTION 37

RESPONSE

Awakening and First Respone of Nature to the Supramental Manifestation	146
First Response of the Inconscient to the Divine Force	148
First Response of the Subconscient to the Supramental Action	146
Response of the Mind to the Supramental Light	21
Response of the Physical Mind to the Supramental Light	21

REST 67

RETURN 74

REVELATION 75

Integral Revelation	75

RICHES (see also WEALTH) 38

Richness of Feelings	93

RIGHT ATTITUDE 66

Aspiration for the Right Attitude	66
Correct Movements	217
Correct Movements in the Vital	217
Right Attitude Established	66

RISING STAR 7

ROAD (see PATH)

Road to the Divine	91

SACHCHIDANANDA 111

SACRIFICE

Divine Sacrifice	204

SEEKING

Seeking for All Support in the Divine	223
Seeking for Clarity	103
Seeking the Light in the Lower Vital	136

SELF-EVALUATION

Correct Self-Evaluation	145

SENSES

Krishna's Light in the Senses	68
Purified Senses	68
Refinement of Sensations	51

SENSIBILITY

Artistic Sensibility	138

SENSITIVITY 157

Vital Sensitivity	165

SENTIMENTAL
Sentimental Remembrance 89

SENTINEL (SENTRY) 63

SERVICE 188
Beauty Offers itself in Service
   to the Divine 213
Power in Service of the Future 125

SILENCE 187
Aspiration for Silence in Mind 95
Aspiration for Silence in the
   Physical Mind 95
Expressive Silence 154
Integral Silence 187
Silence in the Vital 6

SILVER 100

SIMPLICITY
Beauty in Collective Simplicity 183
Candid Simplicity in the Vital 183
Integral Simplicity 250
Mental Simplicity 238
Simple Sincerity 22

SINCERITY
Birth of True Mental Sincerity 160
Emotional Sincerity 22
Mental Sincerity 225
Simple Sincerity 22
Sincerity in the Vital 22

SKILL
Radiating Skill in Work 192
Skill in Emotive Work 193
Skill in Integral Work 192
Skill in Material Work 193
Skill in Mental Work 193
Skill in Physical Work 193
Skill in Psychic Work 193
Skill in Vital Work 193
Skill in Works 192

SMILE
Divine Smile 162
Eternal Smile 119
Smile of Beauty 201
Smile of Nature 201

SOARING
Psychic Soaring of Nature 211

Soaring of Aspiration 63

SOLACE 167
Integral Solace 167
Rest 67
Solace of in the Mind 167
Solace in the Vital 167

SOLICITUDE
Divine Solicitude 158
Divine Solicitude Rightly
   Understood 158

SPECIALISED
Specialised Detailed Energy 60

SPIRIT, THE
Sign of the Spirit 250

SPIRITUAL
Aspiration for Spiritual Intensity 183
Aspiration for Spirituality 218
Joy of Spirituality 219
Matter Consenting to Be
   Spiritualised 218
Power of Spiritual Beauty 125
Power of Spirituality 219
Pure Spiritual Surrender 212
Spiritual Ascension 61
Spiritual Ascension of the Vital 228
Spiritual Aspiration 234
Spiritual Aspiration in
   the Physical 216
Spiritual Atmosphere 25
Spiritual Awakening of the Vital 72
Spiritual Beauty 153
Spiritual Happiness 188
Spiritual Intensity 183
Spiritual Perfume 185
Spiritual Power of Healing 189
Spiritual Speech 21
Spiritual Success 132
Vital Consenting to Be
   Spiritualised 218

SPLENDOUR
Splendour and Opulence in
   the Material Life 205

SPONTANEOUS
Spontaneous Aspiration of
   Nature towards the Divine 59
Spontaneous Beauty 139

Spontaneous Boldness 55
Spontaneous Endurance 256
Spontaneous Joy of Nature 185

SPRING
Spring Purity 76

SRI AUROBINDO
Avatar—The Supreme Mani-
   fested in a Body upon Earth 172
Opening to Sri Aurobindo's
   Force 237
Remembrance of Sri Aurobindo 155
Sri Aurobindo's Compassion 201

STABILITY
Integral Even Basis in
   the Physical 64
Stability in the Vital 28

STEADFASTNESS 203
Solid Stadfastness in the
   Material Consciousness 32
Steadfast Vitality 19

STRAIGHTFORWARDNESS 143

STRENGTH
Quiet Strength in the Vital 251
Strength in the Vital 72

SUBCONSCIENT
Aspiration for Supramental
   Guidance in the
   Subconscient 184
Divine Will Acting in
   the Subconscient 65
First Response of the
   Subconscient to the
   Supramental Action 146
Krishna's Influence in
   the Subconscient 78
Krishna's Light in
   the Subconscient 95
Power of Truth in
   the Subconscient 233
Psychic Light in
   the Subconscient 78
Subconscient Remembrance 83
Supramental Influence in
   the Subconscient 77
Supramental Light in
   the Subconscient 77

SUCCESS
Power of Success 126
Spiritual Success 132
Success in Supramental Work 70
Success in the Most
  Material Vital 109
Successful Future 102

SUCCULENCE
Primitive Succulence 169

SUN-DROP 194

SUPERHUMANITY 85

SUPERMIND
Aspiration for Supramental
  Guidance in the
  Subconscient 184
Aspiration in the Physical for
  the Supramental Light 142
Aspiration of the Mind for
  the Supramental Guidance 147
Awakening and First Response
  of Nature to the Supramental
  Manifestation 146
Beauty Aspiring for the
  Supramental Realisation 171
Beauty of Supramental Love 115
Beauty of Supramental Youth 115
Beginning of the Supramental
  Realisation 38
Body-Consciousness
  Undergoing the Supramental
  Transformation 112
Connection between the
  Supermind and the Physical 45
Consciousness Turned towards
  the Supramental Light 112
Effective Power of the
  Supermind 118
First Response of the
  Subconscient to the
  Supramental Action 146
Future Supramental Centre 47
Intensity of the Consciousness
  in the Full Supramental Light 112
Joy of Vegetal Nature in
  Answer to the New Light 40
Matter Aspiring for the
  Supramental Guidance 179
Matter Prepares Itself to
  Receive the Supermind 96
Matter under the Supramental
  Guidance 110
Nature Aspires to Be
  Supramentalised 137
New World 32
Power of the Supramental
  Consciousness 126
Realisation of the
  Supramental Riches 203
Receptivity of the
  Supramentalised Psychic 105
Response of the Mind to
  the Supramental Light 21
Response of the Physical Mind
  to the Supramental Light 21
Success in Supramental Work 70
Supramental Action 28
Supramental Artistic Genius 112
Supramental Attachment for
  the Divine 214
Supramental Beauty in
  the Physical 127
Supramental Bird 228
Supramental Consciousness 127
Supramental Friendship with
  the Divine 45
Supramental Immortality 108
Supramental Immortalty
  Upon Earth 12
Supramental Influence 91
Supramental Influence in
  the Cells 152
Supramental Influence in
  the Sex Centre 75
Supramental Influence in
  the Subconscient 77
Supramental Invocation 228
Supramental Knowledge 3
Supramental Light in the
  Subconscient 77
Supramental Manifestation 110
Supramental Rain 205
Supramental Riches 221
Supramental Sun 16
Supramentalised Endurance 256
Supramentalised Life Energy 60
Supramentalised Mental Dignity 84
Supramentalised Mind 235
Supramentalised Plasticity 231
Supramentalised Psychic
  Activity 42
Supramentalised Psychological
  Perfection 162
Supramentalised Receptivity 105
Supramentalised Vital
  Transparency 42
Supramentalised Wealth 177
Tranquillity of the Sex Centre
  when under the Influence
  of the Supramental Light 75
Vegetal Goodwill towards the
  Supramental Forces 81

SUPPORT
Seeking for All Support in
  the Divine 223

SUPREME, THE
Avatar – the Supreme Mani-
  fested in a Body upon Earth 172
Steps to the Supreme 157

SURRENDER 212
Detailed Surrender 212
Loving Surrender 212
Mental Surrender 214
Perfect Surrender 212
Pure Spiritual Surrender 212
Surrender of All Falsehood 174
Sweetness of the Power
  Surrendered to the Divine 127

SWEETNESS 167
Gentleness 153
Sweetness of the Power
  Surrendered to the Divine 127
Sweetness of Thought Turned
  Exclusively towards
  the Divine 174

TAPASYA 86
Integral Tapasya 86
Mental Tapasya 86
Perfect Tapasya 37
Vital Tapasya 86

TEAM-WORK
Organised for the Divine 24

TENDERNESS
Tenderness for the Divine 211

THIRST
Thirst for Perfection 31
Thirst to Learn 166
Thirst to Understand 79

THOROUGHNESS	246	
Artistic Thoroughness	246	
Integral Thoroughness	247	
Physical Thoroughness	246	
Psychic Thoroughness	247	
Vital Thoroughness	246	

THOUGHT
Integrally Pure Thoughts 249
Religious Thought 251
Sweetness of Thought Turned Exclusively towards the Divine 174
Logic in Thoughts 201
Thoughts Turned towards the Divine 249

TIMIDITY
Timidity in Attachment to the Divine 211

TRANQUILLITY
Tranquillity of the Sex Centre under the Influence of the Supramental Light 75
Psychic Tranquillity 243

TRANSFORMATION 165
Body-Consciousness Undergoing the Supramental Transformation 112
Obscurity Offering Itself to Be Transformed 236
Transformation Makes the Obscurity Disappear 236
Transformed Sex Centre 39

TRANSPARENCY 41
Illumined Transparency 41
Integral Transparency 41
Psychic Transparency 41
Supramentalised Vital Transparency 42
Transparency in the Physical 42
Transparency of the Emotive Vital 42
Vital Transparency 42

TRIPLE
Triple Protection 35
Triple Aspiration 48

TRUE

Birth of True Mental Sincerity 160
True Action in the Material Vital 72
True Worship 154

TRUST
Aspiration for Trust in the Divine 23
Integral Trust in the Divine 23
Mental Trust in the Divine 23
Trust in the Divine 23
Trust in the Vital Mind for the Divine 24
Trust of the Emotive Vital in the Divine 24
Vital Trust in the Divine 24

TRUTH
Absolute Truthfulness 222
Effort towards the Truth 251
Never Tell a Lie 189
Power of Truth in the Subconscient 233
Surrender of All Falsehood 174

TURNING (see also CHANGE)
Consciousness Turned towards the Light 112
Consciousness Turned towards the Supramental Light 112
Exclusive Turning of All Movement towards the Divine 99
First Turning of the Vital towards the Divine Light 215
Physical Consciousness Turned Entirely towards the Divine 238
Thoughts Turned towards the Divine 249

UNDERSTANDING
Divine Solicitude Rightly Understood 158
Thirst to Understand 79

UNION
Aspiration of the Vital for Union with the Divine 199
Consciousness one with the Divine Consciousness 116
Joy of Union with the Divine 178
Will in Course of Uniting with the Divine Will 129
Will One with Divine Will 129

UNSELFISHNESS 28
Unselfish Prosperity 75

USEFULNESS
Balanced Use of the Integral Power 222
Right Use of the Granted Grace 219
Usefulness of the New Creation 127

VANITY 84

VEGETAL
Joy of Vegetal Nature in Answer to the New Light 40
Vegetal Goodwill towards the Supramental Forces 81

VICTORY 11
Certitude of Victory 51
Joy of Victory 14
Victorious Beauty 128
Victorious Endurance 256
Victorious Love 128
Victory in the Vital 11

VIGILANCE 188
Perfect Vigilance 157

VITAL (see also LIFE)
Aspiration for Conquest of the Enemies in the Vital 247
Aspiration for Vital Purity 92
Aspiration of the Vital for Union with the Divine 199
Attachment in the Emotive Vital to the Divine 245
Attachment of the Material Vital to the Divine 95
Attempt at Vital Goodwill 143
Broadening of the Most Material Vital 222
Candid Simplicity in the Vital 183
Conquest over the Vital Enemies 247
Conscious Vital Immortality 108
Consent of the Vital 36
Conversion of the Vital 131
Correct Movements in the Vital 217
Disinterested Work Done for the Divine in the Vital 76
Distinction of the Vital 161
Endurance of the Higher Vital 256
Enthusiasm in the Higher Vital 191

Entry	Page
Enthusiasm in the Most Material Vital	191
Enthusiastic Vital Consent	36
Fearlessness in the Vital	224
First Turning of the Vital towards the Divine Light	215
Formative Faculty in the Vital	80
Generosity in the Vital	136
Harmoy in the Material Vital	17
Harmony in the Vital	17
Integral Offering of the Vital	10
Integral Progress in the Vital	53
Integral Renunciation of Vital Desires	15
Intimacy with the Divine in the Vital	151
Joyous Enthusiasm in the Higher Vital	191
Joyous Enthusiasm in the Most Material Vital	191
Joyous Vital Enthusiasm	191
Krishna's Light in the Vital	215
Krishna's Play in the Vital	93
Liberation in the Vital	32
Life Energy	59
Life Energy in the Vital	59
Light in the Vital	57
Light in the Vital Movements	189
Offering of the Material Vital	10
Offering of the Most Material Vital	10
Offering of the Vital	10
Opening of the Emotive Vital	27
Opening of the Higher Vital to the Light	237
Opening of the Material Vital to the Light	237
Opening of the Vital to the Divine Love	99
Organisation in the Vital	202
Peace in the Vital	169
Power in the Higher Vital	124
Power of Vital Expression	18
Purified Dynamic Life Energy	60
Quiet Strength in the Vital	251
Radha's Consciousness in the Vital	68
Radiating Vital Purity	229
Renunciation of the Vital Desires	15
Seeking the Light in the Lower Vital	136
Silence in the Vital	6
Sincerity in the Vital	22
Skill in Vital Work	193
Solace in the Vital	167
Spiritual Ascension of the Vital	228
Spiritual Awakening of the Vital	72
Stability in the Vital	28
Steadfast Vitality	19
Strength in the Vital	72
Success in the Most Material Vital	109
Supramentalised Life Energy	60
Supramentalised Vital Transparency	42
Transparency of the Emotive Vital	42
True Action in the Material Vital	72
Trust of the Emotive Vital in the Divine	24
Victory in the Vital	11
Vital Aspiration for Immortality	54
Vital Attachment to the Divine	226
Vital Boldness	55
Vital Centre	47
Vital Consecration	113
Vital Consenting to Be Spiritualised, the	218
Vital Continuity	5
Vital Courage	224
Vital Endurance	256
Vital Enthusiasm	191
Vital Fantasy	232
Vital Governed by the Presence, the	221
Vital Honesty	147
Vital Immortality	108
Vital Impulses	109
Vital Joy in Matter	175
Vital Opening	32
Vital Patience	7
Vital Plenitude	189
Vital Prayer	253
Vital Progress	52
Vital Promise	1
Vital Protection	35
Vital Purity	92
Vital Receptivity	105
Vital Sensitivity	165
Vital's Possibility of Perfection, the	6
Vital Tapasya	86
Vital Thoroughness	246
Vital Transparency	42
Vital Trust in the Divine	24
Vital Will Manifesting in Life	94
Wealth in the Most Material Vital	177
Wealth in the Vital	177
Will to Conquer the Vital Enemies	247

VITAL MIND
Entry	Page
Trust in the Vital Mind for the Divine	24

VITALITY
Entry	Page
Perpetual Vitality	74

WATER 200

WEALTH 176
Entry	Page
Emotional Wealth	176
First Movement of the Riches towards the Divine	238
Generous Wealth	177
Greed for Money	177
Integral Wealth of Mahalakshmi	177
Realisation of the Supramental Riches	203
Riches	39
Splendour and Opulence in the Material Life	205
Supramentalised Wealth	177
Supramental Riches	221
Wealth in the Mind of Light	177
Wealth in the Most Material Vital	177
Wealth in the Vital	177
Wealth under the Psychic Influence	177

WHIPPING
Entry	Page
A Whipping	49

WILL
Entry	Page
Vital Will Manifesting in Life	94
Will in Course of Uniting with the Divine Will	129
Will Manifesting in Life	94
Will One with the Divine Will	129
Will to Conquer the Vital Enemies	247

WISDOM 93
Entry	Page
Integral Wisdom	7
Striving towards Integral Wisdom	39
Striving towards Wisdom	39

Wisdom in the Physical Mind	39	Perfect Working of the Mind	239	Works of Love	136
WORD, THE		Power Aspiring to Become an Instrument for the		WORLD (*see also* EARTH)	
Creative Word	60	Divine Work	187	Blessings on the	
		Psychic Work	51	Material World	221
WORK		Radiating Skill in work	192	Divine Love Governing	
Artistic Work	192	Skill in Emotive Work	193	the World	37
Cheerfulness in Work for		Skill in Integral Work	192	Divine Love Spreading over	
the Divine	74	Skill in Material Work	193	the World	204
Disinterested Work Done for		Skill in Mental Work	193	New World	32
the Divine	76	Skill in Physical Work	193		
Disinterested Work Done for		Skill in Psychic Work	193	WORSHIP	
the Divine in the Vital	76	Skill in Vital Work	193	True Worship	154
Faultless Planning of Work	65	Skill in Works	192		
Mahasaraswati's Perfection		Success in Supramental Work	70	YOUTH	
in Works	209	Working of the Enlightened Mind	76	Beauty of Supramental Youth	115
				Eternal Youth	119

Index of Common Names

Abyssinian sword lily	6	Bloodwood tree	110	Champak	162
Acerola	157	Blue dawn flower	138	Changeable rose	117.128
African tulip tree	226	Blue-eyed African daisy	19	Chenille plant	4
African violet	217	Blue lace flower	239	Cherry-pie	113
Agati	221	Blue sage	218	Chilly pepper	49
Air plant	148	Bluewings	239	China aster	41
Alexandrian laurel	44	Bottlebrush	40	Chinaberry	161
Almond tree	201	Bottle gourd	150	China rose	211
Alpine violet	82	Bouncing Bet	219	Chinese bellflower	194
Amaranth	13	Bower plant	185	Chinese forget-me-not	83
Amaryllis	131	Bowstring hemp	44,219	Chinese-hat plant	133
Amazon lily	98	Bridal-bouquet	200	Chinese lantern	1
Amethyst flower	36	Brier rose	211	Chinese-lantern plant	194
Angel's trumpet	86	Brinjal	224	Chinese lavender	79
Angel wings	38	Brisbane lily	100	Chinese parsley	74
Annatto	32	Broom	103	Chinese pink	88
Annual aster	41	Broom, Scotch	83	Chinese wisteria	250
Annual phlox	192	Burr-nut	239	Christmas flower	99
Annunciation lily	154	Bush clock vine	237	Cigar flower	81
Apple-blossom cassia	51	Busy Lizzie	136	Citronella	33
Ashoka	220	Butterfly bush	37	Climbing lily	107
Aster, China or annual	41	Butterfly lily	111	Clock vine	237
Aubergine	224	Butterfly orchid	94	Clove pink	88
Awl tree	169	Butterfly tree	28	Clover	239
Azalea	208	Butterfly weed	21	Cockscomb	55
Baby's breath	109	Cactus, easter-lily	93	Cocoa-shade, Nicaraguan	106
Baby snapdragon	154	Cactus, hedge	56	Coconut palm	70
Bachelor's button	56	Cactus night-blooming	221	Coffee plant	72
Bael tree	6	Cactus, night flower	56	Conessi bark	132
Balloon flower	194	Calabur	169	Confederate rose	117,128
Balsam	136	Calico flower	19	Conifers	74
Balsam, perennial	136	Calliopsis	74	Copperleaf	4
Balsam-pear	167	Candlestick senna	50	Copper-pod	188
Barbados aloe	12	Candytuft	135	Coral plant	146,216
Barbados cherry	157	Cannonball tree	75	Coral tree, Indian	96
Barbados pride	197	Canterbury bells	44	Coral vine	17
Basil	178	Cape honeysuckle	233	Corallita	17
Basil, sweet	178	Cape jasmine	103	Coriander	74
Bear's-breech	5	Cape plumbago	195	Cornflower	56
Beauty-of-the-night	167	Caper tree	76	Cosmetic-bark tree	169
Bengal quince	6	Carambola	24	Cotton plant	109
Betel-nut palm	19	Cardinal climber	205	Cotton, tree	109
Bird-of-paradise	228	Cardinal's-guard	184	Country rose	212
Bird's-eye bush	177	Caricature plant	109	Crape gardenia	230
Bitter gourd	167	Carline thistle	49	Crape myrtle	151
Bitterwood	205	Carnation	88	Cream fruit	229
Black-eyed Susan	215,236	Carrion flower	228	Croton	71
Blanket-flower	102	Cat's claw	91	Crown plant	43
Bleeding-heart	89	Chalice vine	222	Crown-beauty	134
Blood lily	110	Champa	196	Crown-of-thorns	99

Cup-and-saucer lily	98	Forget-me-not, Chinese	83	Indian cork tree	165
Cup-of-gold vine	222	Fortnight lily	168	Indian laburnum	50
Cupflower	175	Fountain plant	216	Indian laurel	43
Curtain creeper	248	Four-o'clock	167	Indian lilac	161
Cypress vine	205	Frangipani	196	Indian shot	45
Daffodil	171	French marigold	231	Ipomoea, star	205
Daisy, creeping	250	Frywood tree	7	Iris, African	168
Daisy, Dahlberg	238	Garden petunia	190	Ironwood	162
Damask rose	212	Garland lily	111	Italian jasmine	145
Dayflower	73	Garlic-vine	203	Ivy	110
Dill	14	Geiger tree	74	Jacob's coat	5
Divi divi	38	Geranium	188	Japanese flowering cherry	201
Dropseed	227	Gingelly	221	Japanese-lantern	120
Drumstick tree	169	Ginger lily	111	Japanese pansy	6
Dwarf white bauhinia	28	Globe amaranth	108	Japanese snowball	248
Easter lily	154	Gloriosa daisy	215	Jasmine	145
Easter-lily cactus	93	Glory bower	64	Jasmine tobacco	175
Easter tree	132	Glory lily	106	Java cassia	51
Edelweiss	153	Gloxinia	222	Java glory bean	66
Eggplant	224	Godetia	62	Jerusalem thorn	186
Eglantine	211	Golden-chain tree	150	Jewels-of-Opar	232
Egyptian star-cluster	189	Golden-dewdrop	92	Joseph's-coat	13
Elder	219	Golden-fleece	238	Kadam tree	16
Elderberry	219	Goldenrod	225	Kaffir lily	69
Everlasting	112	Golden shower tree	50	Kapok tree	53
Eye flower	230	Golden spider lily	157	Karela	167
Fairy flax	154	Good-luck plant	74	Kashmir bouquet	64
Fairy lily	253	Gourd	80	King's mantle	237
Fairy rose	212	Gourd, ridge	157	Knotweed	199
Fame-flower	232	Gourd, white-flowered	150	Krishna tulsi	178
Farewell-to-spring	62	Grape, cultivated	250	Kurunji	228
Feathered amaranth	55	Green ebony	143	Lady-of-the-night	37
Fennel	100	Groundsel	221	Lady's-eardrops	101
Fiddlewood	61	Guatemala rhubarb	146	Lady's-finger	1
Finger grass	58	Guava tree	203	Lady's lace	194
Fire dragon	5	Guernsey lily	173	La-kwa	167
Firebush	110	Gul Mohur	86	Larkspur	87
Flamboyant	86	Gum tree	97	Leaf cactus	189
Flame lily	106	Gumbo	1	Lebbeck tree	7
Flame-of-the-forest	37	Hawaiian wood rose	162	Lemon tree	61
Flame vine	205	Hawthorn	76	Lemongrass	83
Flame violet	94	Heather	44	Leopard flower	30
Flamingo lily	16	Heliotrope	113	Life plant	148
Fleece flower	199	Henna	153	Lilac	230
Fleur-de-lis	140	Herald's trumpet	28	Lily-of-the-field	14
Floppers	148	Holly	135	Lily of the valley	74
Flora's paintbrush	93	Hollyhock	9	Lily thorn	51
Florist's chrysanthemum	59	Honeysuckle, Japanese	156	Lion's tail	153
Flossflower	7	Hopseed bush	89	Lipstick tree	32
Flowering cherry, Japanese	201	Hyacinth	134	Lobelia	155
Flowering maple	1	Inch plant	251	Lobster-claw	113
Flowering tobacco	175	Indian almond	234	Logwood	110
Forget-me-not	169	Indian coral tree	96	Lotus, sacred	172

Love-lies-bleeding	13	Pagoda flower	65,66	Ridge gourd	157
Lupin	157	Pagoda tree	196	Ringworm cassia	50
Madagascar periwinkle	52	Painted leaf	99	Rock purslane	39
Madonna lily	154	Palm, betel-nut	19	Rose	210
Madre	106	Palm, coconut	70	Rose apple	230
Marjoram, knotted	182	Pansy	249	Rose cactus	189
Mango tree	159	Parasol flower	133	Rose moss	201
Maple	5	Peacock flower	6	Rose-of-Sharon	124,129
Margosa	25	Pelican flower	19	Rose periwinkle	52
Marigold	231	Peony	185	Rosebay	173
Marigold, chrysanthemum	231	Peregrina	146	Rusty shield-bearer	188
Marrow	80	Perennial aster	22	Sage, blue & scarlet	218
Marvel of Peru	167	Perennial verbena	246	Sage rose	242
Medlar	165	Persian lilac	161	Satinwood	169
Mesquite	201	Physic nut	146	Sausage tree	148
Mexican bush salvia	218	Pincushions	221	Scarlet-bell tree	226
Mexican fire plant	99	Pink, clove or Chinese	88	Scarlet bush	110
Mexican palo verde	186	Pin-wheel flower	230	Scarlet flame bean	37
Mexican shrimp plant	31	Poet's narcissus	171	Scarlet orchid	94
Mexican sunflower	238	Poinsettia	99	Scarlet sage	218
Mickey Mouse plant	177	Polyantha rose	213	Scotch broom	83
Mignonette	207	Polyanthus narcissus	171	Scotch heather	44
Mignonette tree	153	Popinac	3	Screw pine	185
Miniature holly	157	Poppy	185	Sea holly	5
Mistletoe	250	Porcelain ginger	12	Senna, candlestick	50
Monkey-pod	93	Portia tree	234	Sensitive plant	165
Moon cereus	221	Pot marigold	39	Sesame	221
Moonflower	44	Powderpuff bush	39	Shasta daisy	60
Moreton bay chestnut	51	Pride of India	151	Shellflower	12
Morning glory	138	Primrose	201	Shrub althaea	124,129
Mosaic plant	100	Puchero	232	Shrub verbena	152
Moses-in-a-boat	209	Pummelo tree	61	Silene saponaria	219
Moss verbena	247	Pumpkin	80	Silk-cotton tree, red	32
Mudar	44	Puncture vine	239	Silk-cotton tree, white	53
Mudilla	28	Purple allamanda	11	Silk-cotton tree, yellow	70
Mungo tree	185	Purple heart	221	Silver-net plant	100
Mussel-shell creeper	68	Purslane, rock	38	Singapore cherry	169
Myrtle	170	Pussy-foot	7	Singapore holly	157
Nasturtium	241	Pussy-willow	217	Sing-kwa	157
Neem	25	Queen-of-the-day	57	Skyflower	92
Nicaraguan cocoa-shade	106	Queen-of-the-night	57	Snapdragon	18
Nittu tree	185	Queen's flower	151	Snapweed	136
Okra	1	Queen's-wreath	189	Snow creeper	200
Old China rose	212	Queensland umbrella tree	35	Snowdrop	103
Oleander	173	Railway creeper	139	Sorrowless tree of India	220
Orange jessamine	169	Rain lily	253	Spanish cherry	165
Orchid	53,88,99,182, 226	Rain-tree	93	Spanish flag	166
Orchid, blue	245	Rama tulsi	178	Spathe flower	226
Orchid, butterfly or red	94	Rangoon creeper	206	Spicy jatropha	146
Orchid, ground	226	Red cassia	51	Spider flower	63
Orchid tree	28	Red-hot cattail	4	Spider ivy	58
Oriental cherry	201	Resurrection lily	147	Spider lily	76,134
Ox-eye daisy	59	Ribbon plant	58	Spiderwort, purple-leaved	209

Spiral ginger	75	Ti	74	Wandering Jew	251
Sponge-gourd	157	Tickweed	74	Water hyacinth	93
Sprenger asparagus	21	Tiger-claw plant	159	Water lily	176
Squash	80	Tobacco, jasmine	175	Wattle	2
Star apple	230	Torch tree	143	Wax flower	134
Starfish flower	228	Touch-me-not	165	West Coast creeper	189
Star ipomoea	205	Transvaal daisy	103	West Indian blackthorn	3
Star-of-Bethlehem	183	Tropical almond	234	West Indian holly	242
Strawflower	112	Tropical crocus	147	White-flowered gourd	150
St. Thomas tree	28	True aloe	12	White popinac	154
Summer snowflake	183	Trumpet bush	232	Windflower	14
Sunflower	112	Trumpet narcissus	171	Winter cherry	194
Sunflower, perennial	238	Trumpet vine, blue	237	Wood rose	180
Sun hemp	80	Trumpet vine, pink	197	Wood rose, Hawaiian	162
Sun plant	201	Tube flower	65	Wood sorrel	183
Surinam quassia	205	Tuberose	198	Woolflower, Chinese	54
Sweet acacia	3	Tulip	242	Yellow alder	242
Sweet alyssum	155	Tulsi, Rama or Krishna	178	Yellow-bells	232
Sweet marjoram	182	Turk's-cap	158	Yellow elder	232
Sweet pea	153	Turk's turban	65	Yellow jasmine	145
Sweet scabious	221	Turmeric	82	Yellow morning-glory	162
Sweet William	88	Umbrella tree, Queensland	35	Yellow oleander	235
Tassel flower	13, 93	Vegetable humming-bird	221	Yellow trumpet vine	14
Teak tree	234	Verbena, shrub	152	Yesterday-today-and-tomorrow	37
Temple tree	196	Violet	248	Ylang-ylang	44
Thistle, carline	49	Virgin's bower	63	Zedoary	82
Thorn straggler	48	Wallflower	58		

The Hibiscus Group

Colour and Details of Petals	Colour of Centre	Size	Single/ Double	Variety	Significance
White, slender or rounded separated petals, erect or pendulous		S-L*	S		Light of the Purified Power
White		V.S*	S	hirtus	Eternal Smile
White, slender or rounded separated petals	bright red, vermilion or magenta	S-L	S		Power of Integral Purity
White		S-M*	D	syriacus	Will One with the Divine Will
White, gradually turning pink		M-L	D	mutabilis	The Divine Grace
Cream-white	pure white	S-M	S		Ananda
Cream-white	dark red	S-M	S		Ananda in the Physical
Cream-white, crinkled or smooth petals	magenta, pinwheel	M-L	S	Hawaiian	Power of Success
Cream-white veined deep pink, separated petals	prominent deep pink centre, orange stigmas	S-M	S	'Sweetheart'	Power to Progress
Cream or pale yellow, crinkled or smooth petals	light pink or white	M-L	S	Hawaiian, 'Cromwell'	Godhead
Cream, deep or pale yellow		M	D		Will in Course of Uniting with the Divine Will
Yellow, light or bright, smooth or crinkled petals	pink, red or light orange	M-L	S	Hawaiian and other	Power of Harmony
Yellow, lemon	light red to deep magenta	M-L	S	Hawaiian and other	Mentalised Power
Yellow, lemon or luminous, crinkled or smooth petals	white or light pink with white aura	M-L	S	Hawaiian	Realisation of the New Creation

When not mentioned the general name is H.Rosa sinensis

* very small = V.S, small = S, medium = M, large = L

Colour and Details of Petals	Colour of Centre	Size	Single/ Double	Variety	Significance
Yellow, cup-shaped with crinkled or smooth petals	large reddish orange firelike	M	S	Hawaiian	Progress of the New Creation
Yellow, splashed orange, crinkled or smooth petals	light yellow	M-L	S	Hawaiian	Concentration of the New Creation
Yellow, light, bright or golden		M-L	D	Hawaiian, 'Daffodil'	Supramental Consciousness
Yellow, golden or ochre, crinkled or smooth petals		M-L	S	Hawaiian	Power in the Converted Mind
Yellow, light or apricot-yellow, crinkled or smooth petals	white or light pink pinwheel with light pink aura	M-L	S	Hawaiian	Sweetness of the Power Surrendered to the Divine
Yellow, ochre or mustard, crinkled or smooth petals	magenta with or without silver aura	M-L	S	Hawaiian	Victorious Beauty
Yellow, rounded outer petals and tufted centre	large fire-red or bright orange	M-L	Semi-D	Hawaiian	Blossoming of the New Creation
Yellow, bright, veined orange-red, smooth or crinkled petals	deep red or bright pink with lighter pink aura	M-L	S	Hawaiian	Firmness of the New Creation
Yellow, golden or orange	red or deeper orange	M-L	D		Power of the Supramental Consciousness
Yellow, golden or orange, crinkled or smooth petals (see Orange)	deep magenta with silver-white aura	M-L	S	Hawaiian	Power of Spiritual Beauty
Orange-pink, or salmon pink, separated petals (see Salmon-pink)	deeper shade or same colour	M	S		Beauty of Supramental Youth
Orange or apricot-yellow, separated petals	red or magenta	M-L	S		Supramental Beauty in the Physical
Orange, all shades, crinkled or smooth petals	various colours other than white	M-L	S	Hawaiian	Beauty of Tomorrow
Orange, crinkled or smooth petals	white with pale pink aura	L	S	Hawaiian	Beauty of Tomorrow Manifesting the Divine

Colour and Details of Petals	Colour of Centre	Size	Single/ Double	Variety	Significance
Orange-red, bright, firm crinkled or smooth petals with light gold on back (*see* Red-orange)	reddish pink	L	S	Hawaiian	Puissance of Realisation
Orange-red, bright, (*see* Red-orange)	deep red	M-L	S	Hawaiian	Power of Perseverance
Orange-red, bicoloured or variegated		M-L	S	Hawaiian, 'Splash'	Manifold Power of the New Creation
Orange or golden-yellow, crinkled or smooth petals (*see* Yellow, golden)	deep magenta with silver-white aura	M-L	S	Hawaiian	Power of Spiritual Beauty
Orange-pink, apricot border, crinkled or smooth petals	deep pink	M-L	S	Hawaiian and other	Effective Power of the Supramental
Salmon-pink or light orange	pink with pale pink aura	M-L	S	Hawaiian	Beauty of Supramental Love
Salmon-pink or orange-pink, separated petals (*see* Orange-pink)	deeper shade or same colour	M	S		Beauty of Supramental Youth
Salmon orange	white stigmas	V.S	S	hirtus	Eternal Youth
Salmon, light or dark with fine red veins	salmon or red	M	D		Agni
Pink, all shades, elongated, separated petals	pink, deep pink or red	M-L	S		Psychic Power in Existence
Pink, very light, lavender-pink towards centre, white border, crinkled or smooth petals	deep magenta	M-L	S	Hawaiian	Ideal of the New Creation
Pink, light to medium		L	D	mutabilis	Victorious Love
Pink, light or deeper with cream border	light red or same coloured	M-L	D		Consciousness One with the Divine Consciousness
Pink, light or deep	white	M-L	S	Hawaiian	Power of Progress

Colour and Details of Petals	Colour of Centre	Size	Single/ Double	Variety	Significance
Pink, deep, crinkled or smooth petals, lighter towards the border	light or deep pink	M-L	S	Hawaiian	Charm of the New Creation
Pink, deep, pale pink on border, crinkled or smooth petals	reddish pink	M-L	S		Beauty of the New Creation
Pink, deep, crinkled or smooth petals	red, magenta or deep pink	M-L	S	Hawaiian	Usefulness of the New Creation
Pink, light or coral		M-L	D		Power of the Psychic Consciousness
Pink, coral, deep pink veins, separated petals	magenta or coral-pink	S-M	S		Enlightened Individual Power
Pink, reddish or deep smooth rounded petals splashed white on one lower edge	dark red or deep pink	M-L	S		Aesthetic Power
Red, light or dark, separated recurved petals, crenate or cut border	red or dark red	M	S		Dynamic Power
Red, all shades		S-L	D		Power of Consciousness
Red, edged white, separated deeply indented and fully recurved serrated petals, pendulous	red	M	S	schizo-petalus	Flame
Red and white, variegated		M	D	alba-variegata	Faith
Red, cardinal, firm petals	red or dark red	M-L	S	Hawaiian	Power of Action
Red-orange, (*see* Orange-red)	deep red	L	S	Hawaiian	Power of Perseverance
Red-orange, bright, firm crinkled or smooth petals with light gold on back (*see* Orange-red)	reddish pink	L	S	Hawaiian	Puissance of Realisation

Colour and Details of Petals	Colour of Centre	Size	Single/ Double	Variety	Significance
Magenta, light, separated petals	similar	S	S	'Lipstick'	Individual Power
Magenta, deep, firm crinkled or smooth petals	dark red	L	S	Hawaiian	Power in the Service of the Future
Magenta, deep, firm crinkled or smooth petals	deep magenta	M	S	Hawaiian	Power of the Future
Lavender-grey, light or deep	pink or magenta	M-L	S	'Sebectini'	Power of Effort
Lavender grey mauve or dark lavender	lavender grey	M-L	D	'Dream'	Controlled Power
Lavender, changing to blue, cup-shaped	magenta white anthers and stigmas	M	S	syriacus	Power in the Higher Vital
Lavender-grey with a ring of magenta to light red, edge of petals dull white, smooth or crinkled petals	magenta	M-L	S	Hawaiian	All-powerful Charm of an Alluring Beauty

Alternative Botanical Names

Alternative Name	Name Used	Alternative Name	Name Used
Althaea rosea	Alcea rosea	Justicia bradegeana	Beloperone guttata
Alyssum maritinum	Lobularia maritima	Kleinia grandiflora	Senecio
Azalea	Rhododendron	Macfadyena	Doxantha
Cacalia coccinea	Emilia javanica	Poinciana regia	Delonix regia
Didiscus	Trachymene	Samanea saman	Enterolobium saman
Dietes	Morea	Sarritea magnifica	Bignonia purpurea
Dillenia suffruiticosa	Wormia bourbridgii	Scadoxus multiflorus	Haemanthus
Dysodia tenuiloba	Thymophlla tenuiloba	Senna alata	Cassia alata
Eugenia jambos	Syzygium jambos	Stenolbium	Tecoma alata
Ipomoea hederifolia	Quamoclit coccinea	Strictocardia beveriensis	Ipomoea beveriensis
Ipomoea alba	Calonyction alba	Thryallis glauca	Galphimia glauca
Ipomoea lobata	Mina lobata	Tradescantia zebrina	Zebrina pendula
Ipomoea quamoclit	Quamoclit pennata	Vinca rosea	Catharanthus roseus
Jacobinia coccinia	Pachystachis coccinia		

REFERENCES:

Unless otherwise stated, the references are taken from the Sri Aurobindo Birth Centenary Library (SABCL) and The Mother's Collected Works (MCW). References are marked with a star for texts given specially for this book.

	SABCL, 26: 185 (Frontispiece)
	MCW, 1: 362 (Frontispiece)
I.	MCW, 8: 25-26
I.	MCW, 3: 72
I-II.	MCW, 5: 243-44
II.	MCW, 3: 132
II.	MCW, 9: 210-11
III.	SABCL, 18: 86-87
III-IV.	MCW, 6: 231-34
IV.	Bulletin Aug. 1990: 68
V.	Bulletin Aug. 1990: 62-64
V.	Bulletin Aug. 1990: 60
V.	MCW, 4: 29
V.	Agenda II, 4-3-1961
V.	MCW, 6: 231
V.	Bulletin Aug.1990: 68
VI.	Bulletin Aug.1990: 66
VI.	Bulletin Aug.1990: 66
VI.	Bulletin Aug.1990: 68
VI.	Bulletin Feb.2010: 34
VI.	Bulletin Feb.2010: 32
VII.	MCW, 8: 25-26
VIII.	SABCL, 22: 499
VIII.	SABCL, 22: 499
VIII.	SABCL, 22: 292-93
VIII.	MCW, 4: 166-67
IX-XIII.	MCW, 8: 36-42
XIII-XIV.	Harmonies of Light 2: 57-58
XIV.	MCW, 3: 132
XIV.	Life in Sri Aurobindo Ashram (1965)
XIV-XV.	MCW, 6: 229-30
XV.	MCW, 6: 231
XVI.	MCW, 4: 167
XVII.	Bulletin Nov.1985: 19
XVII.	Agenda II (4-2-'61)
XVIII.	Agenda II (7-1-'61)
XIX.	MCW, 1: 359
XIX.	MCW, 17: 186
2	MCW, 14: 321 (Work)
3	SABCL, 16: 70 (Supramental Knowledge)
5	SABCL, 21: 537 (Emotions Awake to the First Contact with the Divine)
6	MCW, 12: 56-57 (The Vital's Possibility of Perfection)
9	MCW, 3: 23 (Offering)
10	SABCL, 23: 607 (Integral Offering)
12	MCW, 2: 30-31 (Dreams)
13	SABCL, 20: 1 (Integral Immortality)
14	SABCL, 22: 351 (Light in the Blood)
15	MCW, 1: 354 (Renunciation of Vital Desires)
16	SABCL, 24: 1538 (Mastery of Sex)
19	SABCL, 28: 38 (Inspiration)
21	MCW, 12: 60 (Spiritual Speech)
22	MCW, 14: 67 (Simple Sincerity)
22	SABCL, 23: 560 (Sincerity in the Vital)
23	SABCL, 20: 197 (Trust in the Divine)
24	MCW, 13: 205 (Organised Team-Work)
25	SABCL, 23: 651 (Spiritual Atmosphere)
27	SABCL, 23-606 (Opening)
28	SABCL, 20: 194-95 (Supramental Action)
30	MCW, 4: 16 (Balance)
30	MCW, 3: 23 (Attachment to the Divine)
31	MCW, 15: 186 (Thirst for Perfection)
32	MCW, 15: 388 (The New World)
33	SABCL, 24: 1628 (Protection)
35	MCW, 12: 54 (Organised Material Energy)
36	SABCL, 24: 1309 (Consent of the Vital)
39	MCW, 8: 41 (Perseverance)
40	MCW, 1: 191 (Joy of Vegetal Nature in Answer to the New Light)
41	MCW, 8: 38 (Transparency)
42	MCW, 8: 82 (Transparency)
47	SABCL, 28: 278-79 (Ananda in the Centres)
48	MCW, 1: 75 (Triple Aspiration)
49	SABCL, 25: 28-29 (A Whipping)
49	MCW, 1: 377 (Incorruptible Faithfulness)
51	SABCL, 16: 67 (Mind of Light Acting in Matter)
53	MCW, 3: 23 (The Aim of Existence is Realised)
54	SABCL, 19: 964 (Aspiration for Immortality)
56	SABCL, 28: 277 (Idealism)
56	MCW, 15: 54 (Fortune)
56	MCW, 15: 154 (Fortune)
57	SABCL, 23: 585 (Light)
58	MCW, 7: 112 (Perfect Radiating Psychology)
60	MCW, 7: 347-48 (The Creative Word)
61	SABCL, 24: 1511 (Continence)
62	MCW, 1: 100 (Glad Remembrance)
63	MCW, 4: 343 (Soaring of Aspiration)
64	SABCL, 20: 167 (Integral Even Basis in the Physical)
67	MCW, 9: 65 (Rest)
68	MCW, 15: 224 (Radha's Consciousness)
69	SABCL, 23: 585 (Conversion of the Aim of Life from the Ego to the Divine)

70	SABCL, 22: 13 (Success in Supramental Work)	115	MCW, 1: 251-52 (Agni)
71	MCW, 3: 34 (Power to Reject Adverse Suggestions)	117	MCW, 8: 251 (Divine Grace)
72	SABCL, 20: 51 (Perfect Path)	118	SABCL, 19: 1044 (Effective Power of the Supermind)
75	SABCL, 24: 1508-09 (Supramental Influence in the Sex Centre)	119	SABCL, 23: 971 (Eternal Smile)
76	MCW, 8: 20 (Spring Purity)	119	MCW, 12: 124 (Eternal Youth)
77	SABCL, 24: 1593 (Supramental Influence in the Subconscient)	119	SABCL, 21: 743 (Faith)
78	SABCL, 22: 357 (Supramental Light in the Subconscient)	120	SABCL, 19: 1015 (Flame)
78	SABCL, 24: 1593-94 (Psychic Light in the Subconscient)	123	SABCL, 21: 587 (Power in the Converted Mind)
78	SABCL, 24: 1594 (Supramental Light in the Subconscient)	124	SABCL, 23: 623 (Power of Perseverance)
79	SABCL, 20: 296 (Thirst to Understand)	125	SABCL, 19: 1041 (Power in Service of the Future)
80	SABCL, 24: 1285 (Formative Faculty in the Mind)	127	SABCL, 19: 1067 (Sweetness of the Power Surrendered to the Divine)
81	MCW, 9: 245 (Vegetal Goodwill Towards the Supramental Forces)	128	MCW, 9: 158 (Victorious Beauty)
82	MCW, 1: 11 (Peace)	128	MCW, 1: 161 (Victorious Love)
82	SSBCL, 28: 293 (Scented Marvel)	129	SABCL, 20: 299 (Will One with the Divine Will)
83	SABCL, 22: 151 (Help)	129	MCW, 4: 2 (Will One with the Divine Will)
84	MCW, 4: 29 (Vanity)	130	SABCL, 19: 935-36 (Integral Conversion)
86	SABCL, 23: 596 (Tapasya)	133	SABCL, 17: 215 (Curiosity)
86	SABCL, 15: 138 (Realisation)	134	SABCL, 18: 2 (Collective Harmony)
87	MCW, 15: 198 (Soaring)	135	MCW, 14: 142 (Equanimity)
88	MCW, 13: 379 (Obedience)	138	MCW, 1: 349 (Artistic Taste)
89	SABCL, 29: 709 (Psychic Awakening in Matter)	141	SABCL, 23: 645 (Divine Purity)
90	SABCL, 24: 1467 (Conquest over the Greed for Food)	142	MCW, 3: 130 (Aspiration in the Physical)
91	SABCL, 19: 657 (Road to the Divine)	145	MCW, 14: 156 (Purity)
91	SABCL, 19: 964 (Road to the Divine)	147	MCW, 4: 1650-66 (Psychic Influence in the Emotions)
92	SABCL, 24: 1341 (Aspiration for Vital Purity)	150	SABCL, 17: 3 (Descent of the Light)
96	SABCL, 18: 251 (Beginning of Realisation in Matter)	150	SABCL, 29: 710 (Descent of the Light)
96	SABCL, 18: 258 (Beginning of Realisation in Matter)	151	SABCL, 23: 971 (Intimacy with the Divine in the Vital)
97	MCW, 3: 241 (Abolition of the Ego)	152	MCW, 12: 284 (Supramental Influence in the Cells)
97	SABCL, 24: 1370 (Abolition of the Ego)	153	SABCL, 28: 5 (Spiritual Beauty)
99	SABCL, 20: 304 (Concentration)	153	SABCL, 15: 135 (Spiritual Beauty)
100	MCW, 15: 186 (Application)	154	SABCL, 22: 499 (Expressive Silence)
101	SABCL, 9: 252 (Art)	155	MCW, 16: 430 (Remembrance of Sri Aurobindo)
102	MCW, 3: 180 (Successful Future)	156	SABCL, 20: 102-03 (Constant Remembrance of the Divine)
104	MCW, 14: 155 (Receptivity)	158	MCW, 1: 15 (Divine Solicitude)
104	MCW, 8: 307-08 (Receptivity)	159	SABCL, 20: 492 (Divine Knowledge)
106	SABCL, 23: 825 (No Quarrels)	160	MCW, 8: 398 (Birth of True Mental Sincerity)
108	SABCL, 17: 80 (Immortality)	161	MCW, 12: 56 (Distinction of the Vital)
109	SABCL, 17: 105 (Success in the Most Material Vital)	162	MCW, 8: 40 (Detailed Gratitude)
110	MCW, 15: 104 (Supramental Manifestation)	163	MCW, 8: 159 (Supramentalised Psychological Perfection)
111	SABCL, 18: 92 (Sachchidananda)	165	MCW, 4: 393 (Transformation)
114	SABCL, 15: 215 (Aesthetic Power)	165	SABCL, 16: 392-93 (Patience)
		166	MCW, 12: 129 (Thirst to Learn)
		167	SABCL, 23: 642 (Solace)
		168	MCW, 8: 216 (Aristocracy of Beauty)
		170	MCW, 1: *Preface* (To Live Only for the Divine)

171 SABCL, 20: 4950 (Power of Beauty)
171 SABCL, 15: 128 (Beauty Aspiring for the Supramental Realisation)
172 SABCL, 25: 19 (Aditi)
172 SABCL, 28: 314 (Aditi)
172 SABCL, 13: 155-56 (The Avatar)
176 SABCL, 25: 12 (Wealth)
178 SABCL, 21: 563 (Joy of Union with the Divine)
178 MCW, 1: 19 (Joy of Union with the Divine)
180 MCW, 15: 297 (Integral Gratitude)
182 MCW, 9: 431 (New Birth)
182 MCW, 9: 374-75 (New Birth)
183 SABCL, 20: 52 (Spiritual Intensity)
184 SABCL, 24: 1594 (Aspiration for the Supramental Guidance in the Subconscient)
188 MCW, 9: 22 (Spiritual Happiness)
192 MCW, 14: 328 (Skill in Works)
193 MCW, 4: 404 (Skill in Physical Work)
194 SABCL, 17: 47 (Krishna's Ananda)
195 MCW, 8: 175-76 (Organisation of the Being around the Psychic)
196 SABCL, 23: 554 (Psychological Perfection)
198 SABCL, 16: 378-79 (The New Creation)
199 SABCL, 23: 1324 (Aspiration of the Vital for Union with the Divine)
200 MCW, 6: 183-84 (Joy of Integral Faithfulness)
201 SABCL, 26: 185 (Sri Aurobindo's Compassion)
203 SABCL, 17: 79 (Collective Emotions Open to the Divine)
204 MCW, 7: 37 (Divine Love)
205 MCW, 1: 230 (Opening of the Physical to the Divine Love)
206 MCW, 14: 164 (Faithfulness)
207 SABCL, 25: 33-34 (Order)
209 MCW, 5: 201 (Divine Presence)
209 SABCL, 25: 34 (Mahasaraswati's Perfection in Works)
210 SABCL, 23: 764 (Psychic Love for the Divine)
212 SABCL, 23: 585 (Surrender)
212 MCW, 14: 114 (Detailed Surrender)
214 MCW, 12: 70 (Love for the Divine)
214 SABCL, 29: 632 (Mental Love for the psychic Influence)
215 SABCL, 22: 405 (Krishna's Light in the Physical Mind)
215 SABCL, 23: 798 (Krishna's Light in the Physical Mind)
216 MCW, 3: 130 (Aspiration in the Physical for the Divine Love)
217 SABCL, 18: 1-2 (The Future)
218 MCW, 4: 67 (Aspiration for Spirituality)
219 SABCL, 19: 857 (Power of Spirituality)
220 **SABCL, 20: 407 (Absence of Grief)**
221 SABCL, 17: 79 (The Supramental Riches)
223 MCW, 4: 391 (Seeking for all Support in the Divine)
224 MCW, 9: 74 (Fearlessness)
225 MCW, 8: 337-98 (Mental Sincierity)
226 SABCL, 25: 3-4 (Aspiration for Purity)
227 MCW, 14: 160 (Humility)
230 SABCL, 17: 12 (Mental Purity)
231 MCW, 4: 207 (Plasticity)
231 MCW, 4: 367-68 (Physical Plasticity)
232 SABCL, 24: 1266-67 (Physical Mind)
233 SABCL, 25: 3 (Power of Truth in the Subconscient)
234 SABCL, 25: 9-10 (Renunciation of Desires)
235 SABCL, 19: 645 (Mind)
242 SABCL, 22: 347-48 (Awakening of the Physical Mind)
243 SABCL, 20: 214 (Psychic Tranquillity)
245 MCW, 4: 91 ((Attachment for the Divine)
248 MCW, 1: 62 (Thoughts Turned towards the Divine)
255 MCW, 14: 174 (Endurance)
255 MCW, 9: 255 (Endurance)
259 SABCL, 23: 959 (Symbolism)
260 Agenda II (4-2-1961)
261 *Champaklal Speaks*, pp. 161-68

Glossary

Parts of a Flower

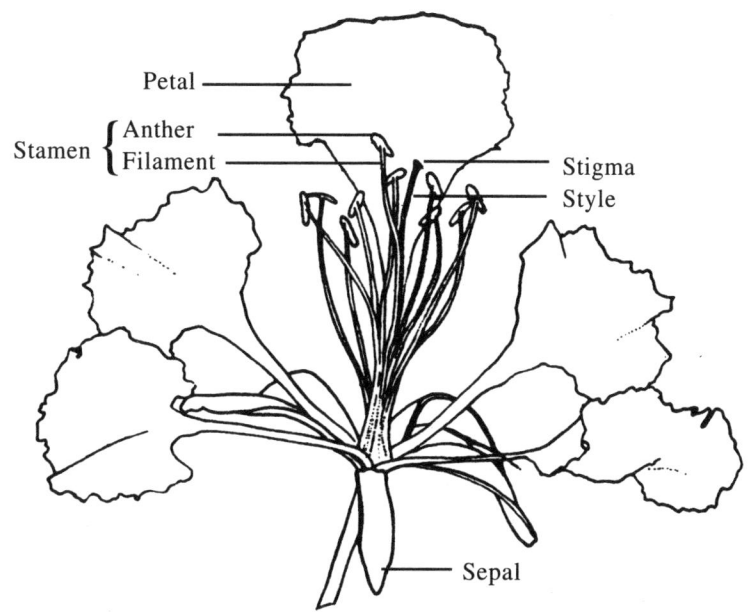

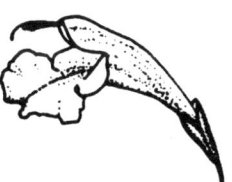

Bilabiate flower:

Two-lipped flower

Bract (Bracteate):

Modified or coloured leaf associated with the flower

Catkin

Cladode:

Flattened leaf-like stem

Campanulate flower

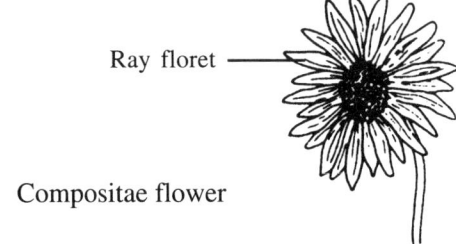
Ray floret
Compositae flower

Corolla 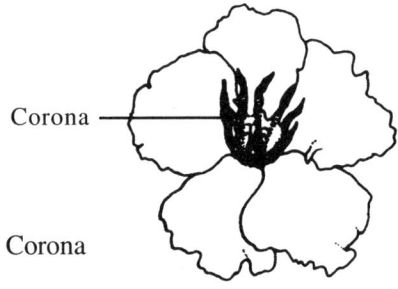 Corolla

Corona
Corona

Corymb

Cyme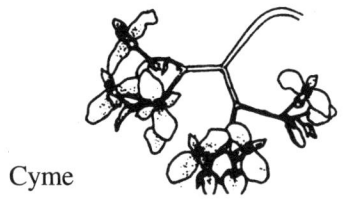

Funnelform flower

Head

Orchid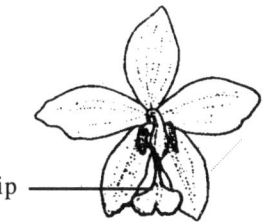
Lip

Papilionaceous flower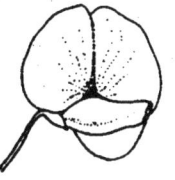

Raceme

Rotate flower: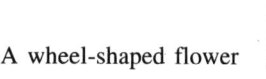

A wheel-shaped flower

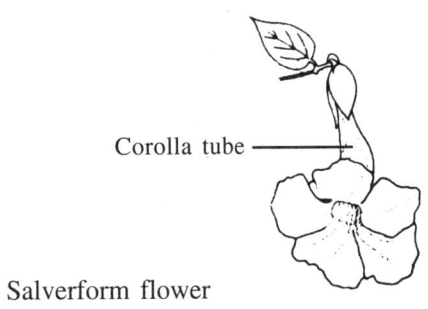

Salverform flower — Corolla tube

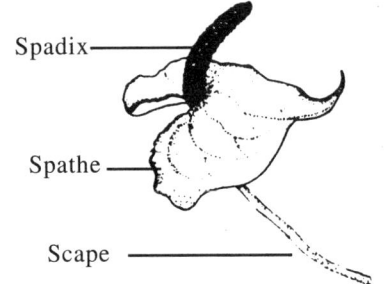

Spathe and Spadix

Scape: a leafless flower-stalk

Spike

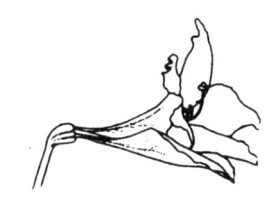

Trumpet-shaped flower

Umbel

Glossary of Philosophical and Psychological Terms

The definitions of the terms below are based upon the writings of Sri Aurobindo and the Mother.

Aditi. The Divine Mother; the divine consciousness; the indivisible consciousness, force and Ananda of the Supreme.

Adverse Suggestions. See **Hostile forces.**

Agni. Fire; the godhead of fire; the fire of aspiration, purification, *tapasya,* transformation.

Ananda. Delight, beatitude, bliss.

Anandamaya. Full of Ananda.

Ashram. The house or houses of a Teacher or Master of spiritual philosophy in which he receives and lodges those who come to him for the teaching and practice.

Aspiration. The call of the being for higher things, for the Divine, for all that belongs to the higher or divine consciousness.

Avatar. Divine incarnation; one in whom the Divine consciousness has descended into human birth for a great world-work.

Bhakti. Devotion, love for the Divine; the delight of the heart in God.

Broadening. See **Widening.**

Calm. A still, unmoved condition which no disturbance can affect; a strong and positive quietude, firm and solid.

Centres (of Consciousness). Centres (*chakras*) of the inner being; centres of consciousness which connect the inner being with the outer personality. These centres are supposed to be attached to the spinal cord, but in fact they are in the subtle body; by their opening through yoga, the yogic or inner consciousness develops and one escapes from the limitations of the surface consciousness.

Chit (*cit*). Pure consciousness, pure awareness; the essential consciousness of the Spirit.

Concentration. A gathering together of the consciousness and either centralising it at one point or turning it on a single object, such as the Divine.

Consciousness. The self-aware force of existence. The essence of consciousness is the power to be aware of itself and its objects; but it is not only power of awareness of self and things, it is or has also a dynamic and creative energy. Consciousness is not synonymous with mentality, which is only a middle term; below mentality, it sinks into vital and material movements which are for us subconscient; above, it rises into the Supramental which is for us the superconscient. See also **Divine Consciousness.**

Consecration. The devoting of all that comes to one, all one's experience and progress towards the Divine.

Conversion. A turning of the being away from lower things towards the Divine.

Divine, the. The Supreme Being from which all comes and in which all lives. In its supreme Truth, the Divine is absolute and infinite peace, consciousness, existence, power and delight. The Transcendent, the Cosmic (Universal) and the Individual are the three powers of the Divine, overarching, underlying and penetrating the whole of manifestation.

Divine Consciousness. The spiritual consciousness to which the Divine alone exists, because all is the Divine. Force, Light, Knowledge and Ananda together make up the higher, spiritual or Divine Consciousness.

Divine Grace. See **Grace, the**

Divine Presence. See **Presence, the**

Divine Will. See **Will, Divine**

Ego. The separative sense of individuality which makes each being conceive of itself as an independent personality. Ego implies the identification of one's existence with the outer mental, vital and physical self.

Emotional (or **Emotive**) **Being.** The emotional vital.

Emotional Centre. The heart-centre of consciousness governing the emotional being.

Emotional (or **Emotive**) **Vital.** The emotional vital. That part of the higher vital being which is the seat of various feelings, such as love, joy, sorrow, hatred, and the rest.

Equality. The capacity to remain unmoved within in all conditions; equanimity founded on the sense of the one Self, the one Divine everywhere.

Evolution. The progressive unfolding of Spirit out of the density of material consciousness; the method by which the One Being and Consciousness, involved here in Matter, liberates itself from matter into life, from life into mind, from mind into the spirit.

Faith. The soul's witness to something not yet manifested, achieved or realised, but which yet the Knower within us feels to be true or supremely worth following or achieving; the soul's belief in the Divine's existence, wisdom, power, love and grace.

Force, the. The Divine Force, the one Energy that alone exists and alone makes universal or individual action possible, for this Force is the Divine itself in the body of its power; in the individual it is a Force for illumination, transformation, purification, for all that has to be done in the yoga.

Godhead. The one supreme divine Being. In His supreme status He is a transcendent unthinkable too great for any manifestation; in His universal status He is the supreme Lord, the Master of works and universal nature; in His immanent status He is the living supreme Soul in all things, the Lord in the heart of all creatures.

Gods, **the**. In origin and essence the Gods are permanent Emanations of the Divine put forth from the Supreme by the Transcendent Mother; in their cosmic action they are Powers and Personalities of the Divine each with his independent cosmic standing, function and work in the universe. In the Vedas the Gods are also the companions and helpers of man; they recognise in the soul of man their brother and ally and desire to help and increase him by themselves increasing in him so as to possess his world with their light, strength and beauty.

Grace, **the Divine Grace.** The help of a higher Divine Force other than the force of Karma, which can lift the sadhak beyond the present possibilities of his nature.

Gratitude. A loving recognition of the Grace received from the Divine; a humble recognition of all that the Divine has done and is doing for you.

Higher Mind. See **Spiritualised Mind**

Higher Vital. See **Vital**, **the**

Hostile forces. **Adverse forces.** Anti-divine, not merely undivine forces that are in revolt against the Divine, against the Truth and Light, and opposed to the yoga.

Illumined Mind. See **Spiritualised Mind**

Immortality. The consciousness which is beyond birth and death, beyond the chain of cause and effect, beyond all bondage and limitation, free, blissful, self-existent in conscious-being; the absolute life of the soul as opposed to the transient and mutable life in the body which it assumes by birth and death and rebirth.

Inconscient, the. The Supreme's state of self-involved, self-oblivious consciousness and force which is at the basis of the material world; this state is the apparent opposite of the Supreme and in it there can be darkness, inertia, insensibility, disharmony and disintegration. Not really inconscient at all, it is rather a complete 'sub'-conscience, a suppressed or involved consciousness...

Inspiration. Something that comes out of the knowledge planes like a flash and opens up the mind to the Truth in a moment; a slender river of brightness leaping from a vast and eternal knowledge.

Integral. Of or relating to all the parts of the being, mental, vital, physical, psychic, spiritual.

Integral Yoga. A union (*yoga*) in all the parts of our being with the Divine and a consequent transmutation of all their now jarring elements into the harmony of a higher divine consciousness and existence; this yoga implies not only the realisation of God but the entire consecration and change of the inner and outer life till it is fit to manifest a divine consciousness and become part of a divine work.

Intuitive Mind. See **Spiritualised Mind**

Kali. The Divine Mother in her aspect of might and strength destroying the ignorance and evil.

Kali Puja. A religious festival in which the goddess Kali is worshipped.

Krishna. As a godhead Krishna is the Lord of Ananda, Love and *bhakti*; as an incarnation he manifests the union of wisdom (*jnana*) and works and leads the world evolution through this towards union with the Divine by Ananda, Love and *bhakti*.

Krishna's Light. A spiritual light of purification and illumination. Its colour depends on the plane in which it manifests.

Liberation. The release of the soul from the outward ignorant existence into the freedom, calm, wideness of the Spirit.

Life-Energy. Life-force, not physical in itself, not material energy, but rather a different principle supporting Matter and involved in it. It supports and occupies all forms and without it no physical form could have come into being or could remain in being.

Light, **the**. Primarily a spiritual manifestation of the Divine Reality illuminative and creative; spiritual Light is not knowledge, but the illumination that comes from above and liberates the being from obscurity and darkness.

Lower Vital. See **Vital**, **the**

Mahalakshmi. The Divine Mother's Power of Harmony. Through love and beauty she lays on men the yoke of the Divine and brings to them her gifts of the spirit's grace, the charm and beauty of the Ananda.

Mahasaraswati. The Divine Mother's Power of Work and her spirit of perfection and order. The science and craft and technique of things are her province. She presides over the organisation and execution of things and assures the material foundation.

Material Vital. That part of the lower vital turned entirely to physical things. It is full of desires and greeds and seekings for pleasure on the physical plane.

Matter. Being manifest as substance; substance of the one Conscious Being. A self-formed mask and robe of the divine Spirit.

Mind. The words 'mind' and 'mental' are used to connote specially the part of the nature which has to do with cognition and intelligence, with ideas, with mental or thought perceptions, the reactions of thought to things, with the truly mental movements and formations, mental vision and will, etc. The ordinary mind has three main parts: mind proper, vital mind, and physical mind.

The **mind proper** is divided into three parts: the thinking mind or intellect, concerned with ideas and knowledge in their own right; the dynamic mind, concerned with the putting out of mental forces for the realisation of the ideas; and the externalising mind, concerned with the expression of ideas in life.

The **vital mind** or desire mind is a mind of dynamic will, action, desire; it is occupied with force and achievement and satisfaction and possession, with enjoyment and suffering, giving and taking, growth and expansion, etc.

The **physical mind** is that part of the mind which is concerned with physical things only; limited by the physical view and experience of things, it mentalises the experience brought by the contact of outward life and things, but does not go beyond that. The mechanical mind, closely connected with the physical mind, goes on repeating without use whatever has happened. Overtopping the ordinary mind, hidden in our own superconscient parts, there are higher ranges of Mind, gradations of spiritualised mind leading to the Supermind.

Mind of Light. A mind capable of living in the truth, capable of being truth-conscious and manifesting in its life a direct in place of an indirect knowledge. There is in it an action of light, of truth, of knowledge in which inconscience, error and ignorance claim no place.

New Creation. The manifestation of a divine life upon earth as the result of the working of the supramental consciousness and force and love.

Occultism. The knowledge and right use of the hidden forces of nature; true occultism means a search into suraphysical realities and an unveiling of the hidden laws of being and Nature, of all that is not obvious on the surface.

Opening. A release of the consciousness by which it begins to admit into itself the working of the Divine Life and Power; the ability of the consciousness on the various levels to receive the descent of the Higher Consciousness above.

Outer Being. The surface being, our ordinary exterior mind, life, body consciousness.

Overmind. See **Spiritualised Mind**

Peace. A deep quietude bringing not merely a release, but a certain happiness or Ananda of itself, a harmony that gives a feeling of liberation and full satisfaction.

Physical, the. That part of the individual nature which includes the physical body and the physical consciousness; by physical consciousness is meant the physical mind and the physical vital as well as the body consciousness proper.

Physical Mind. See **Mind**

Plane. A level of world-existence; a world or level in the scale of being with its own system and ordering of principles.

Plasticity. Suppleness, the capacity to adapt to circumstances.

Presence, the. The sense and perception of the Divine as a Being felt as present in one's existence and consciousness or in relation with it.

Psychic. Of or relating to the soul (as distinguished from the mind and vital). Used in the sense of the Greek word "psyche", meaning "soul", the term "psychic" refers to all the movements and experiences of the soul, those which rise from or directly touch the psychic being. It does not refer to all the more inward and all the abnormal experiences in which the mind and vital predominate; such experiences, in this terminology, would be called psychological (surface or occult), not psychic.

Psychic, the. The soul; the psychic essence; the psychic being.

Psychic Being. The evolving soul of the individual, the divine portion in him which evolves from life to life, growing by its experiences until it becomes a fully conscious being. From its place behind the heart-centre, the psychic being supports the mind, life and body, aiding their growth and development. The term "soul" is often used as a synonym for "psychic being", but strictly speaking there is a distinction: the soul is the psychic essence, the psychic being is the soul-personality put forward and developed by the psychic essence to represent it in the evolution.

Purity. Freedom from soil or mixture. The divine purity is that in which there is no mixture of the turbid ignorant movements of the lower nature.

Purusha. Conscious Soul, Conscious Being; essential Being supporting the play of Nature; the true or spiritual Person.

Quiet. The absence of restlessness or disturbance.

Radha. The maiden of Brindavan in the Puranas; entirely self-given in her love for Krishna, she is the personification of absolute love for the Divine, complete self-giving and total consecration.

Realisation. The reception in the consciousness and the establishment there of the fundamental truths of the Divine; the making real to ourselves and in ourselves of the Self, the transcendent and universal Divine.

Receptivity. The power to receive the Divine Force and to feel its presence and allow it to work, guiding one's sight and will and action. The capacity of admitting and retaining the divine workings.

Revelation. The direct sight, the direct hearing or the inspired memory of Truth. It is a part of the intuitive consciousness.

Sachchidananda (*sat-chit-ananda*). The One Divine Being with a triple aspect of Existence (*sat*), Consciousness (*chit*) and Delight (*ananda*). God is Sachchidananda; He manifests Himself as infinite Existence of which the essentiality is Consciousness, of which again the essentiality is Bliss, is self-delight.

Sadhak. One who practises a spiritual discipline; one who is getting or trying to get spiritual realisation.
Sadhana. Spiritual practice or discipline; the practice of yoga.
Sadhika. Female sadhak.
Samadhi. Sanctuary or tomb of a saint.
Shakti. Force, Power; the Divine Power; the Power of the Mother; the consciousness and force of the Divine; the Mother and Energy of the worlds.
Siddhi. Perfection, accomplishment of the aims of yoga.
Silence. Freedom from thoughts and vital movements – when the whole consciousness is quite still; not only cessation of thoughts but a stillness of the mental and vital substance.
Sincerity. To mean what one says, feel what one professes, be earnest in one's will. Sincerity in the sadhak means that he is really in earnest in his aspiration for the Divine and refuses all other will or impulse except the Divine's; it means to allow no part of the being to contradict the highest aspiration towards the Divine.
Spirit. The Consciousness above mind, the Atman or Self which is always in oneness with the Divine.
Spiritual. Of the spirit. All contacts with the Self, the Higher Consciousness, the Divine above are spiritual.
Spiritualised Mind. Higher ranges of Mind overtopping our normal mind and leading to Supermind; these successive states, levels or graded powers of being are hidden in our own superconscious parts. In ascending order the gradations of spiritualised mind are:

Higher Mind. A luminous thought-mind whose instrumentation is through an elevated thought-power and comprehensive mental sight. In the Higher Mind one becomes constantly and closely aware of the Self, the One everywhere and knows and sees habitually with that awareness.

Illumined Mind. A mind no longer of higher thought, but of spiritual light; here the clarity of the intelligence, its tranquil daylight, gives place or subordinates itself to an intense lustre, a splendour and illumination of the Spirit.

Intuitive Mind. A mind of intuitive reason characterised by its intuitions, its inspirations, its swift revelatory vision, its luminous insight and discrimination; it is a kind of truth-vision, truth-hearing, truth-memory, direct truth-discernment.

Intuition. A power of consciousness nearer and more intimate than the lower ranges of spiritual mind to the original knowledge by identity; it gets the Truth in flashes and turns these flashes of Truth-perception into intuitions – intuitive ideas. Intuition is always an edge or ray or outleap of a superior light. What is thought-knowledge in the Higher Mind becomes illumination in the Illumined Mind and direct intimate vision in the Intuition.

Overmind. Full of lights and powers, the Overmind sees calmly, steadily, in great masses and large extensions of space and time and relation, globally; it creates and acts in the same way. The Overmind is a delegate of the Supramental Consciousness, its delegate to the cosmic Ignorance. The Supramental is the total Truth-Consciousness; the Overmind draws down the truths separately and gives them a separate identity.
Subconscient, the. A nether diminished consciousness which lies between the Inconscient and the conscious mind, life and body. The individual subconscient is that submerged part of one's being in which there is no waking conscious and coherent thought, will, feeling or organised reaction, but which yet obscurely receives the impressions of all things and stores them up in itself, and from it too all sorts of stimuli, of persistent habitual movements can surge up into dream or into the waking nature.
Supermind. The Supramental, the Truth-Consciousness, the Divine Gnosis, the highest divine consciousness and force operative in the universe. A principle of consciousness superior to mentality, it exists, acts and proceeds in the fundamental truth and unity of things and not like the mind in their appearances and phenomenal divisions. Its fundamental character is knowledge by identity, by which the Self is known, the Divine Sachchidananda is known, but also the truth of manifestation is known because this too is that.
Surrender. To consecrate everything in oneself to the Divine, to offer all one is and has, not to insist on one's ideas, desires, habits, etc. but to allow the divine Truth to replace them by its knowledge, will and action everywhere.
Tapasya. Effort, energy, austerity of the personal will; concentration of the will and energy to control the mind, vital and physical and to change them or to bring down the higher consciousness or for any other yogic or high purpose.
Transformation. Not just a change of consciousness, but the bringing down of the higher, divine consciousness and nature into the lower nature of mind, life and body, and the replacement of the lower by the higher.
Truth-Consciousness. The Supermind; the consciousness of essential truth of being (*satyam*), of ordered truth of active being (*ritam*) and the vast self-awareness (*brihat*) in which alone this consciousness is possible.
Trust. The feeling of sure expectation of another's help and reliance on his word, character, etc. The mind's and heart's complete reliance on the Divine and its guidance and protection.
Vital, the. The life-nature made up of desires, sensations, feelings, passions, energies of action, will of desire, reactions of the desire-soul of man and of all that

play of possessive and other related instincts, anger, greed, lust, etc. that belong to this field of the nature. The vital part of man is a true instrument only when its feelings and tendencies have been purified by the psychic touch and governed by the spiritual light and power. The vital has three main parts:

Higher vital. The mental vital and emotive vital taken together. The mental vital gives a mental expression by thought, speech or otherwise to the emotions, desires, passions, sensations or other movements of the vital being; the emotive or emotional vital is the seat of various feelings, such as love, joy, sorrow, hatred and the rest.

Central vital (or **Vital proper**). Dynamic, sensational and passionate, it is the seat of the stronger vital longings and reactions, such as ambition, pride, fear, love of fame, attractions and repulsions, desires and passions of various kinds and the field of many vital energies.

Lower vital. Made up of the smaller movements of human life-desire and life-reactions it is occupied with small desires and feelings, such as food desire, sexual desire, small likings, dislikings, vanity, quarrels, love of praise, anger at blame, little wishes of all kinds, etc. The material vital is that part of the lower vital turned entirely upon physical things, full of desires and greeds and seekings for pleasure on the physical plane.

Wideness. The expansion of consciousness that comes when one exceeds or begins to exceed the individual consciousness and spread out towards the universal; it is felt as a great substantial vastness giving the sense of oneness, free and infinite.

Will. A force put upon a thing to be changed. The power of consciousness turned towards effectuation.

Will, Divine. Something that has descended here into an evolutionary world of Ignorance, standing at the back of things, pressing on the Darkness with its Light, leading things presently towards the best possible in the conditions of a world of Ignorance and leading it eventually towards a descent of a greater power of the Divine, which will not be an omnipotence held back and conditioned by the law of the world as it is, but in full action and therefore bringing the reign of light, peace, harmony, joy, love, beauty and Ananda.

Yoga. Joining; union; union with the Divine and the conscious seeking for this union. Yoga is in essence the union of the soul with the immortal being and consciousness and bliss of the Divine, effected through the human nature with a result of development into the divine nature of being. Yoga is a generic name for any discipline by which one attempts to pass out of the limits of his ordinary mental consciousness into a greater spiritual consciousness.

Nature, the Mother and Flowers

Mirra was her name and she was by nature "a very silent child." Her mother often told her, whenever she complained about the food or some other petty thing: "You know, you are born to realise the highest Ideal." and sent her packing. She was indeed a very matter-of-fact woman and in time proved quite right.

Mirra had clearly from childhood an awakened life, for she could sit by herself in her little chair and "look into things." At these times she often saw a beautiful light above her head and tried to bring it down!

Her sensitivity to plants began early. She enjoyed admiring maiden-hair ferns for hours when she was taken by her parents to certain friends of the family.

Later, at the age of twelve, she spent her free afternoons in the woods at Fontainebleau. Seated at the base of those old trees she could feel their vital strength and would come home refreshed and replenished by the quiet presence of those giant beings.

She went to study for several years at an artists' workshop in Paris at the age of sixteen. There, her artistic talent as well as a new sensibility and appreciation of beauty blossomed. In fact, her motto throughout life was to study, to master herself and to become more conscious. However in her case, everything happened in her life naturally; often experiences came to her unsought.

Mirra was twenty-five when she went to Tlemcen in Algeria to study occultism with two great occultists, Max Théon and his wife Alma. All that we cannot see or touch, all the occult phenomena became clear and visible to her. It was during this period that she became aware too of the subtle power of flowers.

After an intense period of inner spiritual preparation and its outer expression with various groups of elite seekers and forward looking minds, she began, in 1912, to keep a diary of her inner experiences. This was later published as *"Prayers and Meditations of the Mother."* In it we find the most precious, inspiring and intimate contact with the Lord of her being and the Divine Mother upholding all.

In 1914 she came to Pondicherry and met Sri Aurobindo. She wrote in her diary:

"...O Thou whom we must know, understand, realise: absolute Consciousness, eternal Law. Thou who guidest and enlightenest us, who determinist and inspirest, grant that these weak souls may be strengthened and those who are fearful may be reassured. To Thee I confide them, in the same way as I confide to Thee the destinies of all of us..." There was a growing sense of the Divine behind all, as expressed in this prayer written a little after:

"All is beautiful, harmonious and calm, all is full of Thee. Thou shinest in the dazzling sun, Thou art felt in the gentle passing breeze. Thou dost manifest in our hearts and live in all beings. There is no animal, no plant that does not speak to me of Thee and Thy name is written on all I look at."

After a short stay she had to return to France and from there left for Japan. During the four years she was there she lived from marvel to marvel coming close to the beauty in Nature. In her garden where she grew her own vegetables she found that they spoke to her, telling her whether they were ready to be plucked or not. In her diary, she writes of her communion with a cherry tree through its flower.

She returned to Pondicherry for good in 1920 and lived as the other disciples. However, after some years Sri Aurobindo began addressing her as Mother instead of addressing her as Mirra. For he wrote, "we have from the beginning followed the same path and have had the same experiences and realisations." In 1926 when he retired he handed the full charge of the day to day activities of his disciples to her. This was the beginning of the Ashram's development.

All that was unique, beautiful, simple and sincere is what gave the Mother most joy. We do not know at what moment the offering of flowers became the way of expressing the disciple's aspiration and love for the Mother. Of course, she herself set the example showing that subtle way of communion by offering a garland of jasmine to Sri Aurobindo each evening. We know that in India flowers are always used in religious ceremonies and in temples.

Full of joy and devotion the disciple would offer her a flower expressing his surrender and inner need. The Mother replied with a flower bearing her blessing and love. The Mother gave words to the aspiration of the psychic in each flower and formed a spiritual significance, or in simple terms, a message, which bore the force of transformation. As she wrote: "When I give flowers I give states of consciousness."

By the end of 1929 she had already given a spiritual name to more than a hundred flowers. The gardeners of the Ashram began growing as many flowers as possible and tried out growing many new ones too. The Mother was particularly fond of roses! The Ashram artists also began painting flowers or embroidering flowers on material for the Mother's use.

The Ashram school began in 1943 as families with children were accepted by the Mother. Gradually she began to use the name in French for flowers. Besides the flower plates, the Ashram artists made small painted cards with which the Mother played games with some of the children to teach them the significances of the flowers.

By 1953 Lizelle Raymond helped to compile all the names of the flowers named by the Mother (*Le Rôle des Fleurs*). There were more than six hundred! Here is an extract from Lizelle's introduction: "The flower is the psychic consciousness of Nature expressing all that is both the highest and the humblest as well as what is most precious and minute."

The Ashram school grew and by 1952 became what is now the Sri Aurobindo International Centre of Education. Several new significances were given by the Mother, such as the "Thirst for Perfection" and the "New World," representing what she was bringing down, we believe, on the material plane.

Later, between 1964 and 1968, preparations were afoot to launch an international city to express a growing human unity. It was to be called Auroville and situated near Pondicherry. For this "City of Dawn' the first flower she named was "Godhead." Quite a few other Hawaiian hibiscus were designated for this new venture, such as "The spiritual beauty of Auroville," afterwards renamed "The Power of Spiritual Beauty." Symbolically, a little Star of Bethlehem flower was called by her "The Beauty in Collective Simplicity."

It was between 1970 and 1971, with the help of a *sadhika* that the Mother revised all the names and added a short commentary for each flower. At that time she also replied to various questions, which are included in the Introduction. Now there are nearly nine hundred messages that keep alive the presence and the ardent aspiration to realise the new consciousness planted here upon earth through the flowers.

The Mother: A Life Sketch

The Mother was born in Paris on 21 February 1878. Mirra, as the child was named, was the daughter of Maurice Alfassa, a banker, and his wife Mathilde. Her early education was given at home and then at a private school. Later she attended an art studio in Paris belonging to the Academie Julian. She became an accomplished artist and some of her works were exhibited at the Paris Salon. She was also a talented pianist and writer.

Concerning her early spiritual life the Mother has written: *"Between eleven and thirteen a series of psychic and spiritual experiences revealed to me not only the existence of God but man's possibility of uniting with him, of realising Him integrally in a life divine."* In 1906 and 1907, while in her mid-twenties, the Mother voyaged to Tlemcen, Algeria, to study occultism with a Polish adept, Max Theon, and his wife Alma. Returning to Paris, she founded a group of spiritual seekers. Between 1911 and 1913 she gave many talks to various groups.

In 1914 the Mother sailed to Pondicherry, India, and met Sri Aurobindo, Indian patriot, poet, philosopher and mystic. After a stay of eleven months, she returned to France for a year and then went to Japan for a period of nearly four years. Returning to Pondicherry in April 1920, the Mother became Sri Aurobindo's collaborator in his spiritual work. During the next few years the number of disciples around them gradually increased. This informal community eventually became the Sri Aurobindo Ashram. From its inception in November 1926 Sri Aurobindo fully entrusted the full material and spiritual charge of the Ashram to the Mother, while he withdrew to concentrate on his work, which was to bring down a new conscious-ness on the earth. He called this the Supramental or Truth-consciousness. Under the Mother's guidance, which covered a span of nearly fifty years, the Ashram grew into a large, many-faceted community.

The Mother founded the Sri Aurobindo International Centre of Education in 1943 and Auroville, the "City of Dawn", in 1968. This growing township, located twelve kilometers from Pondicherry, is a bold experi-ment in international living with a high spiritual ideal.

The Mother personally supervised the daily activities of the Ashram until the age of eighty-four. In March 1962 she retired to her room, but continued during the next decade to guide the Ashram and receive people regularly. On 17 November 1973, at the age of ninety-five, the Mother left her physical body.